Recommendation from
Dr. John Breeding

Shirley Luxem is on a wonderful mission. Her new book brings a wealth of wisdom and experience to help parents see themselves and their children as real people who can communicate and relate with love and authenticity. She reminds us that we thrive when we are able to live according to our true nature, which is designed for both loving connection and self-determined autonomy. Shirley has a great way of challenging wrong-headed notions of control, power, and submission; instead she shows us how to relate to young people with attention and respect, a way that really works to create an atmosphere of goodwill and collaboration. I love that she debunks stupid ideas like the outrageous diagnosis called "oppositional defiant disorder," and teaches us that we are not "training seals," but relating to awesome human beings! I recommend her book.

John Breeding, Ph.D. Psychologist, family counselor and author of The Wildest Colts make the Best Horses: What to Do When Your Child Is Labeled A Problem by The Schools.

THE NEW PARENTING HANDBOOK

Understanding Why Children
Do What They Do

*To Sophia —
For happy
days ahead!*

SHIRLEY LUXEM

THE NEW PARENTING HANDBOOK
UNDERSTANDING WHY CHILDREN DO WHAT THEY DO

iUniverse books may be ordered through booksellers or by contacting:

iUniverse
1663 Liberty Drive
Bloomington, IN 47403
www.iuniverse.com
1-800-Authors (1-800-288-4677)

Because of the dynamic nature of the Internet, any web addresses or links contained in this book may have changed since publication and may no longer be valid. The views expressed in this work are solely those of the author and do not necessarily reflect the views of the publisher, and the publisher hereby disclaims any responsibility for them.

Any people depicted in stock imagery provided by Getty Images are models,
and such images are being used for illustrative purposes only.
Certain stock imagery © Getty Images.

ISBN: 978-1-5320-6396-1 (sc)
ISBN: 978-1-5320-6395-4 (e)

Library of Congress Control Number: 2018914250

Print information available on the last page.

iUniverse rev. date: 07/27/2019

Dedicated to the memory of my grandfather, Guy Butterfield, who gave me a childhood secure in his unconditional acceptance, and to my sons with their continuous demonstration of the intrinsic goodness and beauty in human nature

ACKNOWLEDGEMENTS

This book could never have been written without Deborah Lacey. She has gone above and beyond in working on the manuscript and in her patience with me. Linda Adams at Gordon Training International and Dr. John Breeding gave me encouragement to keep going. Eleanor Reynolds, who established Mount St. Vincent Intergenerational Learning Center in Seattle, and her successor, Marie Hoover, have been inspirational to me in their Problem-Solving approach to being with large groups of children. And, too, I want to express my gratitude to Eleanor for allowing me to reprint lengthy pieces from her textbook. Fellow P.E.T. instructor Doug Love, parent/activist Anne Siems and, from the world of Montessori, Barbara Hilling, were reliable sounding boards for my questions and frustrations. All along the way I was bolstered by my beliefs in P.E.T and the Attachment teachings of Doctors Maté and Neufeld. Most important of all are the many parents I have been privileged to know and learn from.

A person's a person no matter how small.

~ Dr. Seuss

WHY ANOTHER PARENTING BOOK?

Early in 1900, the American people, including parents, educators, pediatricians, psychologists, and social workers, among others, fell under the spell of a fellow named John Broadus Watson. He promoted a system of child-rearing based on his laboratory experiments with the effects of punishments and rewards on rats. He called his theories Behaviorism and went on from psychology to a successful career in advertising.

He was followed by Burrhus Frederic Skinner who carried out his own experiments with rats, pigeons, and chickens, advancing Behaviorism to the world and adding the promise of Utopia to his claims. Both men made their scientific plan for controlling children seem so simple and feasible that we all fell for it and, as though in a trance, have been trying new and different punishments, bigger and better rewards ever since, always looking for and never finding the magic formula for happily living with children.

They were wrong.

This book will explain to you how they were wrong and what can be done about it now. The findings and teachings distilled here, many from today's brain research, can be your guide into the true happiness of parenthood.

WELCOME!

Welcome to the wonderful world of living with children as you engage in their development with eyes wide open!

Whether you are a new parent with questions about babies or have run into problems with a toddler, a school-aged child or a teenager, you will find many answers in the following pages and discover, for yourself, the limitless pleasures in knowing what you are doing and why you are doing it.

The philosophy and guidance presented here offer you the relationship-building communication skills of Dr. Thomas Gordon's Parent Efectivefness Training[1] along with the most up-to-date understandings in child development and Attachment based on the work of developmental psychologist Dr. Gordon Neufeld[2] and physician Dr. Gabor Maté.[3] You will find references to famous researcher, lecturer, and author of the highly acclaimed Unconditional Parenting book,[4] Alfie Kohn, as well as teachings from other respected writers and researchers, all giving us valuable understanding for living in peace and harmony with our children.

---

[1] Explore the P.E.T. website at www.gordontraining.com where you can read testimonials from other parents describing how P.E.T. helped them. The free newsletter can be ordered here, also.

[2] Read about Dr. Neufeld at www.neufeldinstitute.com. A wide variety of resources are available on this website. The internet offers several video lectures by both Dr. Neufeld and Dr. Maté

[3] Learn about Dr. Maté at www.drgabormate.com. On this website we find a selection of articles about Parenting along with information and teachings from his research on Addiction.

[4] Unconditional Parenting: Moving from Rewards and Punishments to Love and Reason by Alfie Kohn, Copyright 2005, Published by Atria Books, New York, NY.

Alfie Kohn talks about "WORKING WITH" children instead of "DOING TO" them. I use his terminology in this book and heartily suggest getting to know him at www.alfiekohn.org where the website offers his Unconditional Parenting book and DVD, about which one mother commented: *"Women should be required to watch this before going off birth control."*

As we explore the effects of reward-punishment control permeating Traditional family interactions, we learn to replace ineffective, alienating, and damaging control methods with a Problem-Solving approach for facilitating and supporting the growth of adaptable, cooperative, responsible children.

Contemporary culture exerts a serious threat to the vitally important Attachment between children and the adults responsible for them. Dr. Neufeld and Dr. Maté explain what it takes to build and maintain a strong healthy Attachment from infancy through adolescence and into adulthood. You will come to understand the perilous and damaging consequences to children and to society when this bond is weak or missing.

Modern brain imaging gives scientific support to the teachings found in this book. Everything you find here is based on solid research and the very satisfying Parenting experiences of millions of families throughout the world. Nothing is founded on "old-wives tales" or the dangerous mythology driving Traditional approaches to parenthood.

My goal is to give you all the guidance you will need for finding unlimited pleasure and fulfillment in being a parent. Folks who may want to pursue a deeper knowledge will find it in referenced sources and my recommended reading list.

AND NOW, WITH THIS BOOK, I INVITE YOU INTO A WORLD OF ONGOING DELIGHT IN LIVING WITH CHILDREN.

A note on pronouns: To avoid the awkward he/she designation of a child, I will use the word He when writing about children. I do not want to offend the parents of little girls and ask you to understand.

ANCIENT MYTHS

THE NUMBER ONE MYTH ON WHICH THE OTHER DANGEROUS MYTHS ARE BASED:

<u>HUMAN BEINGS ARE BORN EVIL.</u>

Arising out of ignorance and superstition, this myth has been a fundamental source of society's problems for centuries.

Other myths followed from this belief.

<u>A PARENT'S JOB IS TO CONTROL AND CIVILIZE THE CHILD.</u>

Children become compatible, cooperative, and positively self-directed at a very early age when given enough loving non-punitive support, guidance, and attention to their needs.

<u>CHILDREN ARE TO BE CONTROLLED THROUGH A SYSTEM OF PUNISHMENTS KNOWN AS SPARE THE ROD AND SPOIL THE CHILD.</u>

Extensive research proves punishments to be temporary in effectiveness, if at all, and damaging to the critical Attachment between parent and child. Punishments interfere with development of the Self. They retard growth of self-control and self-esteem. Punishments build fear, anger, rage, and aggression. Recent research shows stress from punishments, fear of parental disapproval, and loss of Attachment to be underlying causes of lifelong health problems[5]

REWARDING AND PRAISING DESIRED BEHAVIOR TRAINS CHILDREN TO BE GOOD.

Rewards and praise erode intrinsic motivation and natural cooperation. Rewards lose effectiveness over time if ever useful to begin with. Praise draws a child's attention to a parent's objectives and away from satisfying feelings of personal accomplishment.

THE TODDLER PERIOD IS ACCURATELY DESCRIBED AS THE TERRIBLE TWOS.

Along with teenagers, two-year-olds are the most misunderstood, mistreated, and maligned individuals among us. Difficulties with toddlers are the result of adult Authoritarian attitudes and tactics. Toddlers are happily compatible when approached with goodwill and kindness instead of anger and disapproval.

TEEN REBELLION IS INEVITABLE.

When parents maintain secure Attachments to their children into adolescence, treating them with respect and relating to each child without the usual punishment-reward strategies, working with their children instead of against them, teenagers feel no need to rebel in order to gain individuation and personal independence.

GANGS AND JUVENILE DELINQUENCY OCCUR BECAUSE CHILDREN ARE NOT PUNISHED ENOUGH.

Troublesome children are the result of abuse and neglect in various forms and to various degrees. Some of this abuse is not understood as such by the perpetrators who, following old teachings, have used punishments in attempts to control a child and, have instead, created an angry and destructive individual out of what

---

[5] Explained in the book, Scared Sick: The Role of Childhood Trauma in Adult Disease by Robin Karr-Morse and Meredith S. Wiley, Copyright 2007, Published by Basic Books, New York, NY.

once was a loving innocent baby.[6] Gangs are made up of children suffering from lack of connection to at least one sympathetic significant adult. Flailing about with no emotional ties, they are drawn to other children as rage-filled and starved for Attachment as they, themselves.[7]

IT IS A PARENT'S RESPONSIBILITY TO POINT OUT A CHILD'S FAULTS.

Telling a child what is wrong with him will not prompt him to change. Negative criticism makes people defensive and angry at being judged. Change can only come from within a child, energized by his own volition and supported by caring adults.

CHILDREN SHOULD BE TRAINED TO OBEY THEIR PARENTS.

To advance this belief, children are told that adults know what is best for them. Parents are human beings who can be wrong just like any other person can. Creating a baby did not automatically make them infallible. Obedience is not a sound foundation for a family or for a society. In the 1940s Germany proved this.

IT IS UNWISE TO TRY TO BE YOUR CHILD'S FRIEND.

This belief followed along with the other tenets of Traditional Parenting that are based on the idea of inborn evil. We are told our naturally bad little children will take advantage of parents who do not maintain an Authoritarian distance from them.

CHILDREN ARE AMAZINGLY RESILIENT.

No, they aren't. Believing no matter what cruel, outrageous treatment children endure at the hands of adults they, somehow, survive unharmed in sound mind and body is an underpinning of the disrespect and cruelty adults have taken

---

[6] This developmental process is fully explored in the book, Ghosts from the Nursery: Tracing the Roots of Violence by Robin Karr-Morse and Meredith S. Wiley, Copyright 1997, Published by Grove/Atlantic, New York, NY.

[7] High Risk: Children Without a Conscience by Dr. Ken Magid and Carole A. McKelvey, Copyright 1987, Published by Bantam Books, New York, NY. Chapters 1 through 8.

license to inflict upon children for centuries. Human beings are fragile creatures. The evidence is all around us in our mental hospitals, prisons, and in the numbers of unhappy, disturbed, sometimes violent children and adults making up a large percentage of the general population. Millions of people suffer and die as victims of crimes and wars instigated by individuals unleashing rage accumulated from maltreatment and neglect in infancy and childhood. Although a skinned knee may heal quickly, emotional damage lasts a lifetime and will find expression one way or another.

CONTENTS

I

Fish swim, birds fly, and people feel
~ Haim Ginott

1

WHAT IS PARENT EFFECTIVENESS TRAINING?

Parent Effectiveness Training was developed by Dr. Thomas Gordon as a way for parents to build secure, healthy relationships with their children. We learn how to model and teach Problem-Solving, while supporting the growth of each child's self-discipline, cooperation, sense of responsibility, and strength of character.

THIS ALL ADDS UP TO LIFE WITH CHILDREN BEING PLEASANT, EASY, AND FUN!

Dr. Gordon studied under psychologist Dr. Carl Rogers, who had arrived at a new way of helping troubled patients. Dr. Rogers had come to see the hope for psychological growth and healing to lie within the person seeking help, and he saw his role as the facilitator of such growth. His research and observations with clients and students brought an important breakthrough to therapeutic empathic listening Dr. Gordon calls ACTIVE LISTENING.

The P.E.T. program is built around the foundational belief in each person's knowing best what is right for him. We do not see a child as analogous to a block of marble to be chipped and chiseled to conform to a parent's vision. We see human beings as being born with their unique individual potentials much like a flowering plant. In order for the plant or the child to grow to strong healthy maturity, their inborn qualities and strengths realized, they need a nurturing environment with ongoing support and informed care.

Problems with children have become endemic because of mistaken beliefs about human nature and the Behaviorist goal of control through application of rewards and punishments.

P.E.T. TEACHES US A BETTER WAY TO LIVE!

And here's the exciting news about P.E.T. as developed by Dr. Gordon in the 1960s: Everything he taught is now scientifically confirmed by today's computer brain research. It is as though Thomas Gordon had held in his hands all the results of modern research and had said, *"I am going to take what we now know about the growth of human brains and, with this knowledge, design a system of communication for teaching families and any individuals, working or living together, how to interact in emotionally healthful and constructive ways. Children's brains will become structured for realizing their inborn possibilities. People will know how to get their needs met and how to help others meet theirs. This is the way to PEACE in the home, in the workplace, in the community, and in the world!"* And because Thomas Gordon had this remarkable vision of what human beings are capable of becoming, he was nominated for the Nobel Peace Prize!

Of course, there were no computer images of the functioning brain in the 1960s. Thomas Gordon figured this all out through his research with Carl Rogers, his work with clients, and his genius at understanding what makes people tick. The result was Parent Effectiveness Training and I now pass it on to you!

THE MAJOR P.E.T. COMPONENTS ARE:

- ACTIVE LISTENING
- I-MESSAGES
- WIN-WIN PROBLEM-SOLVING
- AVOIDING COMMUNICATION ROADBLOCKS
- PROBLEM OWNERSHIP

When we are able to incorporate the attitude behind the principles into our personal outlook, and think and act according to the easy-to-understand P.E.T. concepts, we are on our way to a new level of freedom and effectiveness never known, experienced, or attainable with Traditional Parenting. As we learn to communicate our positive regard to the children in our care through this LANGUAGE OF ACCEPTANCE,[8] they engage with us in development of their natural abilities for becoming highly-functional, cooperative, responsible individuals.

Parent Effectiveness Training changed my life in the 1960s when the world was a very different place. Pressures, fears, and stresses for adults, babies, and children were nothing like they are today. As terrorism, mass shootings, social media, and the world's accelerating tempo impact today's families, the relationship insights presented in this book are more urgently needed with each passing day and, along with findings from modern brain research, map-out for parents a peaceful way of life in a chaotic world.

---

[8] From the book, P.E.T. Parent Effectiveness Training: The Proven Program for Raising Responsible Children by Dr. Thomas Gordon, Copyright 1970, 1973, 2000, Published by Three Rivers Press, New York, NY, Member of The Crown Publishing Group, Chapter 3, "How To Listen So Kids Will Talk To You: The Language of Acceptance."

2

ACTIVE LISTENING

Dr. Thomas Gordon introduced the term Active Listening to the general public through his teachings and writings in Interpersonal Communication. It became the popular name for the curative way of listening Carl Rogers had called Reflection of Feelings. The therapy behind the different names is known and used throughout the world for facilitating emotional healing and personal growth, solving problems, and building relationships.

In his best-selling book, <u>The 7 Habits of Highly Effective People: Powerful Lessons in Personal Change</u>,[9] Stephen Covey said, *"Being understood by others is the greatest need of all."*

There is no human interaction in which the need for understanding is so great as in the communication between parents and children.

Active Listening makes understanding possible and provides clear principles for creating a communication of connection. Dr. Gordon devotes four chapters in his P.E.T. book to the art of Active Listening. I suggest reading them for a full grasp of the skill. Also, the internet offers descriptions as well as videos under the Active Listening and Empathic Listening headings.

---

[9] <u>The 7 Habits of Highly Effective People: Powerful Lessons in Personal Change</u> by Stephen Covey, Copyright 1989, 2004, Published by Simon and Schuster, New York, NY.

The goal is to hear the other person without trying to change or evaluate feelings behind the words; not attempting to talk him out of what he is feeling or to give advice. The intent is to UNDERSTAND while allowing the other person to experience and honestly express his feelings without being judged or dismissed.

We remind ourselves: ALL FEELINGS ARE LEGITIMATE. Children are allowed to feel what they feel and to express what they feel. If the feelings being voiced are hateful or obnoxious, it falls to us to remain open to hearing them without judgment. Buried and denied negative feelings do not go away. They fester and simmer, impacting personality, behavior, and physical and mental health in damaging ways.

Active Listening is a learned skill and requires practice. The more we use it, the easier it gets. Our good results motivate us to get better and better at this Attachment-Strengthening and Problem-Solving capability.

Habitual ways of responding are hold-overs from the old myths about changing and controlling children.

When we understand change as coming from within, we can appreciate the beauty of Active Listening as it builds the capacity for solving problems and furthers growth emerging from the child himself.

And so, how do we Active Listen?

First, we show interest by being fully attentive. When a child needs to tell us something, we stop whatever we are doing, enter into the experience, and establish friendly eye contact. If he approaches us needing to talk when we are really too busy to stop and give our full attention, we arrange to hear him as soon as we can. *"Sweetheart, I've got dinner bubbling on the stove right now. I want to hear what you have to say. I can sit down with you in the living room in about ten minutes."*

When we do have time to listen, we become fully engaged and acknowledge his first words by responding in ways to show we are paying attention. We may nod or say, *"Hmm"* or *"I see."* As he gets further into his experience, we put into our words what we think he is feeling. *"Wow, you were really scared!"* We match the intensity of our responses to the level of his feelings. We do not simply parrot his words back to him! We put what we think he is feeling into our own words to help us grasp what is going on with him and leave room for him to correct us if we are not quite getting the picture.

Guarding against using Communication Roadblocks is elemental to the value of the interaction. Any one of them will shut down free expression and leave a child feeling misunderstood, hurt, and frustrated. The ROADBLOCKS are described in a following chapter.

When we allow our child full expression while we Active Listen, he will reveal to himself, as well as to us, underlying questions, doubts, fears, and needs he had been unable to face or take into account, for solving a problem and moving forward.

Here's a shortened and slightly altered version of a true-life episode starting on page 79 in the P.E.T. book:

Eight-year-old Danny had grown increasingly resistant to going to sleep. His mother decided to see if she could put an end to their nightly conflict by doing some Active Listening.

This is what happened:

Mother: *"I'll sit on your bed awhile and rest my feet before I do the dishes."* She takes the book from him, turns off the light, and leans back.

Danny: *"Gimme my book! Don't turn off the light. Get out of here. I'm not going to sleep. I hate you!"*

Mother: *"You're very angry!"*

Danny: *"Yeah, I hate school. I'm never going back, never."*

Mother: *"You're fed up with school."*

She knows he loves school. As he now gets into complaining about it, she Active Listens to all his gripes. This venting about school seems to relax him and Mother tells him good night.

Danny: *"Will you sit with me some more?"*

Mother: *"Uh-huh."*

Danny: Starts snorting and sniffing with much exaggerated clearing of throat and nose. *"Snort, snort, snort."*

Mother: *"Nose really bugs you."*

Danny: *"Yeah."* Snorts with a big sigh of anguish. *"Oh, I wish you didn't have to breathe through your nose when you sleep."*

Mother: Tempted to ask where this idea came from; she sticks to her Active Listening: *"You think you have to breathe through your nose when you sleep."*

Danny: *"I know it. Tommy told me. What if I go to sleep breathing through my mouth and my nose is stuffy and in the night when I'm sound asleep, I close my mouth?"*

Mother: *"You're afraid you might choke."*

Danny: *"Uh-huh. You gotta breathe."*

Mother: *"It simply couldn't happen. Just like your eyes blink automatically, your mouth would open."* She carefully explains this automatic reflex and, understanding, he is finally able to relax.

Danny: *"Well, good night."*

Mother: *"Goodnight, dear."*

This was the end of Danny's bedtime resistance.

Dr. Gordon heard hundreds of reports from parents describing Active Listening uncovering deep-down reasons underlying problem behaviors; reasons they never could have guessed.

In this case, his mother provided the information Danny needed for solving his problem—fear of going to sleep and suffocating—when she listened long enough.

Her bonus was in finding she didn't have a defiant child after all. She had a very worried little boy and was able to dispel his fears by giving him her full attention while he uncovered the source of his troublesome resistance.

Active Listening can move a child through several layers of feelings before bringing to light a deeply hidden burden at the root of a dilemma or a problematic behavior.

Listening empathically is amazingly effective in preventing struggles in day-to-day situations when a child is required to do something he would rather not be doing.

When it is time to leave the park and our child resists, Active Listening to his unhappiness about leaving will help him through the transition. *"You were really having fun! You wish we could stay here all day."* Listening to whatever he is saying with true empathy legitimizes his feelings and his right to express them. Bolstered by our kinship, he is able to muster the inner strength to walk away from the fun he was having without falling apart.

By providing this level of acceptance we are acting as therapeutic agents, expressing and modeling empathy, deepening Attachment, and facilitating Problem-Solving. Hearing our child describe his thoughts and feelings opens our eyes to seeing things from his perspective. This quality of understanding takes us into a whole new world: The World of Our Child.

Children who are listened to and taken seriously when they are small share their thoughts and feelings with us as they get older. They do not become alienated and out of reach as they grow into adolescence. They find no need to turn to peers for acceptance or advice and possible adverse influence. We want a child of any age, with a problem big or small, to feel safe in coming to us without fear of shame, blame, recrimination, or punishment. Whether a new jacket is lost, a teen dents a fender, a coach makes sexual advances on a soccer player, a sixteen-year-old daughter is afraid she's pregnant, an eighth-grader is being intimidated or physically assaulted at school, or a college student is failing a course, we want our kids to know they are safe in turning to us. We are always on their side, will listen, and are ready to help if our help is wanted.

Active Listening must come from a place of love, not to be thought of and used as a novel Control Technique. When you are practicing it for the first few times, it will actually be a technique you are applying in training yourself to replace common divisive language with a healing level of listening. With the ultimate goal of supporting and helping your child, you will gain a sensibility of the unique person here before you as Active Listening becomes a natural way to respond.

When a child has been through a frightening or hurtful experience, Active Listening helps him cope with his distress.

Imagine a three-year-old who has fallen on his tricycle and broken his arm. As we rush to his side, we do not help by telling him to calm down or by trying to distract him from the calamity at hand. We listen to him. We try to put his pain and fear into words for him. *"Wow! You took a real tumble and your arm is hurting something awful. We'll get you to the doctor and have it fixed up right away."* If an event has been unusually frightening or upsetting, a child may bring it up again and again. He may say something about it days or weeks later, at which time we must be open to hearing and empathizing through Active Listening without telling him to forget about it or to stop worrying. Our empathic listening will help him to eventually come to terms with the mishap.

When we settle into the P.E.T. lifestyle, as great as it can be to find ourselves free of the old hassles, this is not the whole story. The most important

changes are taking place completely out of sight inside our child's brain where our listening, our understanding, our empathic support facilitate the wiring of healthy new brain connections, giving him the emotional strength and stability to handle challenges and cope with life's setbacks.[10]

Our therapeutic listening also allows children to own their problems and opens the way for finding their own solutions. In learning to face and solve their unique dilemmas, youngsters grow up with a firm sense of personal responsibility and self-reliance.

While learning to become "WORKING WITH" parents, it is critical to guard against the temptation to see P.E.T. as a new way to manipulate children into compliance.

Control is not our goal! Our hopes and dreams have nothing to do with gaining dominance. Through the ability to listen with true empathy, we are striving to reach a deep union with children and bring about, for ourselves and for them, a harmonious, happy way of life, unreachable through Traditional Parenting.

---

[10] This Integration of Experience by the human brain is described in the first chapter of the book, The Whole-Brain Child by Daniel J. Siegel, M.D. and Tina Payne Bryson, PhD, Copyright 2001 by Mind Your Brain, Inc. and Bryson Creative Enterprises, Inc., Published in the United States by Bantam Books, an imprint of The Random House Publishing Group, a division of Random House, Inc., New York, NY.

3

I-MESSAGES

Children have an emotional hunger to FIT IN with the family they find themselves in. Arriving in our world with no idea how to do this, they need our trust and understanding.

We adults sometimes make fitting in seem beyond reach by frightening and confusing children or inviting defiance with a coercive and disconnecting manner. One way we do this is with our words. Kind words and a friendly tone of voice will help our child gain a sense of belonging. With other words, other tones, we scare him away from trying, or make him so hurt and angry he can only fight back.

Dr. Gordon designed I-Messages as a way of telling another person what we need without stimulating a negative response. An I-Message is created with words to get a need met without blaming, insulting, demanding, or provoking resistance.

If you and your child have been trapped in an antagonistic relationship, it will take a while before his defences melt away under the influence of this different manner of being spoken to. Eventually his natural cooperative nature will emerge as you communicate with him in this non-violent way. Parents are surprised by remarkable results when they replace old ways of talking with the P.E.T. communication skills.

An I-Message has three parts, spoken in any order. Here's how we tell another person what we need:

DESCRIBING A PROBLEM OR A BEHAVIOR

"Toys are on the kitchen floor."

DESCRIBING FEELINGS

"I'm getting worried."

DESCRIBING TANGIBLE EFFECT

"I may trip over them or step on them and break them."

We steer clear of introducing blame into our I-Messages:

"Your toys are on the kitchen floor," or *"You left your toys on the kitchen floor."*

A child who has been treated with respect, not punished, not put into an adversarial position, will take the initiative and pick up the toys. If, until now, you have been using coercive measures to make your child mind, it may be hard to believe this different way of talking can elicit cooperation.

During the transition from being a "DOING TO" parent to a "WORKING WITH" approach, I-Messages may fall on deaf ears. A child deserves the right to either respond to our need or to go about whatever he was doing, ignoring our statement. With protecting the Self in mind, we must allow him this choice. If he is to gain autonomy, he needs the freedom to direct his own behavior.

He may come to the kitchen checking out this new type of communication and be open to making a cooperative effort with a little boost. *"I'm putting the toys in this bag to take to your room."* If his inclination has him reaching for the bag and helpfully going off with it, great! If not, you will, in a matter-of-fact way, trot off to his room with the toys. A guilt-tripping comment, such as *"Well, I guess I'll have to do it myself,"* represents using guilt as a form of coercion, would suggest being in a contest with him, and would stimulate resistance.

"What do you mean? Shouldn't I make him get in here and pick up the toys?"

This customary reaction is based on chauvinistically believing whatever our child may be doing is not as important as what we are doing. *"After all, he's only playing and I'm trying to make dinner."* With awareness and consideration, we see our child's activities to be as important to him as ours are to us. In this case the toys aren't bothering him, so why should he stop whatever he's busy doing to grant us this favor?

In moving forward with your new P.E.T. approach, you will be happy to find granting of favors to be his spontaneous response to your needs. Energized by his sense of belonging, as an active participant in a helping relationship, his help comes freely when needed.

We have been told to give children practice in decision-making by allowing them choices, such as *"Do you want to wear the blue shirt or the yellow one?"* or *"Which game do you want to play today?"* and this is perfectly helpful advice as far as it goes. Children do need lots of practice in making decisions. We also want our kids to grow up appreciating how the things they say and do; the choices they make, affect other people and, ultimately, the world they inhabit with others.

Under the spell of old myths about inborn evil, children are expected to act badly if given the freedom to choose their own behaviors. We now know this thinking is completely contrary to fact. When they are free from coercion, their needs are met, and they are consistently exposed to adult models of cooperation and kindness, this is what they learn. This is what they know. Their helpful responses come naturally.

If your youngster's helping hand has been hard to come by, you will be overjoyed when your I-Messages bring cooperation and a child as young as two or three follows his inborn drive to be a contributing member of the family. When this happens, be alert to viewing his cooperative behavior as a natural outcome of your strengthening relationship and his growing sense of partnership. Remarks such as, *"Oh there's my good boy,"* or *"Look at my big helper!"* dishonor his integrity. A simple response, such as *"Thank you. Now I can get dinner ready quickly and easily,"* will give him the feedback he needs.

Your child's best possible reward comes from his inner feelings of contribution and a gratifying sense of shared responsibility.

I-Messages are powerfully influential in the development of life-affirming values. Without lecturing or preaching, we pass our values on to our children.

DESCRIBING A FEELING

"I am so happy!"

DESCRIBING A BEHAVIOR

"All medical experiments on animals have been stopped at the university."

DESCRIBING A TANGIBLE EFFECT

"This is an important step toward the humane treatment of animals."

Or this:

THE PROBLEM

"Tons of food are going to waste in our country."

THE FEELING

"It disturbs me."

THE TANGIBLE EFFECT

"This same food could be feeding hungry people."

Children adopt the values of parents they admire and like. When we treat youngsters with kindness and respect, they want to be like us and will be strongly influenced to make our values their own.

4

THE TWELVE COMMUNICATION ROADBLOCKS

In the Parent Effectiveness Training book, Dr. Gordon explains how the way we talk either enhances or damages connection and is critical to building good relationships. He identifies twelve ways we shut down listening, cut off cooperation, and threaten Attachment with our words:

- ORDERING, DIRECTING, COMMANDING
- WARNING, ADMONISHING, THREATENING
- MORALIZING, PREACHING
- ADVISING, GIVING SUGGESTIONS OR SOLUTIONS
- ARGUING, PERSUADING WITH LOGIC
- JUDGING, CRITICIZING, BLAMING
- PRAISING, AGREEING
- NAME-CALLING, RIDICULING
- ANALYZING, DIAGNOSING
- REASSURING, SYMPATHIZING
- QUESTIONING, PROBING
- DIVERTING, BEING SARCASTIC, WITHDRAWING

Two important things to know about the Roadblocks and why to avoid using them:

1. When another person has a problem to solve, we can facilitate his ability to find his own solution by Active Listening and leaving out Communication Roadblocks.
2. Traditional language using Roadblocks will eventually destroy a relationship.

On page 13 in his book, <u>For Parents and Teenagers: Dissolving the Barrier Between You and Your Teen</u>,[11] Dr. William Glasser says this about our common divisive words. *"Exhibiting them in any relationship will damage the relationship. If you keep doing so, the relationship will be destroyed."*

The stronger your child's Attachment to you, the more he will look to you for direction. The strength of a parent-child Attachment determines a child's ability to cooperate.

In Dr. Thomas Gordon's words, *"Relationship is everything!"*

Your language will either draw your child to you and strengthen the relationship or drive your child away from you and weaken or break the critical bond. The Roadblocks listed above are certain to damage Attachment and can very likely destroy it completely. This is true for a relationship between any two people, not only between parents and children.

Besides weakening Attachment, Traditional "Parent Talk" undermines a child's self-esteem, stunts psychological growth, and cuts off meaningful dialogue. As a result of the way adults talk to children, by the time many of them are teenagers, parents find them completely alienated and beyond reach.

---

[11] Dr. Glasser defines seven deadly habits of communication on page 13 in his book, <u>For Parents and Teenagers: Dissolving the Barrier Between You and Your Teen</u> by Dr. William Glasser, Copyright, 2002, Harper Collins Publishers, Inc., New York, NY. His list: criticizing, blaming, complaining, nagging, threatening, punishing, rewarding to control.

On my first meeting with new clients, I present them with a printout of the Communication Roadblocks to tape to their computer, the bathroom mirror, the refrigerator door, or some good place in plain sight to help break divisive language habits. At the end of this book, you will find two pages with lists of the Roadblocks to tear out and post or carry with you.

When we eliminate Roadblocks and replace them with empathic Active Listening and I-Messages, the human bond is sustained and strengthened. A damaged or destroyed bond can be reestablished through a heartfelt serious effort at changing the way we talk and by eliminating punishments and rewards.

Here are some examples of the difference between old style Parent Talk and supportive, helpful communicating:

12-year-old girl: *"I hate Miss Armstrong. She yelled at me in class because I dropped a book and it made a loud noise."*

OLD WAY:

"What a terrible thing to say. Don't use the word 'hate' in this house. You should be ashamed of yourself." ORDERING, MORALIZING, JUDGING.

"If you were more careful you wouldn't get yelled at." BLAMING, ADVISING.

"Oh I'm so sorry, honey. How did it happen? Did you have too many books to carry? Do you want me to buy you a bigger book bag?" PROBING, SYMPATHIZING, CONSOLING, OFFERING A SOLUTION.

"Miss Armstrong needs everyone to be quiet so she can do a good job of teaching. You are way too sensitive to get along in this world. Don't worry about it. Everything will look better tomorrow." ANALYZING, JUDGING, REASSURING.

"I'll bet you're hungry. How about a piece of cake?" DISTRACTING, DIVERTING.

"You are such a good girl and an excellent student. She shouldn't have yelled at you." PRAISING, AGREEING.

NOW LET'S LOOK AT SOME USEFUL RESPONSES:

"She really made you mad!"

"You thought she was unfair to yell at you for only dropping a book."

"It felt awful to be yelled at in class."

Can you put yourself in the girl's place and feel the difference between a disconnecting Roadblock response and a Listening connecting one? In an appendix to the P.E.T. book, Dr. Gordon gives us a full analysis of the Roadblocks as they interfere with constructive communication, discourage children, and damage relationships.

In addition to all the help offered in the P.E.T. book for learning how to talk to children so they will listen and benefit from your words, wisdom can be found in Haim Ginott's book, <u>Between Parent and Child: New Solutions to Old Problems</u>.[12]

---

[12] <u>Between Parent and Child: New Solutions to Old Problems</u> by Dr. Haim Ginott, Copyright 1965, Published by Macmillan, New York, NY.

5

WIN-WIN PROBLEM-SOLVING

Parent Effectiveness Training teaches us to resolve a conflict in a way to arrive at a win-win solution. Traditional Parenting has usually settled family disputes in one of two ways:

1. The parent exercises authoritarian power and wins.
2. The parent gives in. Child wins and parent loses.

Either way, one party is left feeling cheated and resentful.

Dr. Gordon's Six-Step Problem Solving protocol is used worldwide in the political arena, the corporate world, in schools, and in families. Conflict resolution experts and professional mediators follow the Gordon model.

Step 1   DEFINING THE PROBLEM

Step 2   GENERATING POSSIBLE SOLUTIONS

Step 3   EVALUATING SOLUTIONS

Step 4   DECIDING ON A MUTUALLY ACCEPTABLE SOLUTION

Step 5   IMPLEMENTING THE SOLUTION

Step 6   EVALUATING THE RESULTS

The P.E.T. book devotes several chapters to this valuable skill. Parents who have incorporated the formula into their way to work out differences find it increases family harmony by eliminating bickering and exhausting hassles common in so many homes.

Dr. Gordon called it the "No-Lose" method for resolving conflicts.

If your children have known the settling of conflicts as being forced to comply under threat of punishment or being persuaded with bribes, they may be highly suspicious when told you are now going to resolve differences with a way to arrive at win-win results.

Here's how Thomas Gordon describes the process in the P.E.T. book:[13]

"Parent and child encounter a conflict-of-needs situation. The parent asks the child to participate with him in a joint search for some solution acceptable to both. One or both may offer possible solutions. They critically evaluate them and eventually make a decision on a final solution acceptable to both. No selling of the other is required after the solution has been selected because both have already accepted it. No power is required to force compliance because neither is resisting the decision."

Like all approaches to avoiding coercion and oppression of children, solving a problem instead of squelching it takes time and thought. The long-term benefits are well worth the time invested in solving a problem without producing a loser. The more we use this method, the less time it takes to reach happy outcomes. Many problems can be solved in a few minutes.

Besides enjoying the happy home Problem-Solving achieves, children acquire a skill they can use all through life.

Note: Marshall Rosenberg, who studied under Carl Rogers, created an organization for teaching a communication process he named Nonviolent Communication, known throughout the world as NVC. He worked with parents, business groups,

---

[13] P.E.T. Parent Effectiveness Training: The Proven Program for Raising Responsible Children by Dr. Thomas Gordon, page 220

and political leaders promoting peace through how we talk to each other. You can learn about his teachings at www.nonviolentcommunication.com where you can also see videos demonstrating Nonviolent Communication. I highly recommend his book, <u>Speak Peace in a World of Conflict: What You Say Next Will Change Your World.</u>[14]

---

[14] <u>Speak Peace in a World of Conflict: What You Say Next Will Change Your World</u> by Marshall Rosenberg, PhD, Copyright 2005, Published by Puddle Dancer Press, Encinitas, CA.

6

ATTACHMENT

Nurturing and protecting the Attachment bond between parent and child is essential at every age, not only in infancy. It is important to think about Attachment in relation to everything we say or do. Will our next actions or next words draw our child closer or will we drive him away and threaten his connection to us?

The language around raising children did not include the term Attachment until the 1960s when the findings of British child psychiatrist John Bowlby and American-Canadian psychologist Mary Ainsworth became known to other researchers who were searching for the missing clues to bringing up emotionally healthy human beings.

Reports of their breakthrough discoveries spread through the professional world soon after Dr. Harry Harlow's publicized results of experiments with Rhesus monkeys, during which he had observed primate infants without affectional ties to a mother or satisfactory mother substitute to be growing up with severe developmental and behavioral abnormalities.[15]

---

[15] Harry Harlow began his experiments with Rhesus Monkeys in1957 at the University of Wisconsin and became world famous for his discoveries about Love and Affection. The internet lists many articles by him and about him along with photos of the mothering-deprived little monkeys.

At the time in our history, when whatever feelings or needs a baby may have were viewed as insignificant, the primate studies, with their implications for humans, were startling.

Not startling enough, however. We remained in our trance. The Parenting revolution Dr. Harlow's work might have sparked did not happen. A Life Magazine article, reporting his discoveries along with a large photo spread of pathetic baby monkeys, deprived of a mother's closeness and obviously damaged, aroused only a passing curiosity.

We continued down the dead-end road mapped out for us by Dr. Watson and Dr. Skinner.

The general public, as well as professionals who worked with children and wrote books, were so enmeshed in the Behaviorist frame of mind that revelations about a baby's need for consistent, warm, dependable mothering were impossible to assimilate in any usable way or jolt us from the course we were locked into until Doctors Bowlby and Ainsworth reported their groundbreaking discoveries. Their firsthand clinical work and research with maladjusted children changed the direction of investigations into personality development. As their revelations became known and verified, the Attachment Parenting movement was launched. In the United States, a campaign to promote breastfeeding was inaugurated and emphasis on physical closeness began showing up as we saw more and more adults carrying babies in slings.

Coming after Dr. Harlow's research, focus on the importance of warmth and closeness between parents and babies opened the way toward building happy parent-child relationships.

Instead, the sunny futures Attachment parents set the stage for do not usually materialize. As soon as a child's feet hit the floor, Moms and Dads of babies who have been slept with, breastfed, and carried in slings, find themselves facing the same conflicts and struggles plaguing conventional parents. Before long, they are commiserating with other adults about The Terrible Twos and the daily battles wearing them out.

Here's why:

This new and better way to treat babies ends up "on the shelf" along with the sling. When the little person starts exploring his world and wanting to do things his way, Attachment loses priority and adults switch into Control Mode, confusing and frustrating their toddler, who becomes increasingly hard to handle as his parents become increasingly demoralized and frazzled.

Attachment Parenting did not replace Behaviorism. It was simply added to it with all the same hurt, anger, and strife of punishment-reward control continuing to contaminate relationships and blight families.

Now, at last, with modern computer brain imaging and brain mapping as research tools, developmental psychologists, such as Dr. Gordon Neufeld, and medical physicians, such as Dr. Gabor Maté, are filling in the missing pieces.

FINDING INDIVIDUAL INFANTS AND CHILDREN TO EACH HAVE UNIQUE EMOTIONAL MAKE-UPS OF INSTINCTS AND INBORN NEEDS AND STUDYING THE RESULTS WHEN SUCH NEEDS ARE EITHER FULFILLED OR UNMET IS A REVOLUTIONARY WAY OF THINKING ABOUT CHILDREN AND HUMAN DEVELOPMENT.

The Behaviorists claimed there was nothing going on in the brains of babies and instructed us to be concerned only with behavior.

The infant brain was described as a BLANK SLATE.

Our only responsibilities were to keep children clean, well-fed, and obedient. Behaviorist John Watson had insisted we would make infants and children dependent by holding, touching, kissing, or giving them any attention at all beyond what was absolutely necessary.

Following Behaviorist dogma and neglecting babies and children by being oblivious to the existence of their feelings and needs, families find themselves lost and floundering in a toxic emotional quagmire.

P.E.T. teaches us: RELATIONSHIP IS EVERYTHING and, today, developmental psychologists are confirming this with their research revealing the workings of the Attachment Brain. In <u>Hold Onto Your Kids: Why Parents Need to Matter More Than Peers</u>, we learn about the importance of Attachment to building healthy relationships and why a child's ability to cooperate is determined by the strength of the Attachment bond and the parent in position as his *COMPASS POINT*.[16]

In the "good old days" Mom was usually at home with her children from the day each of them was born. They were there together with Mom in the kitchen when Bobby or Suzy came in from school. Without television, computers, social media, commercialism's unremitting sensory input, pressure cooker schools, daycare, and myriad activities filling long hours of separation, most parents, without trying, fostered enough connection for their children to be at least somewhat easy to live with no matter how lacking the adults may have been in Parenting Skills.

In today's fast-paced world, it has become increasingly important for parents to be consciously aware of Attachment needs and to make an ongoing deliberate effort to strengthen and secure the bond starting in infancy and continuing through the teen years.

This includes attention to the physical side of Attachment by responding lovingly to physical needs with hugging, holding, embracing, rocking, co-sleeping if we choose, carrying in a sling, patting, cuddling, and holding hands.

---

[16] The importance to a child of finding his compass point in a parent is addressed from a variety of perspectives in the book, <u>Hold On to Your Kids: Why Parents Need to Matter More Than Peers</u> by Gordon Neufeld, Ph.D. and Gabor Maté, M.D., Copyright 2004, 2005, 2014, Published in the United States by Ballentine Books, an imprint of the Random Publishing Group, a division of Random House, Inc., New York, NY, 2006 Ballentine Trade Paperback Edition.

Attention must be given to emotional connection as well by being kind and respectful, listening attentively, avoiding the Roadblocks to communication, establishing a stabilizing routine, and by eliminating punishments and rewards from the parent-child relationship.

ATTACHMENT IS NOW SEEN AS THE MOST FUNDAMENTAL AND COMPELLING HUMAN NEED.

The strength and quality of an infant's Attachment to his mother, or an attuned mother substitute, in the hours, weeks, and months after birth is vitally important to the healthy structuring of his brain. With around 75% of human brain development continuing outside the womb, we adults must take responsibility for providing the best possible conditions in which this can happen. Babies and children need to feel safe and connected to at least one full-time nurturing, aware adult for sound brain development to occur.

With modern brain research making this need perfectly clear, what in the world are we going to do when mothers must work outside the home for financial reasons or for the sake of their own emotional well-being?

Since our modern culture has taken us down a path in complete opposition to supporting early brain development, we, as individual parents, are left to figure out how to provide reliable nurturing care for our children.

If there are two parents, is it possible to adjust work schedules allowing one parent to be home at all times? Can a job be done from home or a career put on hold until kids start school?

Could you arrange your workplace to accommodate having your baby there with you?

Is there a grandparent living nearby or willing to move in and become your baby's long-term nurturer?

As another possibility, I suggest searching for a nanny who will come into your home to take over physical care and meet the long-term Attachment needs of your child. You may find the right person for you through the local Senior Center, an Association for Retired Teachers, a church, or an employment agency.

The hope is in finding someone to care for your child at least until he starts school. Ideally, this person will be with him until he can be on his own. I do not recommend bringing in an Au Pair from a foreign country who will be contracted to care for your baby or young child for 12 months. Losing an Attachment figure after one year is shattering to children of any age and takes a toll on their emotional health.

An option may be found in locating a stay-at-home mom who can use some additional income and would be delighted to take your baby into her home and into her heart.

Most communities have, scattered throughout them, a few women licensed to look after two or three babies in their homes because they love babies and enjoy caring for them.

All such arrangements must, of course, be thoroughly checked out for the safety of leaving your baby in another individual's care and keeping. If this book is resonating with you, finding a caretaker who will be open to understanding and LIVING the P.E.T. philosophy will keep your life running smoothly.

If commercial daycare is your answer, take a few days to stay with your child, giving him time to become accustomed to the sights and sounds in this new and different place, while you orchestrate his connection with each individual worker. Whether your child is a baby or a three-year-old, involve him in your conversations with every employee. Such Match Making, as described in <u>Hold On To Your Kids: Why Parents Need to Matter More Than Peers</u>, is a necessary step in fostering a child's sense of security and belonging during the hours when he is away from you.

Each time you leave him, no matter if a baby, a toddler, or a pre-schooler, make a clear statement about your return: *"I'll be back when I get off work and we'll be together again."*

When you return for him each day, reconnect with firm eye contact, a smile, and a big warm hug. Be acutely aware of Attachment needs. Housework, emails, shopping, and all other pursuits must be way down the list of priorities. Your child's mental health and your future happiness depend on this!

If your situation allows you to be a stay-at-home mom, and this becomes your choice, the information in this book can be your guide for fashioning a life of satisfaction, achievement, and a degree of happiness and pleasure you could not have imagined.

We humans crave and seek firm Attachment all our lives. The need is so potent that children and adults alike may make unwise connections when nurturing, loving ones are not available. The emotional hunger for a tight bond sometimes drives individuals of any age into faulty, unsatisfying and, possibly dangerous, connections.

Because the instinctive need for Attachment is so powerful, children attach to other children in the absence of a satisfying connection to at least one involved adult. When children attach to other kids, they are left without the nurturing guidance and support only adults can provide. The excellent book, Ghosts from the Nursery: Tracing the Roots of Violence,[17] describes how lack of Attachment in the early days, weeks, and months of life predisposes children to a future of crime and violence and how such unattached youngsters find and attach to each other.

As busy as we may be, it becomes imperative to meet our child's need for focused time with us. Somehow, some way, we must whittle out a slice of time each day or each week. A full hour is wonderful. A half hour is good. Any way we can

---

[17] Ghosts from the Nursery: Tracing the Roots of Violence by Robin Karr-Morse and Meredith S.Wiley.

manage it, our child will reap immeasurable benefits from the time he knows we set aside exclusively for him.

Such special time fosters self-esteem while strengthening the bond. Arranged to be spent in the intimate one-on-one involvement a child chooses, this is not an occasion to teach or direct activities. He is nourished when he knows we have reserved this private time for the two of us, following his ideas and plans.

This level of connecting differs from other ways we may engage with children, such as going to a park, taking a walk, or playing catch in the backyard. For this exclusive involvement, we are arranging a more cozy togetherness. One little girl almost always wants her mother to "play dollies" with her. Some children ask to be read to. Others prefer to have their parent watching while they draw pictures or assemble puzzles. On other days, snuggling and talking could be exactly what's needed. This type of closeness presents a perfect backdrop to Active Listening and for building a deep connection between parent and child.

An ideal way to spend regular one-on-one time with a baby or a small child is in a rocking chair, quietly rocking or with singing or talking softly along with the rhythmic movement. In finding thirty minutes each day to rock with our child, holding him closely in our arms, we are setting the stage for happy days ahead.

I do not suggest rocking a baby to sleep. This would interfere with development of his ability to fall asleep on his own. One-on-one rocking is for your awake child, fully aware of the closeness, and soaking it up into the core of his being. And, by the way, you can luxuriate in soaking up some of this soul-nourishing intimacy along with him.

A note about slings: Although carrying a baby in a sling is a lovely thing to do, we must not neglect his need for routine and order, peace and quiet, just because it is so convenient to tote him around this way anywhere, anytime.

And, Mothers, Fathers, Caretakers: talk to little babies! Tell them how wonderful they are. Light the way into their big new world with your loving voice. Tell them about the beauty and joys awaiting them. Make them feel welcomed and cherished. However tiny they may be, they will understand your words long before they know your language.

We must keep in mind our responsibility to treat children with genuine respect. Yelling, punishing, shaming, ignoring, criticizing, and lecturing will drive them away and weaken or destroy the vital connection.

If our behavior toward a child severs the bond completely, his natural inborn impulse to cooperate shuts down and our influence dwindles.

Although a family tie can be broken at any age, it becomes dramatically apparent in the life of a teen when he turns to his peers seeking connection. If his friends happen to be indulging in risky sex, alcohol, drugs, dangerous or illegal behavior, he's headed for trouble. When parents see a child going off in such directions, the most usual response is to become more critical, more demanding, and more punitive; driving the teen further away and more securely into his peer Attachments. A new gang member has not suddenly "turned bad." He has grabbed and is clinging to an Attachment life raft, leaky as it may be, and seeking protection in a frightening neighborhood. Many times, he comes fully equipped with a burden of hostility and rage accumulated during years of violence and abuse in his home.

Our best guide is in knowing that all behavior problems are Attachment problems. This serves as our starting point for addressing difficulties with children of any age. Protecting and securing Attachment to the children in our care must be the number one priority in our responsibilities to them.

Note: The internet offers a 1992 pdf titled: The Origins of Attachment Theory by Inge Bretherton. This account of John Bowlby's and Mary Ainsworth's intellectual journey to their deep insights into Human Nature reads like a good novel. I highly recommend it.

7

MISBEHAVIOR

PRIMARY TO PARENT EFFECTIVENESS TRAINING PHILOSOPHY:

ALL BEHAVIORS ARE SOLUTIONS TO HUMAN NEEDS.

<u>PRINCIPLE 1</u> Like adults, children have compelling needs and they continually strive to meet their needs by doing something.

<u>PRINCIPLE 2</u> Children don't misbehave. Their behaviors are simply actions they have chosen to meet their important needs.

Children are bound to do things parents don't want them to do. New to the world and inexperienced, they will blunder and make mistakes.

Think about such behaviors this way:

They are behaviors children are engaging in to meet their needs. Their particular way of behaving is unacceptable to you. They are not trying to do something to you. They are only trying to do something for themselves. They are not "bad" or "misbehaving," although they may be causing you a problem.[18]

---

[18] As taught by instructors certified through Gordon Training International. To learn about the Gordon Training courses go to www.gordontraining.com.

When we can get the idea of "bad behavior" out of our heads and recognize it as a throwback from ancient mythology, we look at our children with curiosity, interest, and empathy instead of irritation, hostility, and anger. We become alert to seeing troublesome things they do as learning opportunities for us as well as for them.

Approaching children as their loving helpers, Active Listening and seeing things through their eyes, we are open to being emotionally and intellectually available for engaging with them in uncovering the needs behind their behaviors. By maintaining empathy, we penetrate the defences any previous Traditional Parenting techniques may have built up and bring about cooperation, learning, and growth.

In line with today's research, we stay attuned to protecting the Attachment bond. With our position of natural authority depending on the strength of our Attachment, we remember to work with our child and to always be on his side. We must ward off slipping into the culturally-habituated inclination to function as his adversary, weakening crucial Attachment, and leaving him outside our sphere of influence. This uncoupling can happen as early as preschool when an unattached child looks to his peers for cues and his sense of belonging.

Children who run away from home are suffering from missing Attachments to the adults in their lives as a result of neglectful and/or punitive ways in which they have been treated and disconnecting language directed against them.[19]

Their hurt and anger leave them without recourse as they escape from situations intolerable to them.

Gang culture and criminality are extreme manifestations of missing Attachments and common punitive adult responses to unwanted behaviors.

---

[19] Drs. Neufeld and Maté explore the growing problems created by peer attachments in the book, Hold On to Your Kids: Why Parents Need to Matter More Than Peers.

The next time your child's behavior upsets or angers you, stop and think before opening your mouth.

WHAT YOU SAY NEXT WILL CHANGE YOUR WORLD. [20]

However off-track he may be, the child is trying to meet his needs. He may not know what needs he is struggling to fill and you will probably be in the dark, about his motives, too. Whatever needs may be pressing in on him, his behavior, as annoying as it may be to you, is his way of coping with his set of circumstances as registered in his brain. The unwanted behavior is a spontaneous outward sign of his internal struggle. We create our own agitation when we interpret the behavior as the problem and get ourselves all worked up by taking it personally. By approaching him with openness and empathy, the two of you can figure out what's bothering him and find mutual relief from his difficulties.

Your bond will be strengthened by this supportive interaction instead of having been damaged or broken by an angry outburst and a punitive response. With the help of Active Listening and a willingness to take time to uncover the needs behind his behaviors, the Self of him is protected and strengthened while your understanding of your unique child is deepened.

"Oh," you're thinking, *"Who has time for all this? Better to just yell at him to stop what he's doing or send him to his room and be done with it."*

The trouble is, with the yelling or the punishing we are never done with it.

The problems continue and get worse. The unwanted behaviors persist or surface in different forms. Our frustration and anger mount while our child gradually disconnects from us.

The time and energy invested in trying to get control of a child over and over again far exceed the time it takes to do the connecting things, to say nothing of

---

[20] This is the subtitle to the book, Speak Peace in a World of Conflict: What You Say Next Will Change Your World by Marshall Rosenberg.

the fun, peace, and happiness we miss during the fleeting years our children are with us; years when, instead of struggling and fighting, we can be basking in the pleasures of parenthood.

> The effects of Authoritarian Parenting are as debilitating to the adult as to the child. In an adversarial position, we reflexively interpret any unwanted behavior as a threat to our control. This unaccepting way of seeing our child's struggles, in making his way the best he can, becomes who we are. It distorts our entire outlook and our personal sense of Self.

Escaping the old shackles of the Control Mentality and the Behaviorist methods supporting it improves our lives as profoundly as our children's.

I'm not pretending this change is easy to accomplish. Our entire culture is built on a framework of control. Our language developed around this way of thinking, with believing certain people have an unquestioned, automatic right to control certain other people.[21] It takes a strong, deliberate, and mindful commitment to overcome our conditioning.

I give you two key tips to help make personal transformation somewhat easier:

1. Stop and think before responding to unwanted behavior.
2. Keep self-talk in line with protecting Attachment.

It helps to know our babies are born with everything right there inside them for becoming wonderful people.

When we can BE THERE for them, accepting them exactly as they are, ready with our support, helping them meet their needs; we are privileged to witness the unfolding of fully competent new Human Beings as nature intended.

---

[21] See page 18 in <u>Speak Peace in a World of Conflict: What You Say Next Will Change Your World</u> where Dr. Rosenberg addresses the way our language has shaped our thinking.

As much as this may be making sense to you and as determined as you may be to put into practice the concepts you are learning here, if you are like many other parents, there are times when something your child has done sends you into a fury. You yell at him with cruel hurtful words, knowing you are being irrational and self-defeating. Such explosions, all out of proportion to anything a child has done, are now understood as being triggered by buried emotional pain carried with us from our own childhoods.

Here's where DISCIPLINE enters the picture. We must learn how to discipline ourselves in controlling our responses to a child's unwanted behaviors.

Because this intense anger can be such a barrier to progress, researchers have been investigating why it erupts and what can be done about it. In this regard, I direct you to the book, <u>Parenting from the Inside Out: How a Deeper Self-Understanding Can Help You Raise Children Who Thrive</u>[22] by Daniel J. Siegel and Mary Hartzell, where the phenomenon is explained with fascinating examples. Informed by Dr. Siegel's brain research, their advice offers great help in moving us beyond being controlled by our past hurts.

With or without the guidance offered in this excellent book, mastering control of your behavior toward your children is critical to progress. Parents have said the practice of yoga has done this for them. Others have been helped with anger management counseling or books on the subject. Some gain relief with chanting, deep-breathing exercises, meditation, or personal affirmations.

If you find yourself losing your temper without a tried and true way to get control of yourself, leave the room! Make some excuse and get out of there until you settle down and can be with your child in a helpful frame of mind.

---

[22] <u>Parenting from the Inside Out: How a Deeper Self-Understanding Can Help You Raise Children Who Thrive</u> by Daniel J. Siegel, M.D. and Mary Hartzell, M. Ed., Published by Jeremy P. Tarcher/ Penguin a member of the Penguin Group, New York, NY.

As you are coming to understand the cultural attitudes and beliefs underpinning our established parenting practices, this knowledge may be enough to keep you from directing your accumulated anger at your children. Page by page, with new understanding, you can find living with them becoming easier and more fulfilling with fewer and fewer incidents stirring your rage.

Parents create serious difficulties for themselves and lasting harm to their children when their expectations for a child's behavior exceed his physical or cognitive abilities. We can get upset and furious because a child has done something we have told him over and over not to do when, in actuality, he is utterly incapable of following our instructions or obeying our commands. As a common example, we see a youngster punished, sometimes seriously abused, because he has wet the bed or soiled his clothing, when all the while the bewildered little kid is developmentally unable to stay dry.

One very significant way to keep your life as a parent running smoothly is by mindfully accommodating your child's developmental limitations.

I must warn you about a poisonous anti-child narrative woven into our culture and contaminating relationships. I'm talking about an ongoing theme, fueled by the ancient myth of inborn evil, heard in everyday remarks about children. It surfaces in cartoons, in radio and TV commercials, in media portrayals of children of all ages, and in parent training books. A common example is in hearing the comparison between a root canal and a road trip with children. In 2013, a famous movie actor recorded a children's book parody: a profane litany bemoaning his maddening exasperation with settling a child for sleep and an ugly slam at all little kids.

Parents are conditioned to believe children's dysfunctional behavior is "normal" and to expect it. We hear: *"If you think living with a two-year-old is awful, just wait until she's three."* We are told to prepare ourselves for the troubles awaiting us when our child turns into a belligerent, rebellious teen.

Unlike the four-year-old who may throw a toy out of pure frustration or strike out at a parent when overwrought, chronically defiant, hurtful, or malicious behavior is a different thing. Although it has become so common it may be seen as the Norm, IT IS NOT NATURAL! Seriously distressed children—ripping curtains off the wall, destroying property, abusing the family pet, or exhibiting other chronic destructive behaviors—are being thrown off kilter by the adults in their lives. **It is a huge mistake to see what they are going through as "The Way Kids Are."**

Stereotyping children in this way poisons the entire society. Labels like The Terrible Twos and Rebellious Teens are insults to all our loveable and cooperative toddlers and all the responsible, engaged teens living among us.

This stereotyping indoctrinates parents and prospective parents, giving rise to self-fulfilling prophesies and perpetuating problems brought about by the popularized misconceptions.

Complaining about their difficult, unmanageable kids, is a common topic of conversation when parents get together. Without exposure to accurate information about the true nature and needs of children and the role they, themselves, are playing in creating their own problems, they find relief venting with other parents who are struggling with their same dilemmas, never knowing how satisfying life can be; living with happy, cooperative kids.

Children who are firmly Attached, treated respectfully and listened to; who have not become alienated and angry by being punished, disregarded, and manipulated are pleasant to live with. Road trips are fun for the entire family. Bedtime is a lovely time of day. Contented, well-connected children do not destroy property and hurt people or animals.

When children's needs are met and they enjoy the Freedom to live-out their Natural Agendas, knowing they are accepted just as they are and cherished simply because they exist, we find them to be delightful and interesting companions.

8

MY CHILD DEFIES ME

Nothing drives an adult up the wall like a child's defiance.

Right here and right now, we're going to get to the bottom of this most common complaint to find liberation from the antagonism and strife it brings to a home.

Something called **COUNTERWILL** is the culprit. Once you understand it, you will begin to see it everywhere and be struck by the harmful and sometimes dangerous ways parents, teachers, police officers and other well-meaning adults react to it.

Knowing how to keep Counterwill slumbering—or what to do when it wakes up and jumps out at you—will change your life forever!

I'm drawing on the work of developmental psychologist Dr. Gordon Neufeld and medical physician Dr. Gabor Maté. Their findings have been fundamental to my understanding of the developing brain as it determines behavior.

Before being introduced to their research, I had been teaching Parent Effectiveness Training. Although I had experienced terrific results as a P.E.T. parent and, more recently, witnessed gratifying outcomes for other parents, I did not know what was going on in a child's brain to make P.E.T. "work" so well.

Dr. Maté's and Dr. Neufeld's knowledge of brain-directed human behaviors is absolutely transformational to our relationships with children.

They have introduced the word COUNTERWILL into the lexicon of Parenting. Before long, I expect this word will be included in the day-to-day language of parenting and found in most other Parenting books and classes.

I am thinking of the term ACTIVE LISTENING, introduced to the public by Dr. Thomas Gordon in 1962, and now used all over the world as a generic term. Most writers who use it do not credit Dr. Gordon and many probably don't know where it came from. I expect the term COUNTERWIL to become common usage in much the same way. Doctors Neufeld and Maté are clear in identifying Austrian psychoanalyst Otto Rank with having first described the dynamic and giving it a name over one hundred years ago, before his potentially world-changing discovery was lost in the mad stampede into Behaviorism.

Learning about the brain's Counterwill response tells us why we hear or ask the question: What's wrong with today's kids?

Now we find there is nothing wrong with them. Adults in their lives, following Traditional Parenting customs, are kindling stand-offs against an ironclad function of the human brain.

Although we all have the Counterwill instinct, it is most vigorously active during the two times in our development when we need it most: in the toddler period and during the teen years. Both are stages when we are working hard to achieve independence.

This irresistible drive is described on page 74 of the book, <u>Hold On to Your</u> <u>Kids:</u> <u>Why Parents Need to Matter More Than Peers</u>:

"Counterwill is an instinctive, automatic resistance to any sense of being forced. It is triggered whenever a person feels controlled or pressured to do someone else's bidding."

On page 76 in this same book we read:

"The basic human resistance to coercion is usually tempered, if not pre-empted by attachment."

A child's ability to cooperate is strengthened in direct proportion to the strength of his Attachment to the person who is seeking his cooperation. Nature has designed a child's brain to facilitate willing cooperation only with adults to whom he is Attached. The stronger the Attachment, the greater the cooperation.

Everything we learn from Parent Effectiveness Training protects Attachment and tells us how to influence our children without activating their Counterwill.

Accepting the fact of Counterwill as a deep-seated instinct beyond conscious control, we "get it" and know why it is up to us to ABANDON HOPELESS EFFORTS TO FIGHT AGAINST NATURE AND TO WORK WITH OUR CHILD WHEN, AT ANY TIME HE FEELS COERCED, HIS BRAIN CAN AUTOMATICALLY FORCE HIM TO RESIST.

Understanding Attachment to be the key to cooperation, we now direct our efforts to strengthening connection by treating children respectfully, being attentive to their needs, avoiding hurtful words and actions, and, no matter how busy we are, by finding time for them.

Dr. Neufeld and Dr. Maté explain how to engage a child's Attachment instincts with eye contact, a smile, a nod, and, when it feels right, a gentle touch. They instruct us to connect in this way whenever we are seeking cooperation and after every separation, whether thirty minutes, several hours, or after extended periods of being apart. They call this **COLLECTING OUR CHILDREN** and devote a chapter in <u>Hold On To Your Kids: Why Parents Need to Matter More Than Peers</u>, beginning on page 179, to this vital Attachment reinforcement.

Counterwill stays with us all our lives. No one likes being ordered around. We fully appreciate this firmly entrenched instinct by knowing it promotes our child's individuation.

Gordon Neufeld tells us, *"Counterwill is a natural defence against the will of others in order to make way for the discovery of the child's own will."*[23]

When we have told our five-year-old to come to dinner and he's looking us straight in the eye, shouting *"No! You're not the boss of me!"* we are not looking into the face of inborn evil. We are witnessing a young human in the grip of Counterwill. Knowing our precious child is under the influence of an instinct beyond his control, we deflect a useless battle by announcing a sudden need to be elsewhere: *"Oh my gosh! I've got to go stir the soup!"*

Taking time to rethink what happened, we ask ourselves why Counterwill perceived us as an Outsider and clicked in to protect our child. Were we demanding and disrespectful? Did we swoop in, ordering and directing without first Collecting? Has he become exasperated with instructions, orders, and advice? Beneath it all, is Attachment shaky?

We return to the scene of the impasse in a "Working With" frame of mind. This time, as we interrupt his activity, we Collect our busy child with eye contact, a smile, and a nod. A hug, too, if it feels natural and easy. We get down beside him and comment on whatever it is we are interrupting: *"It looks like you're fitting the last blocks into your tower. Let's close the door to keep it safe while we eat."* With our arm around him, we escort him into some giddy fun of engaged handwashing as we lather up, taking his hands into ours.

Responding this way takes reflection and extra minutes of a busy parent's time. Why not simply force the struggling, screaming kid to come to the table and be done with it?

---

[23] Quoted from Dr. Neufeld's DVD lecture, "Making Sense of Counterwill." Dr. Neufeld's lectures on DVD can be ordered from his website, neufeldinstitute.com where you will find many articles and editorials available free of charge to help deepen your understanding of what's going on when you face a rough spot in your parenting journey. The DVDs are also found in some public libraries.

I aim for this book to provide satisfactory answers to this question as readers come to see the bright and shining futures they have the power to design for themselves.

Helping a child escape from Counterwill is a truly empathic way to preserve peace. Knowing what we are up against, we are able to bypass this powerful instinct and find being a parent pleasant, fascinating and fun!

Note: I'm bringing this up again . . . Active Listening, and other applications of the P.E.T. philosophy are not control strategies. They are ways to Connect with another person.

Active Listening is as much about YOU as about your child. Collecting a child is about Relationship, not about gaining the upper hand. Each time you listen with true empathy and each time you look deeply into your child's eyes, eliciting his cooperation, you nourish your own inner being along with his.

Now as you are moving forward toward a richly satisfying relationship with a child or any number of children, we have two fundamental goals to keep in mind:

1. To strengthen and protect Attachment with everything we say and do.
2. To avoid stimulating Counterwill with whatever we say or do.

This is a formula for happy years ahead!

II

External control is a plague on all humanity.
~ William Glasser

1

FREEDOM FOR PARENTS

If you are struggling and sometimes fighting with your children, it is because, like most Americans and many parents worldwide, you have been taught to think about children and about being a parent in certain culturally-implanted ways. It is deep in your bones to see your responsibility and your duty in terms of CONTROLLING YOUR CHILD.

Human beings are all born with a powerful instinct to resist external control. As described previously, **we are working against human nature when we try to control a child**.

Whether we exert pressure punitively with physical punishments, removal of privileges, isolation, yelling, or other harsh methods or we apply a kinder, gentler strategy, using sticker charts, rewards, and praise; all are control methods and all are counterproductive.

CONTROL IS THE PROBLEM!

A new little person entering our complex society must have certain conditions in order to thrive and be fun and pleasant to live with.

Old attitudes prevent us from appreciating our babies and children as our drive for control gets in the way of seeing them as fully human. **Obsession with**

control blinds us and provokes defensive oppositional behaviors in our children.

At times when we could effectively solve a problem that our child has created for us by calling on our empathy, we fail this inexperienced little person by resorting to punishments or bribes, hoping to extinguish unwanted behaviors.

Behaviorist strategies take our focus away from our child, directing our attention only to his behavior. His needs, his feelings, the very "being" of him, are disregarded in a blind drive to control his actions.

When we can abandon authoritarian control maneuvers to focus our attention on understanding our children's needs while being firmly on their side, living with them becomes easy and fun!

We recognize how to remain in charge of the situation without arousing Counterwill through our attempts to control the feelings and conduct of another human being.

See chapters: BE THE PARENT and MEAN WHAT YOU SAY.

Traditional teachings have failed to offer the necessary understanding and information to enable us to meet an infant's or child's emotional requirements, leaving us bewildered and helpless with this new and different responsibility, while only offering new and different methods of control.

When, as new parents, we suddenly have total physical dominance over another human being, we are faced with a unique challenge. We now have a helpless small person right here in our home on whom we can vent our angers and frustrations.

When the little person causes our frustrations, the situation may become dangerous. We will do well to be mindful of one of the most well-known and enduring quotes of all time:

POWER CORRUPTS AND ABSOLUTE POWER CORRUPTS ABSOLUTELY[24]

Note: For a look into a chilling real-life drama exposing the corrupting influence of power, read about Dr. Philip Zimbardo's 1971 Stanford Prison Experiment on his website. Or see the 2015 movie depicting this famous research project. In his book, <u>The Lucifer Effect: Understanding How Good People Turn Evil,</u>[25] Dr. Zimbardo describes the experimental situation ending with power and control running amok.

In the United States, parents are one of the leading causes of death for children under age five when frustrations with not knowing what to do and failed attempts at control explode into violence. Nearly two thousand children die each year because a caretaker becomes overwhelmed by listening to a baby's crying or with trying to make a child do or not do something the adult sees as necessary.

What is commonly defined as child abuse is an extension of accepted cultural parenting practices carried to an extreme. Slapping becomes spanking. Spanking escalates to beating. As frustration mounts, beating becomes more intense. The child still refuses to use the potty or stay away from an ashtray. A parent tries a cigarette burn to the hand or a shove across the room. This time a little head collides with the corner of a table and a toddler is dead.

ALL BECAUSE DEEP-SEATED BELIEFS WERE DRIVING A FRANTIC PARENT TO DO HIS DUTY AND GET CONTROL OF THIS CHILD.

An abusing mother or father may say they were only administering necessary discipline. They tell us they were beaten regularly as children and they turned out "all right." They describe being raised in a neighborhood where all the kids were treated this way; they expected it, accepted it, and "deserved it."

---

[24] 1887 Lord Acton, British intellectual who devoted his life to the study of freedom.

[25] <u>The Lucifer Effect: Understanding How Good People Turn Evil</u> by Philip G. Zimbardo, Inc., Copyright 2007, Published in the United States by Random House Trade Paperbacks, a division of Random House, Inc., New York, NY. Original published in hardcover in 2007 by Random House, Inc., New York, NY.

Here's the problem:

They remember the part about all their friends being treated the same way and adjusting to it as a normal condition of childhood. The part they don't remember is being hurt at an earlier age when they were too young to justify their fear and pain as somehow acceptable.

Or there were later times when what was being done to them, in the name of discipline, was beyond justification. Without cognitive rationalization and/or a caring adult to listen and empathize, the suffering became wired into their brains, stored there as an accumulation of rage to be carried into adulthood, simmering beneath the surface and bursting to break out when frustration mounts, as it now has, bringing them into the news.

Children, because they are small, helpless, and unable to fight back, become available targets for this uncontainable fury. The American culture and many others worldwide encourage the Child-As-Target response, fueled by Ancient Myths about naturally bad children, our responsibilities as controllers and disciplinarians, and the importance of obedience.

When a young father in Tacoma, Washington has beaten his three-year-old son to death for wetting their shared bed and stands before a judge, he is not standing alone. There in the courtroom with him stands our cultural history of attitudes and beliefs about children. The old myths about obedience and control are etched into this father's brain. On this day, combined with rage from whatever pain and suffering he, himself, endured as a helpless child, they became a lethal mixture ending in murder.

The police, the courts, and the general public blame this one man, who is seen as despicable, and they believe locking him up solves their problem.

WAIT JUST A MINUTE! You opened this book to learn about finding JOY in Parenthood and here I am confronting you with this depressing stuff about child abuse.

As disturbing as it may be to read about adults who kill children, all of us must be fully aware of how a murdering parent's ferocious impulses fit into the continuum of our culturally-established treatment of children, where we ourselves fall on this continuum, and how we got here. This knowledge will help move us forward on our personal journeys into living with children in Peace and Happiness, making the world a better place one person at a time.

We can shed the old blaming/punishing frame of mind and become our own relationship experts, knowing how to create an atmosphere of calm in which adults interact with children in ways that never bring them to the boiling point of unbearable exasperation.

When we give up trying to control our child, we are released from an impossible task and huge frustrations.

In place of Control, we are able to think in terms of Attachment, Needs, and Problem-Solving. Now we have something to hold onto and can move forward without the hopeless goal of gaining dominance.

Parents all over the world have embraced the concepts of Parent Effectiveness Training, given up the losing battle for control, and escaped from the trap of punishments and rewards. You, too, can be liberated to enjoy a hassle-free, satisfying, joyful life with children and the marvelous freedom this brings.

If you are entangled in a power contest with a child, you are certain to be carrying around a load of anger, ready to erupt with each new confrontation, and thwarting sincere attempts to change your parenting approach. Today's difficulties with our kids, piled onto old hurts from our own babyhoods locked up in our brains, can bar our escape to freedom. If the information and suggestions in this book are not enough to transform your life, you may want to seek counseling through Gordon Training International, the Gordon Neufeld Institute, or a counselor near you who is trained in Attachment and Interpersonal Communication.

UNHAPPINESS WITH THE WAY YOUR PARENTING LIFE IS GOING IS NOT AN UNCHANGEABLE CONDITION. NO ONE IS DOOMED TO SETTLE FOR THIS UNFULFILLING WAY OF LIFE.

YOU CAN BEGIN YOUR PERSONAL LIBERATION TODAY!

2

TAKING THE WORK OUT OF PARENTING

HELPING A CHILD GROW UP IS A RELATIONSHIP, NOT A JOB!

The word Parenting entered the dictionary around 1960 when the word Parent became a verb. People who had children had always been called Parents and what they did was called Raising children, Rearing children, or Bringing Up children. We didn't Parent children, we lived with them. We cared for them. Being a parent changed from what can be an enjoyable relationship with a small new human into what became the difficult job of controlling an uncivilized creature with a blank brain to be trained with punishments and rewards. We were henceforth said to Parent our children or to be doing a job called Parenting.

As our entire culture adopted the Behaviorist methods and integrated them into an already firmly-enshrined ideology based on ancient myths and misunderstandings, we rendered ourselves incapable of functioning as loving supporters and teachers of children. Instead, we cast ourselves as enemies and controllers of our young.

With all the rules, punishments, and rewards we were busy establishing, monitoring, and enforcing, living with children became complicated and exhausting work.

> Preoccupied with methods of control, we stopped being human. We lost touch with our natural instincts for tenderness and empathy when we took on the role of Official Parent and worked hard at the difficult job of Enforcer in the home.

While we were busy figuring out how many minutes Bryan should spend in Time-Out for not picking up his toys or how many days to ground Jennifer for coming in 30 minutes after her curfew, our children became alienated from us. Our involvement in the big job of Parenting disconnected the entire enterprise from real-life and from the human needs of our children and ourselves. One reason being a parent can be such hard work is because no one likes being treated the way we have been treating our precious offspring.

Our children have been living under and resisting against a form of chauvinism John Breeding calls ADULTISM. He describes it as follows: *"Adultism is the systematic mistreatment of children and young people simply because they are young. The overall conditioning against emotional expression is laid down through Adultism. The pattern is one of massive disrespect. To test whether you are acting as an agent of oppression, apply the following question to any action you take toward a young person: Would you treat another adult the same way?"*[26]

Alice Miller called it *"The Poisonous Pedagogy."*[27]

Punishments, Authoritarian Control, and Behavior Modification exemplify a general disrespect, distrust, and hostility toward the young, weakening the

---

[26] From the book, <u>The Wildest Colts Make the Best Horses</u> by John Breeding, Copyright 1996, Published by Bright Books, Inc., Austin, TX and Copyright May 3, 2009, Published by Chipmunka Publishing Ltd., The Mental Health Publisher, Cornwall, England, UK.

[27] You can learn all about this world-famous and ground-breaking psychoanalyst on her website, www.alice-miller.com, where her books are listed along with a review of <u>For Your Own Good: Hidden Cruelty in Child-Rearing and the Roots of Violence</u> by Alice Miller, Copyright 1983, 1984, 1990, Published in Canada by Harper Collins Canada Ltd, Printed in the United States of America, Designed by Herbert H. Johnson, Third Edition 1990, Sixth printing, 1994. First published in 1983 by Farrar, Straus and Giroux. This edition first published by Noonday Press.

Attachment Bond, driving our children away from us, making it difficult—and sometimes impossible—for them to follow their instincts for cooperation.

Although your experience with children may suggest any sort of predisposition toward cooperation to be non-existent, we all have it in us to derive satisfaction by cooperating with our fellow humans. The toddler struggling against getting into his car seat was born to cooperate!

After the relationship between parents and their children was given the job title: Parenting, along with this new title came a job description: Difficult and Exhausting.

As our children detached from us and relationships turned into struggles, Parenting books and instructors told us to "discipline" our children. When parents became more exhausted and desperate for help, the same experts added new strategies and gimmicks to their control methods, giving us more work to do and leaving us with our same problems.

The way we talk to children, the words we say to them, the things we do to them, our rigid attitudes make being a parent tedious and stressful.

WE DO THIS TO OURSELVES!

The job of Enforcer in our home becomes a tiresome ordeal we grow to dislike and we may eventually find ourselves disliking our children as well.

> Having read about COUNTERWILL earlier in this book, you already understand how we wear ourselves out when we battle against a powerful instinct our child is as helpless to control as we are.

With new awareness we can work with each child's capacity for positive growth, as we gradually release ourselves and our children from the crippling weight of punishments, rewards, and the control mentality enslaving us.

We escape from the tyranny of beliefs and habits rising from ancient myths about inborn evil and our duties as parents. Appreciating the instinctive positive drives all humans are born with, we find delight and deep satisfaction in witnessing each child's ongoing growth in positive self-direction and solid self-discipline.

Watching the natural blooming of a new human being can be the most fulfilling adventure of your life. When you free yourself from the burden of old beliefs about the JOB OF PARENTING, you will know THE FUN AND JOY OF LIVING WITH CHILDREN as you step aside and allow Nature to do her work.

Note: When trying to decide on a title for this book, I thought about STOP PARENTING AND START LIVING. I knew it could give the wrong impression, as though I'm saying, *"Neglect your kids and go out partying!"* However, as you read through everything I have written, I hope you will come to a point when you know exactly what I mean and feel the thrill of Giving Up the Job of Parenting to Start Living!

3

PARENTS HAVE NEEDS, TOO

Your needs are as important as your child's. You are operating against his best interests, as well as your own, if you give up your needs for his.

An exception occurs during early infancy when you will almost certainly give up some of your need for sleep. And, of course, through all the years of growing up, there will be times when a child's health and happiness take priority over an adult's wants and needs.

Recognizing the difference between needs and wants, for both ourselves and our children, is a major factor in making family life run smoothly. When we arrange our time to accommodate the needs of a baby or a child of any age, we are sometimes giving up adult wants to be able to maintain the regularity and order of daily life.

As much as we may want to run out to pick up something from the grocery store, out of consideration for our child, we wait until after he has had his complete nap.

We quite automatically make adjustments to our time and activities to support our child's healthy physical and emotional development.

However, as we live within the family group, we have our own emotional and physical needs, which our children can learn to respect and help us to meet.

When your child is living without accumulated hurt, anger, and frustration, and when he has been allowed to freely communicate his needs, knowing you are there to help meet them, he will spontaneously help you to meet yours.

With I-Messages for stating needs, you will find your child responding positively as a natural part of his stature as a family member. When he has been listened to and respected, he learns to listen to and respect others. This becomes his normal way of life as he adopts the qualities and the helping language the adults around him are modeling.

Children live what they learn and will learn what they have been exposed to. By growing up within a helping relationship, they become helpers themselves. This is the only way they know how to be.

This way of being can be observed in very young children. Maria Montessori, who based her philosophy on "Respect for the Child," wrote about the emergence of self-direction and the contented cooperation of the toddlers who flourished under her influence, free from punishments or rewards.

Your needs are as important as your child's. We would drift off into Permissiveness if we failed to honor this side of the relationship.

4

HOW CAN I GET MY CHILD TO COOPERATE?

To help find the answer to this question, picture this:

Husband to wife: *"Did you pick up my shirts from the laundry?"*

Wife: *"Oh honey, I was so busy today, I totally forgot to go to the laundry."*

Husband: *"I depended on you to do this one thing for me. I'll tell you what. You can get on the phone and cancel our plans for dinner and a movie with the Johnsons Saturday night. You simply do not cooperate and you need to be taught a lesson."*

As silly or abusive as this may sound when we speak of adults, similar scenes are routine and fully accepted in adult relationships with children.

Now back to your question: *"How can I get my child to cooperate?"*

First, it is vitally important to know that all humans enter this world with an **inborn drive to cooperate**. In 1955, the world famous anthropologist, Ashley Montagu, published The Direction of Human Development: Biological and Social Bases,[28] a 315-page book substantiating this conclusion. The citations for his research fill 35 pages.

---

[28] The Direction of Human Development: Biological and Social Bases by M. F. Ashley Montagu, Copyright 1955, Published by Harper Brothers, New York, NY.

How can this be? *"If humans are genetically designed to cooperate, why are we plagued by endless wars and every imaginable form of violence?"*

Dr. Montegu gave us the answer, now confirmed by modern brain research, in the first paragraph on page 247 in his book, where speaking of biological man, he wrote: *"When social behavior is not cooperative it is diseased behavior."* In the next paragraph he goes on to say: *"Combativeness and competitiveness arise from the frustration of his need to cooperate."*

Back to your question, which now becomes: *"If my child was born with a drive to cooperate, why is he refusing to cooperate with ME?"*

Answer: *"It is you, dear parent, who are failing to cooperate with him."*

Along with the drive to cooperate, all humans come equipped with a powerful instinct to protect us from outside influence. Described earlier as the brain's Counterwill, we know, if for some reason, a parent registers in a child's brain, as an outside influence, cooperation is cut off.

Question: *"Are you saying I should give up and let him have his way?"*

Absolutely not. Putting this understanding to work, you can avoid turning on his brain's Counterwill by not issuing orders and by learning to WORK WITH his natural drive. Your child's willingness and desire to cooperate are strengthened in proportion to the strength of your Attachment bond with him. **The stronger the Attachment, the less his Counterwill perceives you as an outside influence. A firmly connected child looks to the parent for direction.**

In our over-stimulating surroundings, calling out a demand or request to a child over all the competition for his attention leads into frustration and conflict.

This is where our COLLECTING comes in; when we elicit a child's attention by establishing connection, as we get into his space with friendly eye contact, a smile, a nod, and sometimes a touch.

Whether you are a parent, a nanny, a grandparent, a teacher, or anyone in a position to want or need a child's cooperation; COLLECTING A CHILD BEFORE ATTEMPTING TO ENGAGE HIM, PARTICULARLY WHEN SEEKING COOPERATION, IS CRUCIAL TO YOUR SUCCESS.

To solidify your ability to bring out the cooperation you dream of, I refer you back to the chapters on Counterwill, Communication Roadblocks, and I-Messages. Everything you find in this book is devoted to a facet of maintaining strong connections to children and to building relationships in which cooperation is automatic because it comes from the heart.

Now, let's look in on a Problem-Solving couple who have no place for punishments in their relationship. When she tells him she forgot to pick up the clean shirts, it can go like this:

Husband: *"This is terrible. I've got to have a clean shirt for the meeting tomorrow."*

Wife: *"You're feeling frantic. I'll wash and iron a shirt tonight."*

Husband: *"No honey, it needs to have the professional laundry look."*

Wife: *"I've got it! Brent is about your size. I'll call Sally and ask her if we can borrow a laundry-finished shirt from them."*

Husband: *"Good idea. Don't call. I'll run next door and check it out myself."*

The problem gets solved with no threat to Attachment by a punishing reaction from the husband. Although the first scenario was an exaggeration, it would not be unusual for some yelling or door-slamming to occur without a Problem-Solving response to such a dilemma.

Problem-Solving prevents ordinary mistakes and misunderstandings from escalating into anger-driven conflicts. Life is good when natural cooperation becomes the response to the needs of others, whether between two adults or between adults and children.

5

VALUABLE TEACHING IN A QUOTE

Dr. Gabor Maté, co-author of <u>Hold On to Your Kids: Why Parents Need to Matter More Than Peers</u>, has also written <u>SCATTERED: How Attention Deficit Disorder Originates and What You Can Do About It</u>.[29] In it, I see the following paragraph on page 145 to be one of the most important ever written for giving us critical insight into the workings of the developing brain and subsequent behaviors.

"Every child with ADD has been wounded by a disruption in the relationship between the caregiver and the sensitive infant. All the behaviors and mental patterns of attention deficit disorder are external signs of the wound, or inefficient defences against feeling the pain of it. If development is to take place, energy has to be liberated for growth now consumed in protecting the self from further hurt. The key factor is cementing the attachment relationship."

I will change the wording as I see this same analysis applying to any child displaying troublesome behavior:

Every child with disturbing behavior has been wounded by a disruption in the relationship between the caregiver and the sensitive infant. All the behaviors and mental patterns of maladaptive responses are external signs of the wound, or inefficient defences against feeling the pain of it. If

---

[29] <u>Scattered: How Attention Deficit Disorder Originates and What You Can Do About It</u> by Gabor Maté, Copyright 1999, Published by Plume, a member of Penguin Putnam Inc. Previously published in a Dutton edition.

development is to take place, energy has to be liberated for growth now consumed in protecting the self from further hurt. The key factor is cementing the attachment relationship.

Let's you and I think about the wise words in this quote as they relate to an exasperating behavior your child continues to display, no matter how many times you have tried reasoning, spanking, Time-Out, ignoring, removing privileges, or screaming at him. We'll say throwing hard toys is the behavior driving you crazy.

According to this insightful paragraph, **throwing toys is the visible symptom of emotional pain**. His action is an expression of Attachment anxieties depleting the emotional energy needed to cope with ordinary childhood frustrations.

Now we know pouncing on him for throwing toys will only increase his anxiety and add to his inability to handle frustration. With our new knowledge, we see things differently. We are not witnessing a Bad Child doing a bad thing. What we are seeing is a Hurting Fellow Human in great need of relief.

So what can we do?

We interrupt the toy throwing in a comforting way, take him onto our lap, and apply our Active Listening skills, *"Wow, sometimes a kid gets so frustrated he wants to throw things. It isn't always easy being a little boy. I'll bet you could go for a smoothie and cuddling up together with a good book. Let's pick out a book and go make our smoothies!"*

You have stopped the unwanted behavior and applied Attachment first-aid. Nothing more needs to be said about throwing toys. He knows you don't approve, and a lecture or attempts at reasoning will only add to his agitation. Now, with day-after-day attention to his Attachment needs and elimination of any coercive or unkind habits you may have slipped into, his feeling of connection expands, Attachment anxieties are relieved and the pressure he feels to throw things or to act out in other violent ways, fades away.

If you are wondering if this approach rewards "bad behavior," recognize this concern as a hangover from Behaviorist thinking when children's feelings are not understood as the drive behind the things they do.

I want to remind you, too, to remember the Communication Roadblocks[30] and the divisive effect they have on relationships. If you have not torn out the printed lists at the end of this book, to keep somewhere in plain sight, now would be a good time to do this. When we are grappling with difficulties, the Roadblocks obstruct our attempts to bring about change.

---

[30] The Roadblocks are described in the first section of this book and in illuminating detail in the P.E.T. book.

6

RESPECT

THE FOUNDATION FOR EFFECTIVE PARENTING IS RESPECT.

RESPECT IS BEST DESCRIBED BY THE GOLDEN RULE. WHEN WE SAY OR DO EVERYTHING TO OUR CHILDREN THE WAY WE WOULD WANT IT SAID OR DONE TO US, ALL OTHER EFFORTS FALL INTO PLACE AND LIFE BECOMES PLEASANT AND EASY.

Every minute your child is with you, he is learning how to behave from how he sees you behaving. You are his model for becoming a contributing member of the family and of society. If you are respectful toward him, he will learn to be respectful. The stronger his Attachment to you, the more he will want to be like you.

A simple equation:

Your level of respect for your child = your child's level of respect for you.

Do not confuse FEAR with RESPECT. Children can be pressured through fear to treat their parents and other adults with a facade of deference. This may involve the requirement to call adults *"sir"* or *"ma'am,"* as in *"Yes sir"* and *"No ma'am."* Some of the most devious children in my experience have been operating under this type of an enforced protocol.

Do not confuse adult respect for children with gushing sweetness and pampering. Treating a child with the same courtesy we extend to treasured friends is what's called for, and not commonly seen in our culture.

The disrespectful and unkind things parents do to a child eat away at his self-esteem, eroding Attachment, and leaving him incapable of following directions or cooperating. Disruption happens in the Attachment brain and is beyond the child's awareness or control.

No matter how hard we may try, a healthy relationship will remain beyond our grasp if we punish, blame, yell at, shame, or in other ways are disrespectful toward our children.

THE FOLLOWING ARE SOME OF THE ORDINARY WAYS ADULTS DISRESPECT CHILDREN:

- Rudeness
- Ordering
- Hitting or yanking
- Name calling, as in "cry baby"
- Teasing
- Shaming
- Uninvited or aggressive tickling
- Forced holding
- Ignoring
- Interrupting
- Not listening
- Bribing
- Punishing
- Yelling
- Stifling expression, as in "stop crying"
- Coaxing or pressuring to eat
- Speaking condescendingly

- Taking a tiny infant into public places
- Interrupting a baby's sleep to play with him, show him off, or take him out on an errand
- Wheeling a sleeping child around in a shopping cart
- Taking a tired or hungry child shopping
- Answering for a child when someone has addressed him.
- Talking about a child as though he isn't there
- Pressuring a child into unwelcome affection
- Telling a child to say please or thank you in front of another person
- Failing to model good manners while expecting them from a child

When you are out in public, notice other adults being disrespectful to children. Being aware of this ADULTISM will increase your sensitivity and help to prevent you from being similarly disrespectful. Becoming sensitive to the widespread maltreatment of children jolts us into seeing how some children develop undesirable characteristics. They are not inherently bad. They are living what they have learned from the treatment they, themselves, have been subjected to. The disregard they exist under squelches the natural human inclination toward kindness, leaving them angry and feeling mean.

> Comment by a four-year-old boy, following a family gathering: *"Uncle Jack and Uncle Max don't know how to talk to kids. All they do is tease."*

How many of us grownups really do know how to talk to children? I'll bet you remember this from your own childhood: *"How old are you now? What grade are you in?"*

We can do better: *"Hi Kathy. I'm so glad to see you again. The last time I was here, you had just learned to swim. Your mom tells me you've been doing a lot of drawing and painting this summer."* Active Listening can take it from there, leaving no place for our hollow questions.

The disconnected relating and blatant casual disrespect of adults toward children is so firmly entrenched in our culture that we fail to see it. Only with eyes wide open can we face the reality of the ongoing relentless disregard and maltreatment of babies and children of all ages and change our unwholesome ways of regarding them.

BEFORE YOU SAY OR DO ANYTHING TO A CHILD, STOP AND THINK: WOULD I SAY OR DO THIS TO AN ADULT FRIEND?

7

STRUCTURE AND ROUTINE

All babies and children thrive on structure and order in their daily lives. The structure we create becomes the foundation of the discipline we endeavor to achieve. If you are having difficulties with a baby or child of any age, one of the first questions to ask will be about the routine and order you have or have not established.

The daily routine we put in place will emerge from the rhythm of our infant's own biological clock. By adjusting our days to his circadian patterns for eating and sleeping, we will eventually find our time falling into a natural flow for our baby and for ourselves.

I like this quote from the book, Simplicity Parenting: Using the Power of Less to Raise Calmer, Happier and More Secure Kids:[31] *"Parental authority is strengthened by rhythms. There is order here and safety."*

Infants and children prosper on routine and predictability. They may become anxious and irritable without the security of a daily rhythm. Without a sense of "what comes next" they grow fretful and unsettled.

---

[31] Simplicity Parenting: Using the Power of Less to Raise Calmer, Happier and More Secure Kids by Kim John Payne and Lisa M. Ross, Copyright 2010, Published by Ballantine Books, a division of Random House, New York, NY.

When we live up to our child's learned expectations of us, he lives up to ours. When parents do what is expected of them, they are models of discipline and anchors of safety for their children.

What should our child learn to expect from us?

WE WILL DO WHAT WE SAY. WE MEAN WHAT WE SAY.

If we have told our child to always hold hands when crossing a street, we do not stand by and yell at him or punish him when he goes into the street. We absolutely do not allow the conditions to exist for him to go into the street without us. We are with him to hold his hand or he is without access to the street. We do this routinely. He can depend on us to keep him safe.

WE WILL FUNCTION AS HIS LOVING COMPANION AS WE MAINTAIN ORDER IN OUR HOME AND IN HIS LIFE.

We establish a routine for him to depend on and expect.

EXAMPLE:

Breakfast and a period of free self-directed play are followed by a long morning walk or interactive activity if the weather keeps us inside. Next, a warm relaxing bath before lunch and the afternoon nap, in this order, every day. A bath can be worked into the routine either before lunch or before bedtime at night. It is best to have no activity at all between eating lunch and settling down to sleep. Just reading a book at naptime can interrupt the smooth transition into sleep when digestion increases blood supply to the stomach and lessens it to the brain, making sleep come easily. We dress him in sleepwear for a daily nap, safe in his crib or bed. We do this out of respect for his comfort and to reinforce the sleep-time aura.

This becomes his lunch and nap routine.

Note: I expect some parents reading this are thinking, *"Are you telling me to undress my three-year-old and put on his jammies in the middle of the day?"* Well, yes. I am. Don't you think a young child's nap will be more beneficial when he's undressed and in his own cozy bed instead of on the sofa fully clothed and wearing his shoes? In writing this book, my goal is to make your child's life and yours **Fun, Peaceful, Interesting, and Satisfying**. I am not saying anything about convenience. Much of what I recommend is not convenient. It is, however, well worth the inconvenience. In this case, a child who is running short on sleep can never be as light-hearted, healthy, and pleasant to live with as a well-rested one.

Bedtime occurs at the same time each night and follows a calming, relaxing sequence lasting about thirty minutes and performed much the same way every night. Our personal electronics are nowhere within sight or sound and we allow nothing to interrupt this important ritual.

A daily routine, including the afternoon nap, should not be disrupted for adult expedience. We arrange other activities to accommodate a child's need for routine and order. Doctor appointments and other necessary commitments can be scheduled before or after naptimes. The fewer disruptions to the established order of things, the fewer problems we have, aside from this being a matter of regard for the needs of a child.

Knowing what our child will be doing, and when he will be doing it, makes our own days predictable. When we know our toddler or preschooler will be sound asleep every day for a predictable length of time, we are assured of having this interlude for doing whatever we want. The choice is ours: a nap, reading, catching up on the computer, making phone calls, or taking on a project.

Our life becomes much easier when we know what to expect.

Our child is happy and cooperative when he knows what to expect.

Regularity and order greatly enhance a child's sense of safety and trust. A predictable environment fosters physical as well as emotional health, making family life smooth and enjoyable. When days follow a familiar rhythm and children know what comes next, tantrums and stressful crying are minimized or non-existent.

If you have been thinking of your child as "difficult" or describing him to others as an "exhausting handful," the routine I prescribe can change your life substantially. Bringing order to his world with daily walks and slowing yourself down to find pleasure in giving your little child a warm soothing bath in the middle of the day will have a stabilizing effect on his nervous system and change your description of him from difficult to delightful.

Although this all sounds fine and good for parents who have chosen to stay at home with their children, what about parents who prefer to work outside the home or who have no choice?

Daycare options are not always ideal in the United States or in many other countries. Although some parents are lucky enough to have a grandparent available to take over their baby's care, this circumstance is becoming increasingly rare in today's mobile society.

You may find a good fit for your family with a senior citizen who can step in and become your child's long-term caregiver. A retired schoolteacher or other healthy active senior living alone, family far away, may miss being around children and be delighted to spend each day caring for your child. With a steady income from Social Security and possibly a pension, too, such a person can establish the security of a long-term lasting bond with your child at a reasonable cost to you and go on maintaining whatever routine you establish.

For folks who can afford the luxury of a professional nanny, finding the right fit for your family may take a little time. If you have embraced the philosophy I've put forth here, it will be essential to find someone who will understand and believe in your parenting values.

> Anyone you pay to come into your home and care for your child must be willing and committed enough to honor the daily plan you want followed, not to include pushing the stroller to the nearest coffee shop to socialize or engage with an electronic device while ignoring your baby.

I caution parents to look deeply into the character and background of any person being considered for taking over the care of an infant or a child of any age.

If daycare becomes the answer to your requirements, you will find most to be following a daily schedule. In this case, a regular routine for the hours you spend with your child will strengthen his sense of security and make life easier for you.

Create a brief everyday ritual for leaving your child as you drop him off at daycare or preschool, such as a good hug, saying similar parting words each day and always mentioning your return.

When you pick him up, force yourself to slow down with a few deep breaths and some soothing self-talk. Children coming out of daycare or school need three main things: connecting, a protein snack, and stress release.

If there happens to be a park on your way home, and weather permits, this can be an ideal place to enjoy a snack and run off stress. At home, children may have fun stretching and bending and/or relaxing into togetherness over cups of a soothing warm beverage.

This enjoyable re-connecting will help set the tone for the evening with the togetherness of a pleasant meal and, later, a well-established bedtime ritual.

Sustaining routine may be quite a challenge when children enter grade school and become involved in a variety of activities. It remains important to their sense of stability and grounding to maintain whatever rituals can be designed into increasingly busy schedules.

Sitting down to eat together as many evenings as possible is well worth whatever planning and effort it takes to make it happen. Adding ritual to dinnertime deepens Attachment and the comfort level of the gathering. Eating by candlelight brings a sense of relaxation and serenity to this time together. Children old enough to light candles delight in being given this responsibility. You may want to go further by having a family member read a poem before meals. Saying grace adds meaningful ritual for some families. And, without question, the dinner table is no place for electronics of any kind.

Children of all ages gain stability from whatever routines and customs we can provide. Some level of bedtime ritual remains important all through the elementary school years.

A teenager will draw security from the simple formality when a parent turns down the bed covers each night with an end-of-the-day comment, such as, *"Sleep well, sweetie. I have blueberry muffins for your breakfast."*

Structure and routine ward off anxiety, a burgeoning threat to the well-being of both adults and children in our modern times.

Rituals and family rhythms help keep the chaos of the outside world where it belongs: Outside.

Note: With all my talk about self-direction and freedom, isn't my recommendation for establishing routine contradictory?

If a family lives on a remote farm or makes their home in the wilderness without television or video games, their children homeschooled and untouched by public school competition, tests, grades, and bullying, or by daycare stresses; perhaps we could leave Mother Nature in charge of their daily rhythms. However, life for urban children has become so unsettled and hectic that one of the best things we can do for them is to give them stability and tranquility through routine.

8

SELF-ESTEEM

We heard a lot about self-esteem in the 60s and 70s when professionals, with their new emphasis on Parenting, were writing about the importance of building a child's self-esteem as a way to prevent the problems more and more children were exhibiting.

This was the time when we started seeing bumper stickers:

Douglas Elementary Honor Student!

Proud Parent of a Gifted Child

I first saw such bumper stickers in Dallas, Texas and could only wonder at the sick irony of cars with bumper stickers, calculated for building children's self-esteem, outside the schools, while inside, kids from first grade to high school graduation were being hit with wooden paddles.[32]

Although advertising about a child's accomplishments is intended to bolster self-esteem, this is not where it comes from. I have known children with real self-esteem who rejected bumper sticker praise. One such young man told his mother he did not want a bumper sticker bragging about him.

---

[32] In 2004, the Dallas Independent School District eliminated paddling as a control method. This change in policy did not change state law. Corporal punishment continues in most Texas school districts.

Praise works against the development of self-esteem, directing attention away from the Self of a child to focus on his accomplishments. Praising children for the pictures they draw, good report cards, or picking up their toys recognizes them as worthy because of something they have done.

I go more deeply into the question of praise in Section 7.

WE WANT OUR CHILDREN TO KNOW THEY ARE PRECIOUS TO US SIMPLY BECAUSE THEY EXIST. OUR DELIGHT IN HAVING THEM IN OUR WORLD MUST NEVER BE CONTINGENT UPON ANYTHING THEY MAY SAY OR DO.

Labels, too, are damaging to self-worth. Whether we tell children they are smart or call them stupid, applaud athletic ability or declare them clumsy, either way; we impose judgment. With our praise, children will come to see our positive evaluations as leaving them open to our negative judgments as well. We overstep the boundaries of individual personhood when we presume to define a child with a label.

Books are written and Parenting programs are based on labels, such as The Strong-Willed Child, Picky Eaters, Stubborn Toddlers. Please restrain yourself from telling a neighbor, asking your pediatrician, or thinking to yourself about your child as identified by any such labels. I expect after reading about Counterwill you now understand what's behind much of this thinking. It comes from folks who are butting their heads against Counterwill and interfering with children's rights to make choices about their own behaviors.

Over the years, each new flurry of articles and campaigns for building children's self-esteem has produced an angry backlash. Traditional thinkers complain and find fault with the entire concept. We hear hateful, disparaging media commentary about efforts to *"protect the psyches of the little darlings."* This is always said in a tone dripping with sarcasm and disgust. I find the attitude to be plainly scary. Aren't children truly our little darlings? If not, what are they? Isn't it important to protect their mental health and emotional development? Well, not if you believe humans are inherently evil and letting our guard down by being too kind and considerate of babies and children invites them to walk all over us.

A large segment of the population sees things this way. The ancient undercurrent of distrust and outright disdain for the young colors the thinking of all members of society, including the few of us who are trying to change.

Children look for the measure of their worth in the mirror of a parent's eyes. What they see there; closeness or distance, warmth or cold, engagement or distraction, acceptance or rejection, determines how they see themselves.

A sense of self-worth flourishes with the freedom to say Yes or No to us and when what we are asking is truly necessary, to have the right to air objections and have them acknowledged and thoughtfully considered by an empathic listener.

Self-confidence is reinforced—and curiosity along with it—when children's questions are taken seriously and are answered honestly with no question rebuffed as something children should not ask about. *"You are too young to know"* is not a legitimate response. If they are old enough to ask, they are old enough to know. We show respect by answering at their level of understanding and stage of maturity. If we don't know how to answer, we can tell them we need time to think about their question so we can give them an accurate answer.

Public library shelves are loaded with books for answering children's questions on just about anything they can possibly ask, at any age, from toddlers to teens.

Answering questions honestly when they come up brings along a nice little fringe benefit for you. It eliminates the Big Sit-Down Discussion for trying to explain "where babies come from."

We keep curiosity alive by answering children's questions and honoring their curious minds. I am thinking of only one situation when we may, possibly, steer away from answering questions. If you sometimes find yourself caught in an unending barrage of *why* questions and, after each sensible answer, you hear *Why?* once again, you are probably there in body only with a kid trying to pull you in on a string of questions. Now's a time to say you've run out of answers, sweep the clutter from your mind and bring your whole self into authentically Being There for your child and deepening communication.

As for curiosity, the internet lists several articles explaining why it is as important as intelligence, along with the Albert Einstein quote: *"I have no special talent. I am only passionately curious."*

When curiosity is respected and personhood is allowed to develop free from the weight of criticism, punishments, rewards, and love-withdrawal manipulations, children can grow up seeing themselves as worthwhile individuals.

Self-esteem thrives when kids know they are accepted just the way they are. They are never required to behave or to perform in certain prescribed ways to earn our acceptance. Being viewed, since the day they were born, as individuals equal in humanity to the adults surrounding them, they can experience themselves as valuable beings and self-worth grows from inside without extrinsic design.

A secure sense of Self blooms when a baby knows the adults in his life enjoy holding him, rocking him, reading to him, playing with him, cuddling him. . . being with him.

It flourishes when he feels firmly connected to at least one caring adult who listens to him and fortifies their bond with understanding and awareness.

The seeds of self-esteem were in him when he was born. They grow and blossom with loving attention to his needs and respect for him as a unique human being.

Self-esteem emerges when, from infancy onward, a child has been allowed to express his needs and voice his feelings. He has learned that the adults he is dependent upon take him seriously and will respond with patience and kindness.

His self-esteem develops along with his autonomy.

Here's what Thomas Gordon tells us on page 40 of the P.E.T. book:

"When parents learn to demonstrate through their words an inner feeling of acceptance toward a child, they can be influential in his learning to accept and like himself and to acquire a sense of his own worth. They can greatly facilitate his developing and actualizing the potential with which he was genetically endowed. They can accelerate his movement away from dependence and toward independence and self-direction."

Our cultural habits provide unlimited ways to wreck a child's self-image and leave him lacking in self-esteem. The destruction is done with punishments, words, and looks eliciting shame.

Janie spills her milk. *"Oh Janie! You are so clumsy."*

Rob is sawing a piece of wood. *"Here, give me the saw. You're doing it all wrong."*

Julia's coat is on a chair. *"How many times do I have to tell you to hang up your coat? Are you too lazy to do this one little thing?"*

Mark brings home his report card. *"There's not an A or B on here. You'll never amount to anything."*

Jacob left his father's tools out in the rain. *"This is unacceptable. You are grounded for a week."*

Our heritage provides a variety of stock responses to any and all types of childish behaviors: *"What's wrong with you?" "What will the neighbors think?" "You'll never learn."*

And the most cutting of all: *"Shame on you."*

Negative criticism and punishments make children feel worthless. We trample on self-esteem when we trivialize or contradict a child's feelings or perceptions:

"Brrrr I'm cold." "How can you be cold? You're wearing your heavy jacket."

"I'm scared, Mama." "There's nothing to be afraid of."

"I'm hungry." "We just ate."

The cost to a society is incalculable when large numbers of a population are lacking in self-esteem and suffering under a load of self-hate with the potential to be expressed in any number of anti-social, and/or self-destructive behaviors.

For their healthy emotional development, children need to feel appreciated. Adult acceptance of them must never have anything to do with their talents, abilities, accomplishments, physical endowments, or their behaviors.

Carl Rogers called this an attitude of *UNCONDITIONAL POSITIVE REGARD.*

Gabor Maté and Gordon Neufeld call it *THE INVITATION TO EXIST IN OUR PRESENCE.*

ADDENDUM TO SELF-ESTEEM

Our expectations have a profound effect on our children and have become an ongoing subject of research since 1963 when psychology professor Robert Rosenthal confirmed his suspicions about this powerful effect in a rat laboratory by posting signs on the cages of the rats, declaring some to be "maze bright" and others to be "maze dull." Although all the rats had no known intellectual differences and had come from the same supplier, in the hands of the unsuspecting lab assistants, performance of the "smart" rats was superior to what the rats labeled "dull" were able to do. With this initial confirmation of his supposition, Dr. Rosenthal, along with his colleague, Lenore Jacobson, went on to set up a similar experiment in an elementary school.

When they gave a list of names of randomly-selected students to the teachers, falsely identifying them as children on the brink of intellectual blooming, like the laboratory rats, the supposedly superior kids lived up to teacher expectations and blossomed.

This famous research study is described in the book, <u>Pygmalion in the Classroom: Teacher Expectations and Pupils' Intellectual Development.</u>[33]

Whatever the lab workers or the teachers did to bring about superior learning, was done unintentionally without their knowing they were doing it.

---

[33] <u>Pygmalian in the Classroom: Teacher Expectations and Pupils' Intellectual Development</u> by Robert Rosenthal, Ph.D. and Lenore Jacobson, Ed.D., First Copyright 1968, Published by Holt, Rinehart and Winston, Inc., Austin, TX.

In applying this knowledge to life with our own children, we can see the difference between telling a child he is "smart" and relating to him the way we would relate to anyone we see as being intelligent.

So we have a problem, don't we? This is not something we can contrive. To be effective, our positive expectations must be deeply held, transmitted unintentionally, and picked up by our child at a subconscious level.

Why am I telling you this if I can give you no formula for deliberately communicating positive expectations?

What I can tell you is this: When children grow up with the freedom to be who they were born to be, accepted as unique fellow humans worthy of our unwavering respect and support; their development will be so fascinating and pleasing to us that the flow of positive expectations from us to them will be as automatic as the beating of our hearts.

III

*If our American way of life fails
the child, it fails us all.*

~ Pearl S. Buck

1

JOANNE SWEENEY

I can almost hear what some readers will say about the ideas in this book. I expect many will think it all sounds like wishful thinking or pie-in-the sky daydreaming to believe kids can ever be as easy to live with as I claim.

I had a taste of this scepticism when my son was growing up under the influence of the P.E.T. philosophy. People would tell me how lucky I was to have such a well-behaved child.

My "luck" was in having been introduced to Parent Effectiveness Training!

I have known one person who was the personification of the P.E.T. way of life without ever having heard about Thomas Gordon or attended a Parenting class of any kind. Her intuitions and her healthy instincts were so firmly aligned with Human Nature that she automatically related to her growing children with respect and unconditional acceptance.

Joanne Sweeney was this person.

When I met her, she and husband Ed had five children. The youngest was four and the eldest was twelve—three boys and two girls. I spent a lot of time with the Sweeney family in a variety of situations. On picnics, play times in parks, in my home or theirs, at large or small gatherings of friends. In homes or on outings, each Sweeney child was delightful to be around. Not once was there discord or unpleasantness of any kind. All interactions between mother and child, father and child, or between the children themselves, were easy and agreeable. Each child could be seen as a living example of responsibility, self-confidence, and congeniality without the bickering, put-downs, and sarcasm common in so many families and among groups of children.

This had nothing to do with luck. Their harmony was the result of the secure, relaxed, easy relationship Joanne had established with each child. There were no punishments or bribes to interfere with their Attachments as they enjoyed being together without struggle or strain.

The enviable lifestyle I describe did not come about by chance. Joanne's five children would not all have been born, "good natured." Their admirable personalities grew under the influence of parents who related to them as equals in their humanity and without manipulations of control.

Some of us, most of us, must make a deliberate effort to overcome deeply-rooted attitudes toward children, the false beliefs supporting them, and the control mentality we have absorbed from the prevailing culture. If we have not yet developed our natural instincts for empathic parenting, we can still be like Joanne Sweeney.

WE CAN LEARN AND WE CAN CHANGE!

2

IS HE A GOOD BABY?

As a new parent, this is one of the first things a friend or neighbor may ask you.

"Is he a good baby?"

The world would be a better place if everyone knew there is no such thing as a "good" baby.

And there is no such thing as a bad baby.

Each baby enters the world with his one-of-a-kind characteristics and full of wonderful innate possibilities, ready to start unfolding according to nature's design.

The friendly questioner is really asking if your baby eats and sleeps when you want him to and isn't "too much trouble."

Some babies are born with an easygoing nature. Others are sensitive and naturally high-strung. Some have difficulties adjusting to life outside the womb. Some settle in easily.

Neither is good. Neither is bad.

By being aware and nurturing a secure Attachment in our baby's first weeks and months, we get to know and appreciate this unique little person and to enjoy him for who he is.

If our baby isn't eating or sleeping when and how we think he should, we find out why and make the necessary adjustments to our expectations or to meeting his needs. This is our responsibility and our baby's days will become regular and peaceful when we can stay friendly and respectful, learning to take our cues from him, while we figure it all out.

The idea of Good Baby or Bad Baby is out of tune with our modern understanding of infants and children. It represents ancient superstitions and beliefs about human nature and dangerous misunderstandings about our responsibilities as caretakers, nurturers, and protectors of the young.

There was a time in our history when babies who cried a lot were believed to be possessed by evil spirits or the devil. Some readers may believe this today.[34]

If anyone in your life is telling you your child is possessed by the devil or demonic forces, I implore you to look beyond such thinking. I can assure you, with the information you find in this book, my other suggested resources or, perhaps, professional help, you and your baby or older child can find peace and happiness living together and forget all about evil spirits.

We create a lot of trouble for ourselves and for our babies if we begin our parenting adventures thinking in terms of good, bad, or evil.

And so, if a well-meaning person should ask this question, we can be prepared with an accurate answer: *My baby is an amazing work of nature with unique qualities and capabilities. I'll be here to help him make the most of them as we live and learn* together.

---

[34] Janet Heimlich explores this way of thinking in her book, <u>Breaking Their Will</u>: <u>Shedding Light on Religious Child Maltreatment</u>, Copyright 2011, Published by Prometheus Books, Amherst, NY. To read about Janet's work on behalf of children, please see her website at The Child-Friendly Faith Project.

3

PACIFIERS

For many years, pacifiers were looked upon with disfavor and babies were rarely, if ever, seen with one through the early 1900s.

Now, as modern life speeds up and parents get busier and busier, it has become quite common to see a baby or an older child with a pacifier. This can be interpreted as a negative consequence of the hectic times we live in.

We can easily sympathize with the benign intentions behind using a pacifier to quiet a fussing baby or to accommodate the pacifier dependence of a toddler or a three-year-old.

Here's the problem:

It is not helpful in the long run to quiet a baby by plugging his mouth with an artificial nipple. He communicates his needs and displays his feelings with the sounds he makes and his facial expressions. By putting a pacifier in his mouth we are saying to him, *"I don't want to hear what you have to say. What you are feeling or trying to tell me is not important. My need for you to be quiet is what's important."*

This object to suck on works for us, as it quiets him and frees us from further immediate involvement with him. It appears as though we have done a good thing for our baby and "made him happy" by quieting him for now.

Appearances can be deceiving. What we really do with a pacifier is distract a baby from his own inner voice by directing his focus to his mouth and his sucking sensations. We shut off attention to physical and emotional signals at a time when nature has arranged for him to learn to interpret them for himself and communicate them to the people in his world.

With this object in his mouth, he succumbs to stifling his emotional signals and becomes disconnected from himself. We may sometimes see evidence of this disconnection in the zoned-out expression of a baby sucking on a pacifier.

Besides shutting a baby off from his inner cues, the pacifier sets up the parents for tuning out their child's early efforts to communicate. By cutting off his attempts to reach them with his vocalizations, parents miss important moments for being there for their baby and, instead, reinforce his helplessness at times when he needs their support for development of his self-confidence through their attuned interaction.

Little by little his early cries, murmurs, grunts, grimaces, smiles, and range of expressions become the language a tuned-in caregiver learns to interpret and respond to. This level of early communication, with adult recognition of his feelings, is fundamental to building a secure bond. Attention to an infant's verbal cues and crying is as consequential to the Attachment process as carrying him in a sling.

Stifling expression is one of the standard ways children have been controlled and their feelings dismissed as unimportant.

As we ignore and shut down a child's expression of needs and feelings with a pacifier, he is conditioned to repress them himself.

Babies have legitimate reasons for crying and fussing. We suppress their natural expression of feelings with pacifiers and with our commands to be quiet. Our control of a child by putting a pacifier in his mouth eventually becomes a method of control he uses for bottling up his emotions himself. His healthy emotional development and sense of security depend on his being able to go through and freely express his feelings, not in stifling them.

Habitual dismissal of feelings and needs, begun in infancy and continued through childhood, interferes with and may block emergence of the autonomous Self.

If a pacifier becomes the addictive companion to a toddler or an older child, family members begin to feel uneasy and may launch into efforts to break the habit. This can turn into a painful ordeal for all concerned. Such a predicament can be completely avoided by not using a pacifier to begin with.

Our goal is to strengthen Attachment and support fluent interaction. To do this, we eliminate all types of manipulation and control. A pacifier interferes with a baby's emerging ability to express himself and the building of his self-worth with acknowledgement of his early efforts at communication.

Pacifiers can be damaging to the emotional and physical health of a child by repressing the important stress release function of crying. Dr. Aletha Solter analyzes the difficulties caused by pacifiers in her book, <u>Tears and Tantrums: What to Do When Babies and Children Cry</u>.[35]

A baby is born with the sucking instinct for taking nourishment to survive. A plastic nipple put into his mouth for adult convenience, not for consuming nourishment, is disrespectful of the natural organism of the child.

If you are pregnant and planning to deliver your baby in a hospital, it will be wise to tell everyone in the maternity ward, from your doctor to the nursery attendants, to not put a pacifier in your baby's mouth. If he cries, he needs feeding or a clean diaper or to be held. They must be responsible for meeting his needs or bringing him to you to take care of. They have no right to repress his natural expressions of distress or needs with a pacifier.

---

[35] <u>Tears and Tantrums: What to Do When Babies and Children Cry</u> by Aletha J. Solter, Ph.D., Copyright 1998, Published by Shining Star Press, Goleta, CA.

If, for his own very personal reasons, your baby needs additional sucking beyond breast or bottle feedings, only he will know this and will find his own very personal solution right there on his hand when he slips his thumb into his mouth. This is nothing for a parent to be concerned about. If you thought it was, please proceed to eliminate it from the list of things to worry about under the heading, Obsolete Old Parenting Job. With loving responses to a baby's physical and emotional needs, the phase usually passes before it becomes a way to stuff feelings and turns into a habit.

Note: In 2014 a new type of pacifier hit the market when a toy company introduced a baby bounce seat with an attached iPad holder. Parent groups, child advocates and professionals in child development are calling for removing it from the market. Whatever happens, this is a clear example of profits taking precedence over the welfare of children and of the toxic environment surrounding them.

Our responsibilities for the care and keeping of our young receive little support from the prevailing culture.

OUR MINDFULNESS IS THEIR BEST PROTECTION.

4

DON'T WEAR YOUR BABY TO TARGET

...or to Home Depot, a shopping center, Trader Joe's, a movie theater, a baseball game, or to any other crowded public place.

The idea of carrying an infant in a sling against the mother's breast has been advanced as a way to get back to our maternal roots. As vital as we now know this closeness to be, wearing babies out and about in today's high-powered urban environments poses a risk to their forming brain circuitry.

Rattling shopping carts, speaker systems, masses of people and the noisy hubbub in busy commercial settings expose a baby to an overload of sensory input. In addition to negative long-term effects from the assault on his senses during this delicate neurological wiring process, treating a helpless infant this way is fundamentally disrespectful.

Tiny and as easily toted about as he may be, this is a human being who deserves our thoughtful consideration. The fact that he is sleeping, or not noisily protesting, is not reason to believe he isn't being stressed. Some infants do protest and we hear them in all sorts of crowded public places. With or without a baby's distress signals, it is unfair to treat him this way when his true need is for quiet, serene surroundings. If at all possible, parents are advised to plan their schedules and make arrangements for the other parent or a sitter to stay at home with the baby when errands are to be run.

Writing this has had me thinking about the introduction of Attachment Parenting, an important development in the world of Parent Training. Only a small percentage of mothers had been breast-feeding and fewer ever thought of carrying an infant in a sling against the body before this movement got going.

Here I must mention a pitfall in Attachment Parenting. The recommendations to breastfeed, carry babies in slings, hold, hug, be accepting and involved have all been tremendously helpful in moving us forward into a more humane, healthy, and satisfying mode. However, risk lies in a parent's thinking that wearing a baby in a sling or sleeping with him takes care of everything and precludes other needs, particularly the need for quiet surroundings. And, too, when out and about, a sling is no protection from the hurt of a baby's needs being ignored while a parent is taking care of business.

Organizing our days and scheduling our time to accommodate the needs of our infant will prevent future hassles and upsets, setting the stage for finding our lives as parents to be enjoyable and peaceful.

In his highly acclaimed book, <u>The Betrayal of the Self: The Fear of Autonomy in Men and in Women</u>,[36] psychoanalyst Arno Gruen presents to us a well-defined picture of the circumstances through which humans achieve autonomy and the importance of protecting infants from overstimulation in the early stages of growth. On page 9 he writes: *"A mother who intuitively protects her child from being flooded by stimuli is planting the seeds from which self-motivated learning can grow."*

We find protecting our child's developing nervous system to be well worth whatever planning it takes to maintain his tranquil surroundings all day, every day.

---

[36] <u>The Betrayal of the Self: The Fear of Autonomy in Men and in Women</u> by Arno Gruen, Copyright 1986, Published by Grove Press, New York, NY.

A calm, stress-free environment sets the stage for the healthy brain development we wish to advance.

Being a parent is easy and fun when our time is spent with a well-settled, contented little person.

5

SENSORY OVERLOAD

Evolution has not prepared a baby's or young child's nervous system for the quantity or quality of sensory input from today's ever-accelerating commercial, electronic, and entertainment worlds.

An infant starts life with a brain constructed and ready to be wired in response to interactions with his caretakers and to his immediate surroundings.

A newborn baby needs, at minimum, a six-month period in a steady, quiet, peaceful atmosphere with one sensitive, aware, and responsive caregiver. **Each additional month and year in a protected, stable environment better prepares him for life.**

Quoting from page 95 in the book, <u>Scared Sick: The Role of Childhood Trauma in Adult Disease</u>:[37] *"Our culture is still largely blind to the sensitivity of the human nervous system, particularly as it is being formatively built."*

To protect this delicate process, we must find ways to shield our infants and children from overstimulation. Many of the venues we have come to see as ordinary and part of daily living are too much for an infant's or young child's nervous system to accommodate in a healthy way.

---

[37] This is an important book for all parents and for everyone interested in new neurological findings about the underlying causes of bad health.

I'm thinking of the confusion and nerve-shattering noise, masses of merchandise, and crowds of people in large stores or huge shopping centers. The overload of sensory input from a big grocery store, a Target, or any busy commercial setting can throw a baby's or any young child's nervous system into chaos with resulting immediate difficulties and/or lasting neurological harm.

Eating in a restaurant can be too much to handle for a small child and may create distress and conflict for all concerned. Taking babies and young children into places where guests are expected or required to sit still and be quiet is unfair to children and to other guests.

Although placing a baby in front of television or occupying children with other electronic pacification may give parents much-needed time for attending to chores, the effect on the brain is in opposition to the healthy development we hope to sustain.

Parents will reap lasting rewards by resisting the convenient sitting services of a TV set, a DVD, or some sort of small screen device when they take their child's developmental needs into consideration and arrange for a sitter or for one parent to care for children while the other attends to various responsibilities or runs errands.

As restricting as this may seem, it is one of the adjustments we can make for the protection of our children's nervous systems and healthy brain development. The more willing we are to make adaptations in lifestyle for the needs of our infants and children, the easier and more problem-free life with them will be as the months and years go by.

Older children, as well as toddlers and infants, need protection from sensory bombardment. Fast-paced games, TV, and DVD visuals jangle nervous systems and interfere with normal brain development and natural disciplined behavior.

Most TV programs and videos marketed to children are much too frenetic for a child's healthful viewing. Such media are not designed with your child's mental health in mind. Rather, they foster addiction, prompting ongoing purchasing of similar products and the compulsive viewing of intoxicating games, DVDs, and TV shows. Your child's brain is being accosted in the service of profits by the manufacturers of video games and DVDs, along with the sponsors of TV programs aimed at kids. Please read <u>Irresistible: The Rise of Addictive Technology and the Business of Keeping Us Hooked</u> by Adam Alter.[38]

Large grocery stores are unfavorable environments for kids. Stacks of products in boxes designed to entice them with cartoon figures and colorful pictures of sugary contents excite the senses and create dissonance. Today's big toy stores and toy departments bombard them with too much sensory input for developing brains to process healthfully.

For a variety of reasons, it is best to leave children at home when we go shopping. If there are two or more adults in the home, life will be easier for children and adults alike when one person stays home to look after the youngsters while another goes shopping. A single parent may be able to trade sitting times with another single parent. A neighbor may be glad to stay with children for a few hours in exchange for help with a chore or an appreciated favor. A senior citizen may delight in the company of youngsters and look forward to helping out for an hour or two. A child may enjoy playing at a friend's house for a few hours while parents are out and about getting shopping done and enjoying a short break from household concerns.

When possible, we can streamline our shopping by going alone while our children are in daycare or school. When it can be arranged, shopping alone gives a busy parent a solitary break, affording a little personal time for browsing or a leisurely cup of coffee before getting back into the day's responsibilities.

A single mother on her own, with no support system and no way to shop without her child or children, may be ready to throw this book out the window! What am I talking about?

---

[38] <u>Irresistible: The Rise of Addictive Technology and the Business of Keeping Us Hooked</u> by Adam Alter, Copyright 2017, Published by Penguin Press, an imprint of Penguin Random House LLC, New York, NY.

Can I make life easier for her?

I feel confident in assuring her <u>she has the power</u> to take much of the stress out of her life. If she is shopping after work, her first step will be to restore connection when she picks up her baby or young child from a caretaker or older children from school. No matter how rushed and pressured she feels, finding a quiet place to hold a baby in her arms or connect with older children for a few minutes to relax into Attaching will ease her stress as well as theirs. Five minutes isn't going to make a difference in the grand scheme of things and will make a huge difference in the here and now. Remembering to meet a child's three pressing needs after a long day of being apart: Attachment, Stress-Release, and Protein, she can minimize possible difficulties by connecting and providing a protein snack. In a store, with her baby in the grocery cart, or an older child or children walking, at the start of any wining or tears, she can stop and make solid eye-to-eye contact along with a bit of Active Listening, *"You wish you were in your cozy chair at home right now. We'll be there soon!"*

Staying attuned and calmly responding to signs of stress is not only essential to a youngster's sense of connection, this level of responsiveness makes life easier for the busiest of parents.

A single mom is subject to a degree of pressure others have no way of understanding. Her screaming six-month-old in a shopping cart is one tiny clue to her daily challenges.

I want to help her to see a screaming child as a small human in dire need, instead of a little tyrant bent on driving her crazy. I want her to know she can change what seems like an impossible situation into an invitation to her empathy and personal fulfillment.

From his seat in the shopping cart, her baby's brain is working at top capacity to assimilate the sights and sounds of this public place and, at the same time, hungering for physical closeness and recognition from a mother just out of reach.

If a baby could put his needs into words, instead of screaming, he would say, *"Help me, Mama! Please pick me up, hold me close and tell me everything's all right! Let me know you'll help me handle this."*

Turning her COMPLETE FOCUS OF ATTENTION to her baby, picking him up and holding him close, letting him know she understands his distress may be exactly what he needs to get him through until her shopping is done. Whatever is going on in his little brain; his well-being is best served by getting him home as soon as possible where he and Mom can both relax.

Let's now consider another common Shopping-With-Baby tableau. I invite you to picture Mother pushing a grocery cart, Father walking beside her with a baby strapped to his chest facing forward. When we first notice them, the baby is happily taking in the experience and returning the smiles of shoppers, some of whom address him with affectionate baby talk and comment on his engaging personality.

Suddenly the baby's mood changes from happy enjoyment to one of squirming and fussing. Mother continues selecting items from the shelves and Daddy begins jiggling and bouncing the baby, attempting to quiet his fussing, which soon turns into full-blown crying.

What has happened? Why isn't this baby continuing to be a sweet attraction for the other shoppers instead of a problem for his father?

I think you know.

He has reached the limits of his ability to cope. Jiggling is not going to help him. What's a father to do? Or a mother?

Assuming this couple arrived here by automobile, one of them can finish buying groceries while the other takes the baby to the car, relieving him of sensory input and allowing his neurological activity to slow down. If they arrived on foot or bicycle, I would hope they can get away from the hubbub of the store in some out-of-the-way spot. Releasing him from the sling, cradling him in loving arms, holding him close, and talking softly in an Active Listening way may help to settle him. If not, we now see his crying as nature's way to drain away the toxins of his stress. Although distracting him with toys or goofy vocalizations may quiet him, without physiological purging through the shedding of tears, the toxins will remain in his system.[39]

I have not taken into account any other possible contributing factors. Mom and Dad will know if he has gone past a feeding or is usually sound asleep by this time of day or night and can respond accordingly. There's no doubt this baby would have been better off if only one parent had gone out to buy groceries while the other remained at home with the little fellow in quiet familiar surroundings.

As much fun as it can be to show off a darling baby, and as much as he may initially enjoy the outing, the assault to his nervous system is too high a price to pay. The cost to his mental health and subsequent consequences to the family are not worth it.

Maintaining regularity and limiting outings with children to times when they are well rested and fed will go a long way toward making any parent's days fun instead of difficult and exhausting. With growing awareness, we see the need to create a calming environment within the home by limiting the number of playthings and belongings surrounding our children and by protecting them from electronic assaults to their senses.

With deliberate thoughtfulness, we can design for ourselves and for our kids, a lovely harmonious way-of-life.

---

[39] The importance of discharging stress toxins through crying is explained in the book, Tears and Tantrums: What to Do When Babies and Children Cry by Aletha Solter.

6

PLAY

Play is the business of your child, and it is the serious business of preparing him for life. As he experiments and explores on his own, his experiences further the ongoing structuring of his brain. As first begun through interactions with the adults in his life and observations of his physical environment, brain development now continues through play.

Free independent play is essential for crawlers, toddlers, and preschool children. Through free play they learn about themselves; what they can do and how to go about doing it. They discover and test their natural abilities while developing self-confidence and competence.

<u>Free independent play structures the brain for academic learning later on, after age six.</u> In Finland, with the most highly-rated education system in the world, formal education is not begun until age seven.

Children become the most deeply involved when free to play in their own way without adult interference, instructions, or warnings. They need only a few age-appropriate playthings conducive to experimentation, creativity, and exploration.

Sturdy wooden cars and trucks, stacking and nesting sets, and a few books made for their age group provide many hours of intense play for a crawler or a toddler.

Dolls, stuffed animals, plastic or wooden figures of animals and people stimulate the imagination.

A good set of wooden blocks in all shapes, sizes, and colors can engage children for days at a time, from toddlerhood all the way into school-age.

A large cardboard box brought home from the grocery store is a fine starting point for all sorts of imaginative play. Boxes of all sizes provide hours of creativity and satisfaction. Starting in toddlerhood, kids can find hours of focused engagement with an assortment of household odds and ends such as the cardboard tubes from paper towels and toilet tissue, bits of yarn, old magazines, scissors, glue and tape.

A collection of discarded adult garments for playing dress-up and a mirror hung at child height afford many hours of pleasurable involvement all through the preschool years.

I recommend avoiding gaudy plastic and electronic toys.

A quality spring rocking horse provides satisfying rocking and good exercise for young children.

Preschoolers and elementary schoolchildren love working with crayons, paints, clay, and colored markers. Easels and chalkboards invite creativity. Toy dishes and building sets such as Tinkertoys® and Legos® offer many hours of deep, satisfying, absorption while advancing cognitive and motor capacity.

Vigorous outdoor play is vitally important with as many hours as possible spent outside. Children who have a safe outside place to play are particularly fortunate. Whether or not they have a yard of their own to play in, kids love going to playgrounds and parks. All children find great pleasure playing in sand, mud, and water and are well-served when we make this possible.

As soon as a baby is crawling, I recommend placing a gate on a doorway, making a room totally safe and allowing him to play just the way he wants without interference. This is a good place to play by himself immediately after breakfast while his caretaker attends to household chores. She can get her work done and he can play without being continually frustrated by being brought away from things he should not be getting into. She, too, is saved from frustration when relieved of monitoring his activities and spoiling his fun by necessarily keeping him away from danger and forbidden objects.

All through your home, firmly anchor to the wall, with screws or bolts, any furniture or electronics a child could climb on and pull over onto himself. A variety of anchoring items for keeping children safe can be found on the internet. Make absolutely certain there is nothing on the floor or within reach to put in the mouth and choke on or any curtains or chords to become entangled in.

A play area of his own provides a baby with the developmental benefits gained through crawling.

If living accommodations do not allow a whole room for a play space, perhaps you can create an enclosed area with a gate and/or pieces of furniture.

If he is afforded this free self-directed play in his enclosed space every day after he first learns to crawl, he will be perfectly happy, by himself, free to play and to enjoy his toys in his own way. He needs only a few items at a time to engage his interest and facilitate healthy brain growth. Being surrounded by too many playthings would be distracting and interfere with his ability to focus on and deeply engage with any single one. By a few, I mean four or five.

The adult will look in on him from time to time to briefly join in his play and give a hug. We would never leave him alone past the time when he needs our companionship. We want him perfectly contented with this arrangement.

As contented as he may be, we must remain aware of what's going on. Leaving the house, taking a shower or a nap would put him at risk.

Babies and toddlers settle perfectly into having their own playtime. They remain happily engaged until the adult enters the scene to socialize or get ready to go outside for a walk. When habitually seen as "the way we do things," a happy home is the result.

Maximum developmental opportunity comes from free self-directed play. This well-known fact exposes the ignorance and disregard for children's welfare behind the idea of HOMEWORK for kindergarten children. As I write this, school districts throughout the United States are planning to bring children into the system at age four so they can start training them in academics. In the mad rush toward "achievement" and the foolish ideas behind the importance of Testing and Test Scores, more and more young children are being robbed of the opportunity for natural development of their inborn capabilities through free play.

Parents who enjoy playing with their children bring a priceless gift to the relationship. Crawlers and toddlers delight in having us down on the floor watching them work. If they ask for help, we are pleased to accept their invitation without imposing instructions beyond what they ask for and letting them take the lead. Being there is what's important.

We enhance our parent-child connection when we initiate play. Let's offer invitations to play before our children ask or come begging.

We give of ourselves when we enter into play with a baby or a child of any age. From the peek-a-boo stage into their teen years, children flourish from our playful involvement. Little children love running, chasing, tag, and hide-and-seek. Kids find great delight in playing dress-up and sometimes performing for an appreciative audience. Riding on a parent's shoulders, touching the ceiling or outside reaching for the trees makes little people feel big, while giving them the physical closeness they crave. Board games and puzzles are perennial favorites. Catching, throwing, kicking, rolling, or bouncing balls can involve any number of players, building coordination and giving everyone a workout.

Some children like being tickled and most enjoy wrestling. We appreciate wrestling as an embellishment to healthy development and family bonding when we see the young of other mammals playfully wrestling in preparation for life. Wild animals as well as domestic puppies and kittens, spend a lot of their time climbing all over each other, wrestling and tumbling with their litter-mates, sometimes involving a parent.

This is a great way to have fun with kids.

However, both wrestling and tickling bring with them a risk of harm to the child and to the adult-child relationship. An adult must be acutely sensitive to a child's physical and emotional boundaries when engaging in this sort of play.

With tickling, it is hard to know when to stop. A child's laughter is not a reliable indication of what's really going on because tickling stimulates an uncontrollable reflexive laughter unrelated to enjoyment. The only safe way to tickle is in short bursts while paying close attention to the child's reactions and honoring the first plea to stop.

Wrestling presents the same dilemma: When is it fun and when has it crossed over into disrespect for a youngster's boundaries? Again, the adult must be well-attuned to the child's responses. If wrestling becomes a contest instead of an enjoyable tussle, a boy may conceal his fear and discomfort to avoid looking weak or being seen as a "sissy." A boy or a girl may go past their comfort zone to hold onto precious involvement with a parent.

One of the dangers in pushing children beyond their healthy tolerance levels is in what it communicates to them about the sanctity of their bodies or lack of it. *"If adults can do this to me, if this is something I am expected to put up with because I'm just a kid with no right to object, I guess all I can do is keep my mouth shut and go along with it."*

This has been the fate of children for hundreds of years and has them being forced to eat foods they hate, required to kiss auntie when they don't want to, and, among countless other violations to Selfhood, are used and abused sexually.

Every child must grow up knowing he has the right to say *No*:

"I don't want to be tickled."

"Leave me alone!"

"Stop!"

Here and now, you and I can make some little difference in the way the world is going by ensuring that our children grow up knowing they have the right to back away if their physical or emotional boundaries are being crossed by anyone at any time. Not Mommy or Daddy, Uncle Joe, a priest, a neighbor, a trusted coach, a beloved grandparent, a teacher, nor ANYONE AT ALL has the right to take advantage of them.

From their earliest months until they walk out the door headed into life as young adults, we can be there for them in the development of their autonomy while finding pleasure in making available, or joining in with, the many ways each individual child finds delight and growth through play.

ADDENDUM TO PLAY

Research studies in 2015, by the Brookings Institution and Vanderbilt University, found Tennessee four-year-olds, trained in academics in Pre-K classrooms, to have lost their gains by third grade, where kids who were not enrolled in Pre-K scholastics are better learners. The researchers are puzzled by this. Only with being blinded by their personal agendas and/or by being stuck in the No Child Left Behind mindset could they possibly miss what's going on with the regressed Pre-K youngsters.

For at least the past hundred years, play-based learning before the age of six has been acknowledged as ESSENTIAL to preparing the brain for learning academic skills. The internet lists study upon study confirming this. I recommend reading an article in the November 2013 New Scientist titled, "Too much, too young: Should schooling start at age 7?" and a summary of the book titled, <u>Crisis in the Kindergarten: Why Children Need to Play in School</u>,[40] from the Alliance for Childhood.

In ignorance or complete disregard for children's developmental requirements, school districts throughout the United States are bringing four-year-olds into the classroom for academic training. Now, in addition to abusing kindergartners with homework assignments, we have this added violation of children's developmental needs as they are force-fed the ABCs while being deprived of the free play necessary for healthy neural structuring and the natural unfolding of their unique cognitive capabilities.

---

[40] <u>Crisis in the Kindergarten: Why Children Need to Play in School</u> by Edward Miller and Joan Almon, Copyright 2009 by the Alliance for Childhood, College Park, MD.

Dedicated teachers who have been able to operate under the radar to shield children from bureaucratic pressures are so burdened with paperwork, testing, and unreasonable institutional demands; they can no longer protect kids. Many are leaving the teaching profession or taking positions in private schools. Parents, trying to be the best they can be, are faced with compulsory education practices working against them.

My recommendations?

If you can afford private education, seek out a school where children's needs are understood and honored. Some private schools charge a lot of money to do a dressed-up version of public school with smaller class sizes being one of a few real advantages. You will want to find a learning environment offering individualized instruction where children are treated WITH GENUINE RESPECT AND RELATIONSHIP IS A PRIORITY. In a good school, learning is deeply engaging and enjoyable through all the grades. In such a school, there is no place for punishments or control through fear.

Or homeschooling may fit into your lifestyle and be the perfect answer. There are many books on the subject, with one of the best being Teach Your Own: The John Holt Book of Homeschooling[41] by John Holt and Pat Farenga. The internet offers a large selection of websites with information on homeschooling.

You can also find online articles to answer every possible question about this growing trend along with curriculums and extensive resources for folks who want to educate their own children.

If public education will continue to be a part of your life, staying attuned to what's going on in the classroom, knowing what children are coping with and being on their side, as always, will help them meet their day-to-day challenges.

---

[41] Teach Your Own: The John Holt Book of Homeschooling by John Holt and Pat Farenga, Copyright 2003 by John Holt Associates, Published by DaCapo Press, a division of the Perseus Book Group, Cambridge, MA.

7

BACK OFF!

"I need my space" has become a popular expression.

And this is true. There are times when we simply need to be left alone to rest, to think, and to just do our own thing, whatever it may be.

Children need their space, too.

They have a lot of learning to do and it is done best without intrusion by adults. We can provide the opportunities, the physical settings, the toys, and resources to make learning possible and get out of the way, allowing them to follow the inner voice directing their unique pursuits and learning styles.

Emphasis on Attachment may lead a parent to believe adults should be involved in everything a child is doing: helping, directing, encouraging, praising, coaching, supervising, and keeping an eye on things. This would be a misinterpretation of Attachment needs.

Much of the time it is in a child's best interest for us to be pursuing our own desires while he follows his. As Thomas Gordon points out, we show acceptance when we allow children to engage in activities without intruding with our questions, advice, or comments. He writes on page 43 of the P.E.T. book: *"Keeping hands off when a child is engaged in some activity is a strong nonverbal way of communicating acceptance."*

Backing off from unnecessary involvement gives us the space we need, too, and eliminates a lot of what has become the "work" of Parenting.

The media have given names to this over-involved, modern parental behavior. They call it Helicopter Parenting or Hovering.

I suspect the hovering urge comes from an uneasy inkling of weakening Attachments and the belief that supervising and directing will make up for the deficiencies.

Real Attachment strength comes from the depth and comfort of the relationship. As much as our children need our closeness and focused attention, there are many hours when they need to be left alone. We show respect by allowing them their personal space.

On the other hand, on occasions when we are involved with our child, it is essential to BE THERE. In today's busy families, outside pressures intrude on the moments moms or dads find for engaging with their children.

Parents are urged to spend "quality time" with each child. One of today's greatest threats to this important quality time is the devotion of adults to their cell phones and other electronic devices.

When you are at the park with your child, BE THERE, not fiddling with your electronics. When you are pushing your baby in a stroller, BE THERE, not talking on a phone. If you are playing with your toddler, BE THERE, not scrolling for tomorrow's weather or following your mind as it wanders off to your unread emails.

> A child's healthy emotional development depends on knowing he's important to us. If we are in a world of our own during his time with us, our distance is registered in his acutely receptive brain and impacts his neurological development in negative ways.

And if our five-year-old is building a fort of cardboard boxes in the living room, our eleven-year-old is working on a science project, or our teenager is planning a party, we can "be there" for them in a different way by keeping our ideas to ourselves and allowing them the space to do it their way without supervision, help, or advice unless asked for.

Adult talking is another common intrusion into a child's life. Much of what we say to children is needless instruction, questioning, and just plain "butting in." The next time you are ready to direct words at your child, stop and ask yourself if what you are about to say is really necessary. Much of the time you'll find it isn't and life will run much more smoothly when you have trained yourself to cut out useless chatter.

Parents are not the only intruders into a child's space. Too much of everything is raising stress levels, stifling spirits, and suppressing the creativity of modern children. Too many activities, too much entertainment, too many video games, too many toys, too many classes, too much television, too many team sports, too many play dates and too much rushing around are taking a toll on developing nervous systems. Adult pressures and demands bombard children from all directions. Among many other requirements, schools want high test scores and obedience. Parents want accomplishments and cooperation. Are children who are involved in team sports or taking music lessons motivated by their own interests or are they fulfilling parental visions of how a child should be?

Kim John Payne of Simplicity Parenting[42] calls all this commotion *"A war on childhood."*

---

[42] Please read <u>Simplicity Parenting: Using the Extraordinary Power of Less to Raise Calmer, Happier, and More Secure Kids</u> by Kim John Payne, M.Ed. with Lisa Ross. Simplicityparenting.com offers a video of the author summarizing Simplicity Parenting along with many other interesting features, including the free Simplicity Parenting Starter Kit.

Besides backing off ourselves, let's back off the world from intruding into our children's lives. Let's give them the priceless gift of free, open, unpressured time for daydreaming, gazing at clouds, or just doing nothing.

As we allow kids the freedom to do their own thing, we open up more time for pursuing our own interests. Respecting each person's time and space becomes automatic and natural. The child who knows we are always there for him will recognize and honor our need for space as we honor his.

8

TOO MUCH STUFF

A good starting point for reducing problems with children is with an evaluation and weeding out of the quantity of playthings and possessions surrounding them.

Many American kids are smothering in masses of stuff.

Let's eliminate a confusing and overwhelming array of toys, with many purchases determined by the latest TV commercials. It is in the best interest of a child to shelter him from commercialism for as long as possible and to avoid exposure to the novel appeal of gaudy plastic attractions and the highly-marketed electronic creations coming from large retail outlets.

The longer we can keep toy stores and toy departments out of our child's experience and awareness, the happier our family will be.

Preschool children need only a few playthings to stimulate their imaginations and creativity and to develop cognitive and motor skills.

A two-year-old will find satisfaction and learning from two or three empty boxes, a few toy vehicles, and a good set of wooden blocks, well beyond anything he could assimilate or enjoy from a large assortment of expensive playthings. You have probably seen a toddler unwrap a toy, only to be found a few minutes later playing with the box the toy came in instead of the toy.

Some of the toys surrounding and overwhelming children are payoffs for a parent's guilt. Without realizing what they are doing, parents may spend money on "things" when they aren't spending time with their children. No amount of toys can fill the void of missed parental companionship. By the same token, an unhappy child will not find contentment with new playthings.

Parents can fall into the habit of bringing home a toy every time they go shopping until their child learns to expect it. I strongly advise against developing this habit and the resulting welcoming calls of: *"What did you bring me?"*

When youngsters come to regard the treasures we give them as evidence of our love, times when we are too rushed to pick out a gift or, for whatever reason, arrive home empty-handed, can produce disappointment or feelings of rejection.

Neither children nor adults feel secure or at peace when their self-worth is tied in with the gifts they receive or the possessions they accumulate.

Your child can be perfectly happy without seeing shopping with a parent as an occasion for buying a toy or a treat. If, on entering a store with you, he asks for something, state calmly and clearly why you are there. *"We are here only to buy groceries," "The only thing we're buying here is a birthday gift for Aunt Karen,"* and so on. When, in a composed, easygoing manner, you define shopping as not being a time for buying a toy or a treat, your child can relax and take in the experience. When not focused on what's in it for him, his intellect is free to observe and learn from his surroundings. He can fully enjoy being out and about with you without the unsettling tension and jitters associated with Wanting Something.

This is not to say we should never give children something new to delight them and capture their interest. With a gift coming as a rare treat instead of meeting a habitual expectation, the gesture takes on a sweet significance.

With too many things surrounding them, children become distracted and unable to focus. In the overabundance of toys, nothing holds their interest long enough to engage them deeply and stimulate their creativity. A profusion of objects diffusing their attention, with no one thing fully drawing them in, leaves them unsatisfied and wanting more.

A mountain of toys will not stave off discontent.

Being surrounded by playthings adds to today's ongoing sensory overload, presenting a confusing overabundance of choices, building agitation and heightening stress.

Kim John Payne's Simplicity Parenting program shows parents how to remove clutter from their children's lives for cutting out turmoil, and in some cases, the resulting drug-free elimination of ADD and ADHD.

Weeding out a large collection of toys to reduce sensory bombardment helps to create an aura of calm and affords children healing relief from the pressures of Too Much Stuff.

IV

Fear is the inseparable companion of coercion.

~ John Holt

1

THE N BOMB OF DISCIPLINE

NO!

This one little word, two little letters, creates a barrier to the development of a quality relationship essential to successfully nurturing happy cooperation.

It can "Blow Up" your hopes and dreams about the joys of being a parent and turn life with your child into a daily struggle.

Some parents describe their relationship with a child as a war.

You can prevent this from happening in your home. Or if it already has, please know you can eliminate the turmoil and create a relaxed enjoyable life for you and for your child. If this is the help you are seeking, great happiness is on your horizon through a different way of thinking about your life as a parent.

So, here we go!

When our helpless infant becomes mobile, we are faced with entirely new responsibilities. At this critical juncture, if this one little word, NO, gets us off on the wrong foot, we can enmesh ourselves in an antagonistic relationship with the possibility for continuing all the way into the teen years and beyond.

Let's get down to how NO can lead to your frustration, anger, and helplessness beginning from a toddler's point of view.

Picture this:

Our eighteen-month-old toddler is contentedly playing with blocks in the middle of the living room floor. We smile at him from time to time when he turns to us from his play. It only looks like play. He is really doing his work; the fun and immensely satisfying work of structuring his neural pathways.

Now he happens to spot the TV controls; a new lure to experimentation for following nature's plan; very different from his toys, and irresistible. In a flash, he is across the room and satisfying his curiosity about this unexplored discovery.

This is where Traditional Parenting has us saying NO and this is when our troubles begin.

Question: Why would this bright, inquisitive little person stop investigating a fascinating new discovery because you want him to and because this NO sound is coming out of your mouth?

Answer: He wouldn't.

Now what do we do? The Traditional way is to exercise our advantage in size and strength and scare him into complying. An angry NO and a slap on the hand, or in some homes, a real spanking, have been accepted responses for a long, long time.

During this frightful confrontation he has only his trust in us and the strength of his Attachment to help him. Our confusing and frightening actions have struck a blow to his trust, leaving him bewildered and his Attachment to us undermined.

He could not begin to comprehend the situation as it relates to all the hours we worked to pay for this TV set. To him, it simply looks like another inviting source of investigation and learning.

Since he was a tiny infant, we have smiled and exclaimed when he reached out for a new toy. Now his reaching out brought this scary face and hard, loud voice, alarming him and assaulting his senses.

> We have taken a first step in drawing him into a contest. Now positioned as his adversary, we have started down a treacherous road. We have embarked on the path of control through punishment and fear.

A toddler has no way of comprehending why this big person who takes care of him, holds him, feeds him, and plays with him has a strange look on her face, with frightening sounds coming out of her mouth, and is hurting him.

Although we may scare him enough, or inflict enough pain to interrupt his behavior, we have contaminated the core of his relationship to us. Instead of working with his natural inborn need to fit in and cooperate, we are now exploiting his fear of the loss of our love and at the same time creating in him a reservoir of hurt, anger, and resistance.

Part of his attention now turns away from learning how to settle into his place in the family. His newly activated Counterwill, focused on protecting him from control, stimulates within him a new feeling and a new reaction to go with it: DEFIANCE. Instead of spending his time pursuing learning and development of his Selfhood, a certain amount of energy will be spent on staying out of trouble, outwitting adults, and hiding his activities.

When this early stage of activated Counterwill progresses to a full-blown power contest, a parent may find a bowel movement in her best shoe or big black crayon marks on her bedroom wall. Instead of asking ourselves what emotional injury has triggered such disturbing behavior, the usual response has been punishment. Spankings, beatings, severe shakings are not uncommon measures used in attempts to stop this sort of instinct-driven behavior. Little children are abused each day because of terrible misunderstandings about their reactions and motivations.

As a defiant child gets older, he may find satisfaction in seeing how much he can get away with. While we frantic adults are trying to "make him" cooperate, his inborn Counterwill is doing the job of protecting him from outside influence.

Engaged in a power struggle, we look for new ways to gain control when the old ones stop working. Scolding and yelling bring no improvement and Time-Out escalates to locking him in his room. We may slap or spank harder. We try removal of privileges, withholding treats, lecturing and grounding for an older child, all the while fuelling his anger and resentment. Beneath his feelings of humiliation and rage lie deep pools of hurt and despair. Our punishments and expressions of anger slash away at Attachment, the foundation of his emotional security and his ability to cooperate.

Somewhere along this road we may try using rewards to control him, only to find our sticker charts, ice cream cones, and new toys eventually lose their effectiveness, if they ever worked in the first place, and we wonder what to do next as our frustration and anger escalate.

Because he is being treated as though he is bad, he may come to see himself as deserving of this treatment and take on the "bad child" role. Accepting the adult view of him as his own, his self-image is distorted.

Or a sensitive child may lose all sense of Self as he simply gives up the quest for autonomy.

Our way out of this unhappy situation is to abandon control, relax into our natural position as a reliable companion and escape from the punishment-reward trap ensnaring us along with our child.

It is never too late! Our new focus becomes "WORKING WITH" instead of following old patterns of "DOING TO."[43]

To begin this transition, our first goal will be to strengthen Attachment by treating our child with genuine respect as we steadfastly abandon any and all control tactics.

As for the word NO, it can continue to cloud happiness as our children grow to school age and into their teens.

Overheard exchange between two young boys at a playground:

Boy one:	*"You could come with us. It'll be fun."*
Boy two:	*"I don't know."*
Boy one:	*"Go ask your dad."*
Boy two:	*"I don't want to."*
Boy one:	*"Why not?"*
Boy two:	*"He'll say no. He always says no."*

And so it goes. In our position as parent with a capital P we become accustomed to arbitrarily tossing out the word NO. Without a compelling reason to deny a request, can we stop and think before allowing an automatic NO to pop out?

Let's stop treating children this way and make the word YES our response when at all possible.

---

[43] I credit Alfie Kohn again for his concept of "WORKING WITH" instead of "DOING TO" as he explains in his book and DVD on Unconditional Parenting.

2

TIME-OUT

This very popular method of control is one of the most damaging to a child's emotional health and to the relationship between parent and child.

TIME-OUT IS A DIRECT ASSAULT ON ATTACHMENT.

Child-rearing books, magazine articles, friends, neighbors, pediatricians, parent educators, relatives, and all sorts of well-meaning people have been promoting this control tactic for years.

Parents who do not want to punish their children by hitting them, have enthusiastically embraced forced isolation as a harmless method of control. Besides losing effectiveness over time, as other punishments do, Time-Out is far from harmless.

Adults have been persuaded to believe Time-Out is not a punishment and to see it as a "quiet time" for a child to settle down and reflect on his behavior. The problem with this thinking is in how different it is from the child's living reality.

For the youngest child, Time-Out exploits his deep fear of loss of acceptance and Attachment, assailing the vital bond and building rage.

No child will be sitting in his room or on a special chair seriously planning to improve his behavior. He will be feeling shamed, hurt, angry, and resentful. An older child will be plotting revenge against the parent or sibling who brought about his banishment and figuring out how to avoid getting caught the next time, while the hurt and anger are being internalized to wear negatively on his character, personality, physical health, and emotional well-being.

Some children express their rage and desperation by breaking things, ripping up clothing or curtains, writing on walls, or destroying books and toys. In the punishment-oriented home, such explosions bring more hurt down on them.

The exasperated parents enter into a war with their own offspring, grasping at more severe punishments, determined to gain control. Caught in this downward spiral, they see their child as bad and strong-willed.

<u>Their child is not bad. Their child is not strong-willed. Their child is filled with Counterwill and an anger fueled by hurt, humiliation, and fear of losing connection to the adults he looks to for love and approval.</u>

Time-Out is punishment no matter how we may try to fool ourselves.

Isolation—removal from social contact—is the exact opposite from common everyday demonstrations of cooperation, Problem-Solving, and constructive interpersonal relating within the family.

The act of sending a child to Time-Out is mindless and void of empathy. *"Go to your room!"* requires no understanding of the needs motivating his actions.

If you are thinking, *"Oh, he just wants attention,"* ask yourself what could be more important. Trying to reinforce Attachment is a perfectly logical reason why a child may provoke your involvement because he legitimately needs your attention.

Or he may be confused about what is expected of him and lacking a clear understanding of the requirements of a situation. Please see LIMITS and MEAN WHAT YOU SAY!

A child may cause a problem with fighting and aggression because he needs help in learning negotiating skills. Knowing aggression to be fuelled by frustration, we can furnish relief by reducing demands, pressures, and stressors in his daily life.

He may be modeling a behavior he has seen in the family or outside the home. Parents can be shocked to see their sweet, innocent child coming home from his first week in preschool with an obnoxious behavior they find intolerable, when he's only trying to be like the other kids.

Research shows exposure to violence or frenetic screen images on TV or DVDs leads to aggression and violence in children. Could this type of media input be contributing to your child's problematic hitting and fighting?

"Your whining and pouting are driving me crazy. Go to your room and don't come out until you have a smile on your face and can stop bothering me." Yes, children are talked to like this and the need behind the whining and gloom remains undisclosed and neglected. In being mindful, we can take our child onto our lap and do some Active Listening. *"Things don't seem to be working right for you today."* Asking ourselves if our child is getting enough sleep may uncover the source of a chronically gloomy mood. Family changes or upsets can cause anxiety and/or depression.

Forced isolation will not fix any of this.

A child may emerge from Time-Out with a smile plastered on his face when we have managed to control his behavior without identifying his needs. Meanwhile he has learned a lesson in suppressing his feelings and displaying a false face.

Parents will tell us Time-Out works because they see proof of it when their child emerges from isolation with a sweet and loving disposition. They are not really witnessing the behavior of a child reformed from his "evil ways." They are seeing an insecure and frightened youngster trying to win back a parent's love and restore Attachment.

No punishment can address an unfulfilled need, unfavorable modeling, or a child's confusion. Disguising a punishment with a nice-sounding name will not lessen the damage to the child and to the family dynamics.

Sending a child away from us displays our unwillingness or our inability to confront and solve problems as they come up. We demonstrate avoidance behavior.

WHEN DIFFICULTIES ARISE, THE ADVOCATES OF TIME-OUT TELL US TO BECOME HELPLESS AND EVADE ENGAGING OUR CHILD IN SOLVING A PROBLEM BY SENDING HIM AWAY FROM US IN AN INTERPERSONAL EXCHANGE COMPLETELY DEVOID OF EMPATHY.

Our shamed and hurt fellow human is sitting in his room alone and detached while the problem remains and the need behind it undisclosed, whatever it may be. We have lost an opportunity to take the lead, be in charge, and to work through a problem by being the strong empathic grownup who can be depended upon and trusted.

Instead, we act as a helpless punitive enemy to be feared, avoided, and deceived.

When we try to see the world through a child's eyes, we find engaging with him to identify the source of a problem to be a valuable learning experience for both of us.

It is a discouraging sign of our times to find Parenting books on the market recommending Time-Out and to see websites selling cutesy Time-Out accessories. Businesses operating to profit from the distress of children expose the sickening level of pathological ignorance and exploitive commercialism contaminating our culture.

Before I leave the subject of breaking Attachment in the name of discipline, I want to bring up a contrivance, you may hear about, for gaining the upper hand.

There are folks teaching Parenting and writing books who prescribe IGNORING and SHUNNING as tactics for bringing a "misbehaving" youngster into line.

They instruct us to turn off all acknowledgement of his existence, to shut him out, and pretend he isn't there until he shapes up. We are told to turn away from him, refuse to speak, and to guard against showing any facial expression. We are also told this is hard to do. Of course it is! It goes against human instinct to ignore a child in distress. A child who needs us.

Hearing about this advice being taught to parents reminds us of the long way we must go, as a culture, in respecting and meeting the needs of our young. We have been walking around with our eyes closed, unconscious to the wondrous joys in mindful relationships with children, as we distance ourselves from them with adult tricks like Time-Out and ignoring.

Dr. James Kimmel called our cultural norm for mistreating babies and children SOCIOPATHIC PARENTING. I urge you to read his articles on the Natural Child website.

3

HAVE YOU TRIED REASONING?

If you have, I expect it hasn't worked. You talk your head off and nothing changes. This advice became popular, along with the wide promotion of Time-Out, when parents were looking for ways to control children without spanking them.

Parents who follow this advice eventually find their patient monologues to be useless and exhausting.

Trying to explain our requests to a child of two or three is a waste of time. The social system and family customs we want him to fit into are far too complex for him to begin to comprehend.

With very young children, our responsibility is to go about meeting the requirements of a situation lovingly and cheerfully while leading our child along with a brief description of what's happening: *"We've got to go and bring sister home from school."* This may involve taking him affectionately into our arms and physically moving him through the needed behaviors, such as getting out the door or into a car seat.

Older children appreciate a bit more information: *"In about fifteen minutes, after I finish cleaning up the kitchen, we'll be leaving to pick up grandma at the airport."*

When a young child is engrossed in play, connecting to him with eye contact, a smile, and Active Listening, will ease him through a transition: *"It looks like you're having fun with your cars. Let's bring one with us going to pick up Daddy. Here's your sweater to keep you warm in the car."* This is said as we are looking affectionately into his eyes, smiling, and helping him into his sweater.

Our courtesy is the most important part of the interaction. If we call to him from another room, ordering him to put on his sweater or we swoop in, harsh and demanding, expecting resistance, a child will fulfill our expectations. Our disrespect will activate Counterwill and the resistance we anticipate.

If we bombard him with a lot of talk, justifying and explaining, we undermine his confidence in us as competent grownups in charge. Some little unarticulated voice inside him is anxiously asking why we need to account for and defend our requests to an inexperienced little kid. His sense of security is fortified by believing the adults around him know what they are doing in taking care of him and meeting the requirements of daily life.

So let's leave out such litanies as, *"We have to go pick up Daddy now. You can play with your cars when we get back. If we don't hurry, we'll be running late. I have to get back and start dinner. You want Mommy to have time to make your good dinner, don't you?"* And on and on with the reasoning, building stress for our child and for ourself.

The old advice to use persuasive logic to gain cooperation directs us to try talking a child into doing something he would rather not do. This is simply another form of coercion. Our stream of words creates the very resistance we hope to avoid. The answer to this dilemma is to stop imposing our will on children when not necessary and, when it is necessary, to be as kind and respectful as we would be to an adult friend, prepared to Active Listen to objections.

COUNTING is similarly non-productive as in, *"I'm counting to three for you to get your shoes on."* Or as a threat, *"By the time I count to three, you had better have your shoes on."* Counting announces our lack of faith in our child's willingness or ability to cooperate and weakens our position in knowing what's called for and having the confidence to get on with it. This counting business is just one more grossly disrespectful way we treat children, compared to how we relate to grownups. Imagine saying to a friend: *"George, dinner's ready. I'm counting to five for you to get to the table."*

If our child objects to a necessary request, we remember the importance of allowing emotional expression while we put his exasperation into words: *"You're really mad for having to stop your block building. You were having such a good time and I came and spoiled it for you. What a bummer."* We calmly proceed with whatever needs doing without explaining, apologizing, or mollifying. We do not attempt to pacify or bribe. *"Stop crying and you can have a cookie"* is never helpful in the long run. However, if we must routinely interrupt a child's play to go somewhere in the car, a nutritious snack can be an established regular part of the trip: *"We're getting ready to leave. Here's your baggie of apple slices."*

A well-meaning parent can get into trouble by asking, *"Do you want to?"* when the time has come for something to be happening: lunch, nap, go outside, come inside, put on a sweater, buckle into a car seat. If the answer is *"No,"* we are now stuck in an argument, which could have been avoided by simply proceeding graciously. AND, since there was no choice anyway, *"Do you want to?"* was misleading and dishonest from the start.

Sometimes trying to control a child with words takes on a form of badgering. We may hear this in the grocery store: *"What are you doing? Stop touching things. Stop running around. Keep your hands to yourself. I told you to stay with me. Get over here, now! Get down from there. You're going to break something."* Words, words, words.

This child is deaf to what his mother is saying. The words have no meaning to him. They do, however, have an impact on his nervous system, creating a painful level of stress. If you have been a witness to or a participant in this common occurrence, you may have seen it culminate in the little kid's screaming meltdown.

Badgering is not always done in an unkind way. An involved father has taken his 11-yeqr-old daughter to buy a gift for her mother. She's looking for a pretty scarf and if you happen to be nearby, you may hear something like this: *"How about this red one? Did you see the black and white one over here? This shade of blue would look good on her, sweetheart."*

As you walk away, the man's continuing advice ringing in your ears, there the young girl must remain, caught in the oppressive orbit of a loving father's good intentions and the unspoken inferences he's communicating:

"You're not smart enough to decide on a gift by yourself."

"You need my help in making choices."

"You are too young and inexperienced to choose on your own."

<u>Our relationships with children improve immediately when we cut out the reasoning, ordering, directing, suggesting, and advising.</u> A child, relieved of tension from external pressures, may become cooperative overnight or in a few days following the suggestions in this book. For others, change may take a week or a month.

Be assured, every human on earth was born with the seeds of cooperation within him. Our patience and respect, along with a firm Attachment, will find us as happy observers to the blossoming of cooperation and the satisfaction our child finds in being a participating member of his family.

4

MEAN WHAT YOU SAY!

THINK BEFORE YOU SPEAK.

EXCLUDE THE AUTOMATIC NO.

AVOID GIVING ORDERS.

ELIMINATE UNNECESSARY REQUESTS.

BE PREPARED AND AMENABLE TO CHANGING A NO TO A YES WITH NEW INFORMATION OR CHANGED CIRCUMSTANCES.

In addition to the repressive dimension in issuing orders and responding with a NO when YES would have been perfectly workable, parents get themselves into all sorts of trouble when they make a request or demand compliance when it isn't really necessary and are talked out of it.

The best course of action is to avoid giving orders and to say YES when at all possible.

We find issuing orders on our list of Roadblocks and WE CERTAINLY GET INTO TROUBLE WHEN WE ORDER A CHILD TO DO SOMETHING WHEN WE HAVE NO WAY TO BRING ABOUT COMPLIANCE as in, *"You're going to sit there on the potty until you do poo-poo.* Many a child has developed a severe case of constipation when adults have attempted to take over the inner wokings of his body around the issue of "Toilet Training."

At the potty age, or any other age, a direct order is an invitation to opposition. No one likes being told what to do and a child's natural push toward autonomy, energised by Counterwill, renders him powerfully resistant to taking orders.

Instead of issuing orders or making demands, we produce far better results when we collect our child with eye contact, a smile, and a nod as we state our need with an I-Message.

In the preschool years, we maintain our position of trust by sticking to a decision once we have announced it. Giving thought to our decisions helps us avoid falling into the habit of responding negatively when a positive answer would have been perfectly workable.

Example:

Our four-year-old asks us to play a game. We say we are too busy to play because we had planned to pay bills during this time. When we tell him this, he cries and begs. Feeling sorry for him, we give in and play the game.

By not sticking to our word, we have created unnecessary problems. Our child has been encouraged to whine to change our mind. It worked this time! Not being protective of our plans, when we turned the course of the evening over to him, weakened our position as the strong adult our child needs to know he can depend on.

When we really did have time to play and responded with an Automatic No, we became vulnerable to being talked out of our response. It helps to ponder a bit before answering to a request. We can always say we need time to think about it.

When he tries to talk us out of our refusal to play another evening, we may be seriously pressed for time or in a different mood. When we say we are too busy to play with him, he wonders if we really mean it and starts to beg. To reinforce our refusal, we become stern and angry, applying the old Traditional tactic of using anger as a control device. He has no idea what's going on and comes away hurt and confused.

This fooling around to get us to change our mind is a waste of his time and ours. He could be getting on with his own activities. His energy can be applied to developing and pursuing his own interests when not being spent on struggles with a parent.

When children come up against something they are unable to change, they face what Dr. Neufeld and Dr. Maté define as THE WALL OF FUTILITY. Facing and accepting an unchangeable fact of life is a critical step in the development of adaptability[44] and the process of maturation. Individuals who do not learn to accept the futility of some of their efforts and wishes never fully grow up.

One of the biggest steps we can take toward building trust and supporting cooperation is in MEANING WHAT WE SAY!

Take your time before saying *"NO"* to any request. Whether your child is asking for a cookie or if he can stay longer at the park, state your reasons briefly, Active Listen to any distress your answer may cause, and move on. Do not get drawn into arguments.

"We're leaving now. Daddy's waiting for us to pick him up." If our child objects or starts to make a fuss, we call on our empathy and bring in Active Listening: *"I can see how much fun you were having and know you would love to stay much longer. All day if we could!"* Some children are helped through a transition of this sort with one advance announcement, such as *"There's time for two more slides before we leave to pick up Daddy."* And we stick to what we said. Two more slides it is!

There's no more talk about staying or leaving and nothing to be gained through persuasion.

---

[44] The process of adaptation, critical to maturation, is described beautifully on pages 221-223 in <u>Hold On to Your Kids: Why Parents Need to Matter More Than Peers</u> by Dr. Gordon Neufeld and Dr. Gabor Maté.

Or about the cookie question: *"No more cookies today. Your body has had all the sugar it can handle."* This ends any discussion about cookies, excluding a long string of words about sugar being bad for us, giving us diabetes, and making us fat or sick. Active Listening is the helpful response to begging or whining: *"You wish you had a giant bag full of cookies to munch on all day long!"*

Explaining, justifying, or apologizing weakens our position as the strong, competent adult in charge of running things. Our child's sense of security is undermined when we get into explaining ourselves to this little kid who looks to us to take care of him. Confusion over when and if we mean what we say, will keep him unsettled, continually fishing around for a secure anchor, anxious, and unable to fully relax.

What if you are trying to put my recommendations into practice and your child has not discovered the satisfactions in cooperating. On this day, you have announced time to leave the park and he's screaming in protest, refusing to budge. What you do not do is plead, coax, and bargain. What you must do is maintain your position of the in-charge adult and carry your screeching, struggling little kid to the car. This is a time for taking a deep breath and resisting any urge to exert your adult advantage by becoming physically rough with him. Remember! You have Counterwill, too! If you allow it to move you to anger and enter into battle, your natural authority is lost. **Your child's Counterwill is in control of him. Do not let yours take control of you.** Such a standoff calls for taking charge of the situation without becoming combative. This is a time for your self-discipline to take hold as you remain composed and, with calm self-confidence, get him into the car. An Active Listening statement along the lines of, *"You absolutely did not want to leave the park,"* will let him know you can see things from his side.

Nothing more needs to be said. It was time to go, and he has lived through a real-life step in becoming adaptable. Before long, with your support and example, he will grow to find deep pleasure in following his natural drive to cooperate.

Teaching a toddler not to play with certain objects, we must always remove and redirect while explaining briefly, *"This is not to play with. Here's something for a little boy."* We show we mean what we say by lovingly removing and redirecting EVERY TIME until he absorbs two facts of life in this household: some things are not to be played with and WE MEAN WHAT WE SAY.

Standing on the other side of the room and shouting, *"No"* is ineffective in teaching a toddler how to fit in. Also, it models using the word *NO* as we are trying to get our way; a tactic he will quickly imitate in application of *NO* to serve his own wants and needs.

If a child cries or throws a tantrum when his wishes are not granted, we lose our position of natural authority when we become angry and punishing toward him. He has a right to his feelings and the freedom to voice them. His distress is his problem. Not ours. We maintain the Attachment bond and our position of Adult-In-Charge by being calm and supportive, remaining in control of the situation and proceeding according to our needs or the needs of the circumstances. **We empathize with his disappointment by Active Listening and allowing him to express his frustration without his tantrum causing us to change our mind or influence us into becoming angry or coercive.**

Our Active Listening puts us in his shoes, seeing things from his perspective and serving our "Working With" frame of mind.

We can mean what we say and be kind about it! Parents sometimes put an angry tone into their voice or yell to show they mean it.

The way to SHOW we mean it is to MEAN IT.

A lot of turmoil is eliminated when we stop making unnecessary demands. It is easy to fall into the habit of arbitrarily telling a child what to do. Many times a parent has no good reason for making a particular request, or refusing one, and becomes a source of unnecessary frustration. Or the parent's position is weakened when an Automatic No leaves room to give in to whining and begging.

There will be times when you have to quickly change what your child is doing: Linda is sitting on the light beige carpet drawing with permanent markers and you shout, *"Linda! Get the markers off the carpet! Take your art project to the table."*

You were so alarmed you didn't think about Collecting your little girl or coming up with an I-Message. Now her Counterwill is in gear. Ignoring your command, she continues her drawing and says, *"I don't want to."* Because you mean what you say, you calmly gather up the markers yourself. You will beware of becoming confrontational as you maintain a congenial disposition while taking control of the situation and demonstrating reliability in meaning what you say.

You look into her eyes and smile with a statement, such as *"Here we go, sweetie,"* as you set her up at the table. You protect your carpet without explaining or apologizing. She knows why you moved the markers. It would weaken your position as the competent adult in charge to say anything like: *"I'm sorry I had to move you. I was just so worried about stains on the carpet."* Instead, you secure Attachment by sitting at the table with her for a few minutes in conversation about the art project.

This was not about winning a contest with your little girl. It was about taking care of your home without turning the interaction into a counterproductive battle with Counterwill.

When Counterwill takes over a child's behavior, neither the parent nor the child can control it. The parent can, however, take charge of the situation.

What if moving Linda's artwork has set her off into a rage?

I expect, after having read this far, you would know what to do. You realize Linda's healthy development depends on her right to express her agitation. You will know, too, this is one of the times when she learns she will not always get her way as she faces this wall of futility. Your part in furthering her growth is in Active Listening to her distress and drawing out her tears without any attempt to shut down her expression of feelings: *"You were all settled on the floor and hated being moved."*

Presenting the self-assured adult your child can depend on and look to for guidance is central to his confidence in you and to the flourishing of his drive to cooperate. One way parents sabotage this natural process is by adding OK with a question mark to their requests and directions as in, *"We're leaving the park now. OK?"* You are the competent adult. You know leaving the park at this time fits into the smooth orchestrating of today's events. You do not need his permission or approval. If he objects, you are there for him with your Active Listening as you are leaving the park.

In meaning what you say, as children get older, there may be occasions when negotiation and Problem-Solving will work well for all concerned.

If you have established safety restrictions on where your son may ride his bike and he comes to you saying it isn't working for him, this will be a time when you sit down together and Problem-Solve for working out a mutually agreeable solution to his biking needs and your safety concerns.

Or, after declaring something to be out-of-bounds, according to your family values, you may acquire new information and change a *NO* to a *YES*.

Example: Your child has asked to go to a movie with friends. You believe this particular movie unsuitable for an eight-year-old and will not allow him to go. The other mother calls to say she has seen the film, describes it, and assures you it conforms to your standards, which are much like hers. Now, you can give your child the go-ahead to see the movie, making it clear how new information has changed your decision.

As children become more responsible, there are more opportunities for negotiation and Problem-Solving; skills they find immensely valuable as they grow into adulthood.

With a child's gaining in independence, we must be on guard against falling prey to the mythology about parents knowing what's best.

A long running TV show called Father Knows Best was a great hit in the late 1950s.

Now, in this new century, the premise could not be more misleading. With change taking place at unprecedented speed, the world today's children inhabit is vastly different from the one we grew up in. We know little or nothing about the complexities they face. To provide the support they require, we will need to stay alert to keeping any vestiges of Traditional thinking from seeping in and contaminating our perspective. Peer pressure is unrelenting in today's culture and secure Attachments to caring adults are critically important.

When reaching for independence, kids become increasingly sensitive to the disconnecting language of the Roadblocks. Active Listening keeps communication open. With Six-Step Problem-Solving as our guide, inviting any and all input, we can work together to find solutions to problems and enjoy observing each child's journey to independence.

As children grow toward maturity, Collecting them continues to be integral to maintaining a secure connection. By remembering to engage their Attachment instincts at every opportunity, we firm-up their sense of security and help them to stay anchored, ready to face life's challenges.

Collecting children of every age in the morning, before launching into the world's hustle-bustle, gets each day off to a good start.

5

STICKER CHARTS

The first thing to know about sticker charts is this: If you enroll in a Parenting class or read a book on Parenting and it includes directions for setting up sticker charts, you are in the wrong place. You are reading the wrong book.

Strategies for manipulating children with gold stars, ice cream cones, stickers, or any other form of payment for desired behavior are primarily disrespectful. Our goal is to establish a mutually cooperative relationship in which offering a gold star or an ice cream cone for "good" behavior would be out of tune with the harmony and mutual respect on which the relationship is grounded.

> We want our children to do the right thing because they feel the right way, not to gain some extrinsic reward in the service of another person's control over them.

To appreciate the whole picture on rewards and bribes, I recommend Alfie Kohn's book, Punished by Rewards: The Trouble with Gold Stars, Incentive Plans, As, Praise and Other Bribes,[45] and the article, Five Reasons to Stop Saying "Good Job!" on his website, www.alfiekohn.org.

---

[45] Punished by Rewards: The Trouble with Gold Stars, Incentive Plans, As, Praise and Other Bribes by Alfie Kohn, Copyright 1993, Houghton Mifflin Publishers, New York, NY.

The P.E.T. book examines this control method and gives us a clear picture of the damage we do when, sincerely wanting to be good parents, we innocently believe rewards to be useful and harmless alternatives to punishments. Setting up a sticker chart tells our child we lack faith in his ability to control himself unless there's a reward to be gained. Because we believe he is inadequate to control his own behavior, he adopts the same belief. Both self-discipline and self-confidence are undermined.

Sometimes a sticker chart will "work" to get results for a while. Most parents find any success to be short-lived, with stickers losing their charm eventually. Other parents find stickers to be useless from the beginning. There's a simple reason for this. A sticker chart represents the adult agenda, not the child's. When we contrive to advance our agenda over our child's, whether with punishments or rewards, we stimulate Counterwill and our efforts meet resistance.

What about the child you may know who appears to be successfully trained with rewards? This is likely a little girl who happily complies; pleasing adults and being rewarded. She gets completely into the games they are using to manage her behavior. She loves the puppy and kitten stickers to put on her chart when she picks up her toys or goes to bed without a fuss. She buckles willingly into her car seat and is quietly cooperative as her mother shops for groceries, knowing the reward for her compliance will be a cookie to eat in the car or a puppy sticker when she gets home.

Her parents wouldn't think of spanking her or intentionally hurting her feelings. They show their love for her in many ways. How could there possibly be anything wrong with this?

What's wrong is in her not knowing, and possibly never knowing herself. She is disconnected from her own needs and feelings as she satisfies adults to gain the rewards they hold out to her.

She is being deprived of fully living her genetically endowed agenda. She has little or no experience exercising her inborn drive to cooperate and is unaware of her natural abilities for directing her own behavior. She could control herself perfectly well within a Working With relationship.

Her parents are deprived, too. They are missing out on enjoying the natural unfolding of their unique little girl. They are, as she is, blocked from experiencing her natural capabilities for engaging in mutually enlightening collaboration. The sticker chart, and whatever other rewards they may be using, are barriers between their real Selves. Her parents have feelings and needs unknown to her. She gets a kitten sticker for following directions without knowing how her behavior may affect others, one way or another.

It would be impossible to guess how many adults are walking around in this state of disconnection from their true Selves. The germinal Self we were born with may never have gained autonomy as we grew up coerced and manipulated into following directions, fulfilling expectations, and satisfying the needs of the adults who held power over us.

The state of our world suggests this number to be a high percentage.

To quote Arno Gruen in the introduction to <u>The Betrayal of the Self: The Fear of Autonomy in Men and in Women</u>:

"The type of personal integration we attain—or the effective lack thereof—depends on what possibilities our life situation offers us for the development of autonomy."

Besides the adverse effects bribes and rewards have on a child, and ultimately on the entire society, sticker charts are an unnecessary burden on parents. The entire enterprise requires time-consuming monitoring and enforcement, usually accompanied by ongoing frustration.

Please, let's forget about sticker charts and enjoy our children for who they are instead of contriving to fit them into our molds and making unnecessary work for ourselves.

6

PAYMENT PLAN DISCIPLINE

Let's look at Payment Plan Discipline in action. In the following illustration, a child decides to pay for failure to follow through on a commitment, thereby clearing his account:

As Mom drives 12-year-old Jason to school, she says, *"Jason, the Martins are coming for dinner tonight and I need your help. The family room is a mess with games and snack dishes scattered around. Please clean up in there and vacuum the carpet before I get home from work."*

Jason is sincere when he says he will do this.

Walking home from school, his two buddies tell him they are headed to the vacant lot to work on their tree house. One friend says, *"If we work on it today and tomorrow, it'll be finished."* This is a fine tree house and building it has been a big part of their lives. Jason is caught in a dilemma. He told his mother he would help her and now his friends want him to work on their tree house. He knows what will happen if Mom comes home to the messy family room. She'll impose the established punishment of locking up his computer games. For a big violation like this, she will probably take them away for a month. He weighs the options and finally decides to PAY THE PRICE. He will go with his friends to work on their big project. It is worth giving up his games in exchange for finishing the tree house.

Punished children weigh the pleasure of doing what they want against the cost in terms of the punishment they will suffer, whatever the punishment will be. Spanked children, grounded children, children sent to their rooms, children deprived of privileges, come to think in terms of cost/benefit evaluations as they make decisions about their behavior.

Consideration of others is not called upon in Payment Plan Discipline. Ethical perspectives involving empathy and loyalty as a member of a working-together family are missing when a payment plan is operating.

As mad as Mom will be, Jason is hoping he may get her to go easy on him if he apologizes and tells her how sorry he is. Apologizing is a common component of the Payment Plan. Our culture puts great stock in the word SORRY. Children and adults alike can do outrageous things to each other and wipe the slate clean by saying they are sorry.

Being sorry is a common ingredient in wife abuse. A husband visits his battered wife in the hospital, hangs over her black and blue face crying and telling her how sorry he is. She forgives him, goes home to him, and two weeks later he beats her up again. What did he mean when he said he was sorry? He has learned, oh so well, how to play his role in the sorry/forgiveness ritual, clearing his debt by saying the word "sorry" and moving on to do the same thing over again.

A payment plan parent-child relationship retards character growth by interfering with development of responsibility.

When a child has "paid for" his transgression by suffering whatever punishment was imposed or by saying how very sorry he feels, he is off the hook with no further thought to whatever responsibility he may have toward others. He did the deed and he paid the price. The entire episode requires no contemplation.

There is yet another component to a payment plan relationship and an easy one for parents to fall into, as the following example will make clear: *I've told you to pick up your toys three times and they're still scattered all over. I took you to the park to play and stopped for ice cream on the way home. Is this how you thank me?"*

Oops! We manage to throw in a dose of guilt with this payment due notice. In support of our child's growing strength of character, we do not want him to satisfy our needs to avoid feeling guilty or because he owes us something. Our goal in a Working With relationship is to have him do what we ask because he feels himself to be a part of a mutually-caring alliance and derives personal satisfaction from his contributions to it.

It is hoped we are taking him to the park because he has fun there and as involved parents we have fun watching him enjoy himself, not ever to use this outing against him as a debt he owes us when we want something from him. To establish the unconditional love and acceptance critical to a healthy relationship and our child's optimal growth, he must never believe he has to **earn** our love and life's pleasures.

Another popular parenting maneuver could be called PUTTING A PRICE ON IT and goes like this: *"If you do not meet my demands, I will make you pay."*

To a five-year-old: *"If you don't pick up your toys right now, you can forget about going swimming today."*

Or to a twelve-year-old: *"Turn off the TV and get out there and cut the grass or I'm locking up your bike for a week."*

This practice of using what a child values against him corrupts a parent-child relationship, reducing it to cheap tit for tat transactions, ripping away at Attachment and positioning adults as bullies in their own homes.

In a Problem-Solving family, without interference by a parent's manipulations of his behavior, a child's emotional energy and intellect are free to observe the way things work in a helping relationship instead of being absorbed with figuring out his maneuvers within the controls imposed upon him.

Without his attention directed to staying out of trouble or managing damage control with the least unpleasant consequences, he becomes open to learning from examples of teamwork and dependability in his home life.

"I'm going to need help in the yard this weekend. Let's put our heads together and decide on a good time for both of us."

He enjoys the intrinsic rewards from involvement in a collaborative relationship. In an emotional environment of trust and positive expectations, your child will soak up your code of responsibility. If you want your child to become a responsible person, be responsible yourself within a helping relationship and his sense of responsibility will automatically bloom.

Contrary to folk wisdom, children do not learn to be responsible by being lectured to, forced to pick up their toys, or from being coerced into doing chores.

7

BE THE PARENT!

Parents sometimes fall into a trap of doing almost anything to "keep the peace."

If Johnny rejects the food on his plate and demands chicken nuggets, Mom will get up from the table and put chicken nuggets in the microwave to get him to eat and/or prevent a blowup.

It is not unusual for children, both boys and girls, to tell their parents what to wear. To avoid a hassle, Mom will take off her red dress and put on the blue one her son is demanding. She may justify following his directions by telling herself she is allowing him opportunities for making choices.

We have children suffering from sleep deprivation because parents, dreading bedtime battles, allow them to stay up as late as they want, usually falling asleep on the floor or on a sofa in front of television; television they watch way too much of, as it is being used as a pacifier. Their parents fear any attempt to limit screen time would provoke the tantrums they bend over backwards to avoid.

Before they know what hit them, parents may find their young child running the household.

Do you know such a child? Do you live with one?

If you do, I understand the desire to avoid conflicts and upsets.

Here's the problem:

Running a household, being in charge, and making family decisions add up to a big responsibility. It takes growing up, life experience, and adult physical size and abilities.

It is too much for a child. He knows this and is unhinged by what he has stumbled into. He has no idea what's happening. It will be up to you to get things back on track with you there running the show and with him in his natural position of the taken-care-of child.

Drs. Neufeld and Maté call such a child an Alpha child. Dr. Neufeld's YouTube lectures and DVDs on the subject are tremendously helpful to parents struggling with and exhausted by this unworkable role-reversal. Chapter two in <u>Hold On to Your Kids: Why Parents Need to Matter More Than Peers</u> describes the workings of the brain in such skewed Attachments. They tell us, a child taking charge of his parents can never feel taken care of himself, keeping him in a state of chronic anxiety.

This unhappy situation usually develops gradually and, before they realize what's happening, Mom and Dad are catering to a five-year-old's demands, hoping and praying they can get through the day without an explosion.

Along with our other parent-child difficulties, the increasing occurrence of this predicament can be seen as a product of our fractured culture, the pressures it exerts on parents, and subsequent malformed Attachments.

If you have been away from your child all day, of course you want your time together to be happy. One way you may find yourself trying to do this is by "giving in" to everything your youngster wants, whether or not what he wants is in your best interest or his.

This is not to say stay-at-home parents are immune to this anomaly. It can happen in any family.

Pandering to a child's demands is a common response arising out of the difficulties of a divorce. When parents have prescribed times for being with their children, they may do whatever they believe necessary to make their hours together "happy." In attempting to accomplish this, children are allowed to violate a parent's needs and boundaries and automatically slip into an unhealthy position of power.

When a youngster's controlling behavior gets to be all a parent can take, and the situation escalates to an adult's loss of temper—yelling or striking out—the bewildered child now has fear added to his confusion.

If the parent changes tactics, attempting to gain control with rewards instead of punishments, this further highlights the adult's agenda, feeding Counterwill, demonstrating the parent's personal helplessness, and magnifying the child's feelings of power.

Punishments, angry responses, or bribes weaken connection, diminishing a parent's influence and compounding the problem. If the parent increases threats, warnings, removal of privileges, or various forms of love withdrawal, the child's anxiety can reach explosive levels, erupting into the violence or tantrums overindulgence was aimed at preventing in the first place. Now, if the parent backs down and gives in to restore peace, the child remains firmly in charge.

Besides throwing family functioning into chaos, meeting a child's unreasonable demands interferes with the development of Adaptability, a necessary step to maturity. As explained earlier, your child needs to know he will not always get his way. This must be a fact of life he learns about and adapts to at an early age. When knowing he will not be getting what he wants in a particular situation brings him to tears, the lesson is complete and he has taken a vital step toward growing up. Our part in his transformation is to acknowledge his distress and support him in his unhappiness. We retard his movement forward if his crying changes our

No to a Yes. Remember! We can maintain a restriction and still be kind about it. Sticking to our position is what counts in furthering his growth.

Everything you read in this book can keep you in your place as natural authority in your home. If this chapter strikes a note, you may want to stop here and go back over the first sections of the book as well as the chapter titled MEAN WHAT YOU SAY!

Peace and Harmony can be yours. To further assure this, I'm inviting you to visualize a typical problem and a solution to it.

After picking up three-year-old Dustin from preschool, Mom took the time to stop in a park to push him on the swings and sit on a bench with him to read a favorite story. Now they are in the kitchen together. She's hurrying to make dinner and Dustin is right under her feet crying and begging her to play with him.

She can scream, *"Get out of the kitchen and leave me alone!"*

She can say, *"We stopped at the park and I read your favorite book to you. Now please let me cook dinner."*

Will this work? *"If you don't hush up and stop bothering me, I'm sending you to Time-Out."*

How about this? *"I'm trying to cook dinner. Go play with your toys, sweetheart."*

Or this? *"Are you asking for a spanking?"*

There are many such things she could say, none of which will address what is happening in this kitchen.

To maintain her place as the natural authority who keeps her home and her life as well as her child's life running smoothly, she must recognize what's going on and respond effectively, not lash out or give orders. Knowing how ALL BEHAVIOR PROBLEMS ARE ATTACHMENT PROBLEMS, here's a way this mother can take charge of the situation and bring harmony into her home:

No matter how much time she spent in the park today, right now, while she's totally occupied with making dinner, Dustin feels abandoned and rejected; feelings he has no way for putting into words. Mom "gets it" and realizes she must direct attention to firming up Attachment during the coming weeks.

To handle the immediate difficulty, she will take Dustin into her arms, hold him closely, and say something along the lines of, *"You missed me all day. I missed you, too. Before I get back to making dinner, I'm going to find something fun for you to do here on the kitchen table so we can visit together while I cook."*

Now, instead of shutting him out, she has drawn him in, giving him support for playing independently while she prepares the meal without giving in to his demands or giving up her own need to make dinner.

Evaluating the possibility of a late-day dip in blood sugar throwing him off balance, she may give him a snack.

There are, of course, hundreds of similar scenarios, all of which could be addressed in hundreds of different ways. In real-life circumstances, similar to my example above, a father who cleaned up after dinner each night, while his wife was putting their baby to bed, was being constantly pulled on and increasingly annoyed by his three-year-old boy. He changed the tone of his responses, did some Active Listening, and gave his son something interesting to play with on the kitchen table. After the first evening's happy results, he filled a small box with several favorite toys, put it on a kitchen shelf, and brought it out each night before starting to clean up. Now, instead of feeling left out and abandoned, while Mommy was engaged with the baby and Daddy was busy cleaning up, the little boy felt included. Having been brought into the fold, his anxiety relieved, he was able to relax into a spirit of camaraderie. This arrangement went on as one of the best times of the day for both father and son, chatting back and forth, each busy with his own activities, there in the kitchen together.

Responding in understanding and caring ways takes the work out of being a parent. The above approach is not hard to follow. The hard-to-do part is changing old habits. You will be pleased to find the results to be well worth the effort.

8

WHAT'S GOING ON HERE?

An adult, whom we assume to be a mother or a father, enters a restaurant with a child. There may be two parents or some other combination of grownups; a mother and a grandmother perhaps. The child may be a boy or a girl, between the approximate ages of three and ten. Sometime during the meal or before they have started eating, the child starts running around or crawls under the table.

There are variations on this scene with the child running around and only crawling under the table after an adult has called out an order to *"Come back over here and sit down."* Sometimes the adults eat their entire meal with the child crouched under the table or running around.

I've seen this painfully awkward situation a few times. From my work with parents, I now recognize it as fairly common. Knowing families who have been in this embarrassing spot, I will assume some readers will have been there, too.

One of the most puzzling things to other guests is seeing the parents ignoring the disruptive antics. As their child runs around or crawls under the table, they eat their meal as though nothing is happening. The other diners are wondering, *"Why don't they do something?"*

If the parents knew what to do, they would do it!

They are afraid that any attempt to get their child seated at the table will result in a physical battle, a screaming meltdown, or both. They sit abashed, gulping down their food and hoping they can get out of there without precipitating a bigger scene.

There is no simple answer to the question of, *"What's going on here?"* because each such incident brings with it a combination of chronic relationship ills and any number of other immediate contributing factors.

One thing we can be certain about and one not subject to a quick solution: part or all of this child's dysfunction lies in shaky Attachments to the adults in his life. The restaurant behavior is set in motion by the weight of this day's bundle of challenges making demands on emotional reserves already over-taxed by Attachment anxieties.

Annoyed observers who are saying, *"All this kid needs is a good spanking"* could not be more wrong.

For folks caught in the embarrassing dilemma, I offer here a few helpful things to do in the heat of the crisis, as follows:

Ask the waiter to put your food into take-out containers. For the sake of the other diners, and for your child's sake as well, an immediate exit is your best move.

Whether he's under the table or running around, make eye contact, put a hand on his shoulder, and make a statement of fact: *"We're going home now."* Nothing is gained by telling him you are leaving because he has ruined the evening, he's embarrassed you terribly, or he's a bad boy.

Take your child to the car and buckle him in with an empathic comment, such as *"Things went way off track for you in there."* Take time to Active Listen to anything he may say and head for home.

You may never know why he went over the edge, here and now, and your child has absolutely no idea what motivated his disturbing performance.

There is no way in the world he could answer questions, such as *"What's wrong with you?"* *"Didn't you see all the other children sitting down enjoying their food?"* *"When are you going to learn to behave yourself?"* Questions of any kind, including sympathetic inquiries, such as *"Did you have a bad day at school?"* only add to the emotional overload already throwing him off balance.

Blaming him for spoiling our dining experience and ruining our day, we could administer a dose of guilt: *"If I make him feel miserable enough about acting up in the restaurant, he'll think twice before behaving like this again."* This way of seeing a child can only damage our relationship to him and his feelings about himself. As far as "thinking twice" goes, his restaurant conduct was beyond rational thought.

There are numbers of possible pressures impacting his behavior on this day and our best help is in simply being there for him.

Of course, you and I know overwrought children are not only seen in restaurants. We may see a stressed-out child just about anywhere. I recently saw a sobbing little girl of about six, stretched out flat on her stomach on the floor of a grocery store, clutching her father's ankles.

In our restaurant example, the child may have entered the establishment already off-balance after missing a nap or from some combination of unsettling challenges. He may have been worried and frantic about meeting expectations for his behavior inside this public place. Anticipation of the unbearable frustration with finishing his food and having to remain seated and immobile, waiting for the adults to finish, may have pushed him beyond his developmental capabilities.

Possibilities are endless.

Getting to the heart of the matter, we go back to basics and remember: All behavior problems are Attachment problems. If his emotional energy is depleted in pursuing Attachment security, a child may be without reserves of inner vitality for facing novel challenges such as eating out.

An ongoing power struggle is a common ingredient in the restaurant tableau. Flowering of the natural drive to cooperate may be obstructed by a struggle for power against at least one important adult in the life of the child who's running around a restaurant.

If this troublesome drama occurs in your family, recognize it as a call for help, prompting you to become more intimately involved and firmly connected to your child. As you move forward to eliminate a possible power struggle, also do whatever you can to reduce the frustrations, pressures, and sensory input bombarding his growing brain.

Besides taking a child out to eat only after he is well rested, we can help make the experience enjoyable by including him in our table conversations and bringing along something for him to do while waiting for his food or waiting for us to finish at the end of the meal. A coloring book and a few crayons, or an engaging item, such as a kaleidoscope or a magnifying glass, may be all it takes to make eating out pleasurable for him and for us. I vigorously advise against handing him your Smartphone before the meal or if he starts to behave inappropriately. The growth we aim to support is impeded by such pacification. Additionally, electronics have no place at the dinner table; at home or when eating out.

9

OPPOSITIONAL DEFIANT DISORDER

This is a label assigned to children who have nothing wrong with them.

The behaviors it addresses are perfectly natural responses to our common everyday control techniques. All humans resist being bossed around and the usual demanding manner in which adults approach children activates their Counterwill.

A child's defiant reaction to an adult's attempts to control him is instinctive, brain-directed behavior. IT IS NOT A DISORDER.

When a "professional" pins this label on our child, we parents feel we are off the hook. We can breathe a sigh of relief and tell ourselves *"There is something wrong with our kid. There's nothing we can do about it ourselves. Drugs will fix him."*

Or some sort of expensive therapy, aimed at this particular "illness," will get him to behave properly.

Because we know how coercion activates a child's brain, forcing him to defy us, we reject seeing him as disordered. We focus on being on his side, securing his connection to us, and get out of the way, allowing his inborn propensity toward cooperation to move him forward.

When troubling behaviors are, indeed, symptoms of real problems, such as a learning difference, ADD, or Autism; children unsettled by them will benefit from the unconditional love and acceptance outlined in this book. Drugs are limited to acting upon symptoms of distress. The only real help comes about through solid, safe Attachment to at least one attuned adult, changes to the emotional and physical environments, and freedom.

Again, I emphasize the importance of vigorous outdoor activity and regular sufficient sleep as vital to children's well-being. A child seen as hyperactive may be jumping out of his skin because he's living a sedentary life of long, boring hours sitting in school followed by hours submerged in electronics at home.

As for sleep, all humans suffer in a number of ways when sleep requirements are not met. For children, adequate sleep is a prerequisite to healthy bodies and brains.

Sometimes behaviors similar to ADD and ADHD symptoms can be smoothed out with changes to a child's diet. Junk food, artificial colors and sweeteners, sugars, preservatives, pesticides and chemical fertilizers threaten our health and are particularly toxic to children.

Food allergies and sensitivities to environmental pollutants can throw a child's system out of balance.

> Young children are under extreme pressure to learn concepts their neurological circuits are not prepared to process. They are being pushed beyond endurance by impossible cognitive demands, and at the same time, they are being deprived of physical activity and free play their bodies and brains must have. For many kids, their resulting anxiety and agitation show up in behaviors the adults around them interpret as symptoms of Attention Deficit Disorder and Hyperactivity.

We would all be a lot better off if the word DISORDER had never been introduced to describe children's difficulties in coping with the circumstances of their lives.

Early experiences affect the structuring of infant brains, giving some children short attention spans. Others seem to have an over-abundance of nervous energy. Can we just describe their behaviors without calling them "disordered" and, worse yet, having them see themselves as disordered?

In the book, <u>Scattered: How Attention Deficit Disorder Originates and What You Can Do About It</u>, by Dr. Gabor Maté, you will find a complete picture of ADD and ADHD, telling us how the syndromes develop, the difficulties they cause for children and parents, and how best to cope with, live with, and progress beyond simply grappling with unwanted behaviors.

Many children "diagnosed" with various disorders are, in fact, perfectly fine—or would be, if the adults around them understood what their children are up against and could help them. Their problematic behaviors are reactions to relentless coercion, unbearable suppression of their natural physical and emotional needs, debilitating encroachment on their time and space, disrespect, and lack of secure Attachments to the adults in their lives.

Another non-existent disability is called Anxiety Separation Disorder. I recommend Chaley-Ann Scott's internet article, "Anxiety Separation Disorder Debunked."

It is entirely natural for babies and little children to become anxious when connections to their primary Attachment figures are broken. The younger the child, the greater the impact on brain systems regulating emotion. Some children react loudly and vigorously.

They get labeled.

In the 1970s, giving schoolchildren drugs to make them compliant became a fad. Booming expansion of a hugely profitable pharmaceutical industry soon followed and grows larger by the day as more and more children are prescribed pills from a growing assortment of chemicals aimed at a growing list of labels.

The drug corporations have school administrators and teachers, politicians, medical doctors, and parents in the palms of their hands as they churn out psychotropic compounds for subduing childish behaviors.

Energetic little kids are required to sit still and be quiet for long periods of time in exact opposition to their real needs. Human bodies are designed for strenuous activity, and lots of it—particularly growing human bodies.

Note: Over the past several years, elementary schools throughout the United States have shortened or completely eliminated recess. For a look into the damaging effects of this development, I highly recommend the January 2013 Academy of Pediatrics Policy Statement titled, "The Crucial Role of Recess." You can find it on the internet. I urgently suggest reading it as an ideal supplement to what I am saying here.

For schoolteachers, who want acquiescent children to work with, drugs are a welcome panacea. Who can blame them? The teachers are facing the same impossible institutional demands as the children.

Our young pay a heavy price, physically and emotionally, as they cope with the stresses of our accelerating, chaotic society and the dictates of the oppressive schools they are compelled to attend.

Medicating children is simply one more way, and a very dangerous one, of controlling them and subduing their natural responses to the context of their lives.

Non-functional behavior is not a medical condition.

Responding with pills to behaviors we don't like is analogous to silencing a shrilly-signaling smoke alarm while we ignore the fire.

Dr. Peter Breggin tells us on page 274 of his book, <u>Reclaiming Our Children: A Healing Plan for a Nation in Crisis</u>: *"From infancy to old age, human relationships are the most powerful healing force for psychological and spiritual suffering of every kind."*

Before following the advice of a teacher, school counselor, or medical professional who claims your child needs treatment or medication for a behavior disorder, I urge you to read at least one of the following books:

<u>Scattered: How Attention Deficit Disorder Originates and What You Can Do About It</u> by Gabor Maté, M.D., Copyright 1999, Published by Plume, a member of Putnam, Inc., New York, NY. *This is a book for all parents, not just folks struggling with ADD.*

<u>The Wildest Colts Make the Best Horses</u> by Dr. John Breeding, Copyright 1996, Published by Bright Books, Austin, TX and Copyright May 3, 2009, Published by Chipmunka Publishing Ltd., The Mental Health Publisher, Cornwall, England, UK. *The Wildest Colts website offers invaluable information about the reckless medicating of children and the labels assigned to non-existent disorders along with a treasure of Parenting advice.*

<u>Son Rise</u> by Barry Neil Kaufman, Copyright 1964, Published by Warner Books, New York, NY. *Barry Kaufman describes in fine detail how he and his wife Suzie brought their toddler son out of isolation in his world of severe autism, with an attitude of unconditional love and total acceptance.*

<u>Reclaiming Our Children: A Healing Plan for a Nation in Crisis</u> by Peter R. Breggin, M. D., Copyright 2000, Published by Perseus Publishing a member of the Perseus Book Group, New York, NY. *In the United States, Dr. Breggin is the most vociferous voice against the drugging of children. You can find information about him and read about his work on several different websites.*

Whatever may be going on at home or in school, each of the above books can be a great help in providing vital insight for moving forward to better, happier days.

ADDENDUM TO OPPOSITIONAL DEFIANCE DISORDER

If you have taken this book to heart and applying my suggestions is failing to bring peace and harmony to your life, you may be grappling with an undiagnosed real developmental anomaly such as autism, ADD, or a learning problem, with dyslexia being the best known.

I'm thinking of a youngster struggling to fit in, fighting over homework, unable to complete assignments, and, day by day, growing increasingly frustrated, angry, and difficult to live with. Because such children are usually highly intelligent and exceptionally creative, the inability to conform may be interpreted as bad behavior by adults who try, without success, to force them into the mainstream mold and get them to "behave properly."

I want the information in this book to free you from parenthood headaches.

A youngster's unrecognized atypical way of processing written and spoken language, integrating experience, or misinterpretation of social cues will erode relationships and sabotage your liberation.

Here's what I suggest:

Do take seriously the concepts I put forth. Meanwhile, if you see your child overwhelmed by schoolwork or unable to cope with life, become informed by researching websites and gathering information from educators, books, articles, and other parents. I do not like the term, "Disabilities" when referring to the different ways children may assimilate information. I prefer to think about Learning and Developmental Differences, which look like disabilities, when kids are being related to and taught in ways incompatible with their personal information processing styles.

If a reputable diagnostician finds your child to be learning in an uncommon way, finding teachers trained to work with unusual learning styles is critical to a happy outcome. As you may well imagine, this has become a profitable open field for experts and amateurs alike. Diligent research is the best course of action for finding dependable guidance.

10

FAMILY RULES

When you have created a Problem-Solving home, you will be surprised to find yourself living without rules. The need for a set of rules has disappeared! Parents and children enjoying relationships built on mutual respect, open communication, and solving problems together have no need for rules.

We can see the pitfall in generating rules when we think about prescribed punishments for breaking the rules. Establishing penalties for breaking rules tells children we have little faith in their ability to follow them—a belief they incorporate as their own.

With our understanding of Counterwill, we see how a direct order invites defiance. A rule is simply a formalized order about a particular behavior.

When Counterwill has been activated, a rule can serve as a dare.

In following the P.E.T. philosophy, you will look around one day and find your family functioning beautifully and living happily without rules. In a Problem-Solving family, we come to agreement and understanding about conflicting expectations. When agreement is difficult to reach, a solution is found through No-Lose Conflict Resolution.

Everyone in the family, children and parents alike, find living much easier and happier when no one is worrying about rules.

Along with questions about the establishment of rules, parents are usually looking for answers about giving children chores to do.

I'm not big on the notion of teaching responsibility through the assignment of chores. I don't believe this is how responsibility is learned. In families where Attachment and mutual respect are firm, kids are willing to help out when needed. Telling a ten-year-old you are giving him the responsibility for taking out the trash can stimulate Counterwill. How much better when we look into his eyes, smile, and say, *"Honey, it will help me a lot if you grab the trash on your way out."* Isn't this the way we would ask an adult to do something for us? You may be the one headed out the door when the next bag of trash has accumulated. Taking it out yourself is only logical.

Without formally establishing a rule, we can just plain "tell" our child, kindly and respectfully, how much it will help us if he takes his dishes to the kitchen sink after each meal. When the relationship is caring and Attachment is firm, he will be perfectly happy to help out. There's no reason to make a "big deal" about it. If he needs reminding until it becomes a habit, our reminders can be given cordially and with good humor. Why not?

We have been making life with kids terribly and unnecessarily complicated and unpleasant. Everyone in the family, children and adults alike, find life much easier and happier when no one is worrying about rules or fighting about chores.

V

What is done to children, they will do to society.
~ Karl Menninger

1

TRAINING A SEAL OR RAISING A HUMAN BEING?

For many years, most Parent Training programs have been designed around the control methods of Behaviorism. Although some may use the language of a humane approach with various examples from brain research mixed in, they invariably fall back into reliance on authoritarian methods of punishments and rewards for manipulating children.

If we are to move forward as the human race, it is imperative to our advancement to learn to treat children with FULL RESPECT and to progress beyond Behaviorism in our relationships with them.

Many readers are familiar with references to Pavlov's dogs. In the late 1800s the Russian physiologist had been investigating digestion in dogs by analyzing their saliva when he discovered, what he named, a Conditioned Reflex. He had inadvertently found the dogs to salivate when they knew food was coming. Fascinated by this finding, he went on to condition his laboratory dogs to associate the sound of a bell or other signals with the imminent arrival of food.

The American Behaviorist movement was born in the early 1900s when psychologist John B. Watson devoted his work to conditioning animal reflexes in the manipulation of their behavior.

John Watson applied his findings to his teachings about raising children. His total focus was on behavior without consideration for, or the possibility of, any inborn characteristics of a child. He was convinced everything we need to know about a person is there to be seen in observable behavior, and this behavior can be **shaped** with rewards and punishments.

Watson became the American Parenting Expert of the day. He claimed there were no feelings or emotional needs within a child and warned against closeness between parents and their children. His advice was exactly opposite to all we have learned since his time. With knowledge from today's brain studies and our understanding of Attachment, we now know his recommendations were wrong and dangerous.

Think of it! He told parents to never hold, hug, or kiss their babies and <u>to touch them only when necessary.</u>

His own children, by the way, were severely troubled all their lives and alienated from him until his death, as a recluse. His granddaughter, the actress Mariette Hartley, describes her miserable dysfunctional family in her book, <u>Breaking the Silence</u>,[46] and says this about having been raised according to John Watson's Behaviorist principles: *"Grandfather's theories infected my mother's life, my life and the lives of millions."*

Psychologist B.F. Skinner adopted Watson's beliefs and promoted them widely from his position at Harvard during the 1950s and 60s where he performed experiments with rats, chickens, and pigeons.

Skinner advocated against punishment and recommended control through rewards and withdrawal of rewards. Today, Love-Withdrawal is the method many Parenting writers and coaches recommend for controlling children. They call it Time-Out, Ignoring, and Shunning.

---

[46] <u>Breaking the Silence</u> by Mariette Hartley and Anne Commire, Copyright 1990, Published by G.P. Putnam's Sons, New York, NY.

When you attend shows of leaping dolphins or dancing dogs, you are witnessing the results of B.F. Skinner's work. The performing animals have been trained through a carefully designed system of rewards he called Operant Conditioning and Shaping.

B. F. Skinner and John Watson were well-intentioned when they saw their behavior modification methods as being applicable to child rearing, as are today's Parent Educators who espouse the techniques.

However, serious problems with their approach to children's behaviors derive from being based on three false premises:

1. Humans are born with blank brains.
2. Human behavior can be shaped and controlled by the same methods used on animals in scientific laboratories.
3. There is no emotional factor in a child's behavior.

Behaviorism was the foundation of most, if not all, Parenting advice until the 1950s when Dr. Carl Rogers, advancing beyond Behaviorism and influenced by Psychologist Alfred Adler,[47] came to comprehend and appreciate the importance of each individual's unique intrinsic qualities and potentialities.

Both men, through their clinical work with disturbed and distressed patients, discovered resources within the individual: inborn strengths, drives, feelings, and emotions motivating observable behavior. They found that by working with a patient's inner resources they could facilitate healing and growth.

Dr. Thomas Gordon studied under Carl Rogers and designed Parent Effectiveness Training for nurturing each individual child's unique combination of inborn

---

[47] The well-known S.T.E.P., Systematic Training for Effective Parenting, was developed by followers of the Alfred Adler Theory of Individual Psychology. This Parent Training course is much like P.E.T. except for the recommendation of what they call, "Logical Consequences." I, myself, as well as Thomas Gordon, Alfie Kohn, and others who have grown beyond Behaviorism, see Logical Consequences to be another name for Punishment. We see no need for enforcing consequences of any kind and find them to be a threat to the crucial parent-child Attachment while retarding the development of autonomy, empathy, and self-esteem.

strengths and characteristics to support him in the development of positive qualities of character and personality while, at the same time, making the parent's undertaking easy and fun.

Beware of books, classes, and coaches who will tell you to TRAIN your child through Operant Conditioning the way you would train a seal to balance a ball on his nose.

An unavoidable problem with Operant Conditioning is this: You have to keep doing it. Your subject, in this case your child, needs continual monitoring, rewarding, and reward withdrawal for you to gain any level of temporary control over his behavior. This involves exhaustive time and effort, accompanied by alienating frustration and anger for both you and your child.

> Watson and Skinner trained animals to perform through carefully controlled laboratory conditions impossible to produce in the home and inapplicable to children.

When we follow the P.E.T. philosophy and work with the Whole Child, he develops and maintains his own self-control because it comes from within him and grows from his one-of-a-kind combination of strengths, aptitudes, and needs. There is a huge difference in the quality of family relationships, and in life as a whole, when our focus is on our child and his needs instead of on his behavior.

After centuries of believing children would run wild without vigorous adult control, based on the old myth of inborn evil, changing our Parenting paradigm to one of Support and "Working With" is a considerable challenge.

Doubters can come up with examples of children behaving badly when left to their own devices. Kids running around and tearing things up as soon as an adult leaves them alone are children who are growing up oppressed.

Chaotic wild activity feels like freedom to children who have lived without experiencing the true freedom of controlling and directing their own behavior.

Lucky parents, who have learned about P.E.T. and similar approaches to parenthood, come to see the mythology deep in our beings, pitting us against our young. By recognizing a jaundiced belief system, we are able to overcome the hold it has on us and reach out for life-affirming ways of living with children. When we accommodate Human Nature on a child's behalf, life is good!

2

THINKING ABOUT PUNISHMENT

With our new knowledge about Counterwill, we understand how the defiance it stimulates sabotages our attempts at control through punishment.

Now, let's look at the big picture.

Everything we have learned from the study of Developmental Psychology and human behavior points to the harmful effects of punishment.

Punishing and neglecting the needs of children are at the root of most, if not all, of society's problems.

Before I explain the reasons for my stand against punishment, I want to share with you a real-life story from my distant past.

A neighbor struggled in daily conflict with her three-year-old boy. One of her many battles revolved around getting him to stay in bed and go to sleep. She had given up on daytime naps and both parents grappled with him every night until long after midnight. One day this exhausted mother said to me, *"I spanked him last night until I could not raise my arm and he still would not stay in bed."*

What can we learn from this mother's plight?

PUNISHMENT WILL NOT BRING THE RESULTS WE WANT.

Unlike the experience of my neighbor, punishment will "work" to bring short-term results sometimes.

At what cost?

For a little boy who would stay in bed after the first spanking, what has it cost him? What has it cost his parents?

Punishment threatens, weakens, and can destroy the critical Attachment bond. A child will not be drawn to an adult who makes him suffer either physically or emotionally. As punishers, we cast ourselves as our children's enemies to be defied, avoided, feared, and deceived.

Punishment fails to address the unmet needs motivating troublesome behaviors. When a need remains unfulfilled, the symptomatic unwanted behavior continues or reappears in a different form. One week, troubling symptoms may show up as hitting and biting. The next week, in addition to a child's physical assaults, he may be throwing tantrums or throwing toys.

If we gain any leverage at all through punishment, it will be temporary and leave us searching for new and better methods of control.

There are children who buckle under to authoritarian pressures and become conforming model children at home only to surprise parents when they start acting up at school. Mom and Dad are shocked when the school principal calls to report and complain about their perfect little kid's unacceptable antics in the classroom.

And we all know about the "nice" twelve-year-old next door who gets into outrageous mischief when his strict parents aren't looking.

A submissive child may be able to contain his anger and his hunger for freedom until teen Counterwill kicks in and he flies off into the behavior we have come to know as Teenage Rebellion or Delinquency.

One of the saddest outcomes of a punitive environment is in the permanently submissive individual who loses all sense of Self and goes through life as a hollow person, never knowing who he is or what he might have been.

When a parent assumes the role of punisher, a child falls into the role of punishee and performs in such a way as to "deserve" punishment. He takes on the behaviors to fit the role assigned to him through punishing. Seen by his parents as needing punishment, he views himself in the same way. Not having been given support for development of self-control, he adopts the parent's belief system and relies on the punishments he endures to serve as payments for his transgressions.

Finding it perfectly functional to raise delightful, self-disciplined children without punishments of any kind, it is tragic to see the inhabitants of advanced societies routinely punishing children from babies to teens.

To folks who ask what to do to children instead of punishing them, the answer is, "*Nothing.*" This is like being asked, "*When you remove a cancer, what do you put in place of it?*"

With the latest brain studies proving otherwise, there are still some professionals, regarded as experts, writing books claiming positive outcomes from control through the application of various combinations of punishments and rewards. Some such writers and Parent Trainers have begun to feel uneasy about punishment and, not knowing how to give it up, fool themselves and parents seeking advice by assigning punishment a new name.

THEY CALL IT CONSEQUENCES.

We are stumbling in the dark when, by following our cultural habits, we mete-out physical and emotional pain to babies and children. Coming up with new names for what we do, like Time-Out and Consequences, keeps us in darkness.

Children, who live under the constant threat of punishment, or so-called consequences, are living with a continual undercurrent of fear. Fear of parental disapproval and loss of love undermines all facets of healthy development. John Holt, in his book, How Children Fail,[48] explained how fear blocks learning.

Fear distorts a growing child's perception of the world and contributes to pathologies culminating in personality disorders, aggression, violence, and criminal activity.

Parents use fear and anger as their go-to weapons. Screaming, shouting and threatening scares children into compliance: *"Hurry up. Daddy will be mad if we're late. You don't want to make Daddy mad do you?"*

Today's developmental psychologists describe the effects of fear on the hormonal and immune systems of babies and children. Recent research into the workings of the brain has revealed how early fears set us up for later health problems, including obesity, diabetes, hypertension, and Alzheimer's disease as well as mental suffering, such as anxiety and depression. The stress children accumulate living within a punitive environment has lifelong effects on their health, as demonstrated and reported in January 2012 by Dr. Jack P. Schonkoff at Harvard's School of Child Health and Development.[49]

For an in-depth study of the ways in which childhood fears generate into adult illnesses, please read Scared Sick: The Role of Childhood Trauma in Adult Disease.[50]

There are families, schools, preschools, and entire communities where a nearly tangible cloud of fear hangs over the young and where, when you find yourself near a group of children, before long you will hear the word *"trouble."*

"I got in trouble in math class today."

"I'll be in trouble with my Mom if I'm late to dinner."

---

[48] How Children Fail by John Holt, Copyright 1964, Published by Pitman Publishing Co., New York, NY.

[49] Please read about this research in Pediatrics: The Official Journal of the American Academy of Pediatrics for the 12-26-11 article on "The Lifelong Effects of Early Childhood Adversity and Toxic Stress."

[50] Scared Sick: The Role of Childhood Trauma in Adult Disease by Robin Karr-Morse with Meredith S. Wiley.

"You'll get in trouble with the park guy if you climb on the fence."

Many kids carry around a crippling burden of fear, stifling their freedom and stunting growth of an authentic Self. Emotional maiming of the young, the adults of the future, retards advancement of the entire culture.

Now, with computer studies of the brain, along with research documented in the books I have cited and others like them, are we entering an intellectual and emotional revolution when we will turn away from the destructive ideas behind our historical mistreatment of children?

Let's hope so.

3

SPANKING

The purpose of this book is to offer parents a way to live in peace and freedom, to take the work out of living with children, and to make family life satisfying and enjoyable with children becoming self-confident, happy, productive individuals.

This may sound like an impossible dream for parents caught in a power struggle, worn out by arguments, or faced with other long-standing difficulties. Many parents feel helpless and hopeless. When they see other families grappling with their same problems, it appears as though the difficult behavior wearing them out is natural for all children and their only recourse is to put up with it.

A child's difficult behavior is not natural and not something to be coped with. By this time, having read this far, perhaps you are seeing bright new possibilities.

And, if you have been spanking, reading about the damaging effects of punishments may have you questioning whether using physical pain to control your child has been a good idea.

Let's take a thoughtful look at it.

Spanking carries with it the dangers of other punishments with this added problem:[51]

CHILDREN TREATED VIOLENTLY LEARN TO BE VIOLENT.

The modeling effect brings with it the fear and anger children internalize from experiences of being physically hurt by the adults they love and depend upon for nurturing and protection.

As very young children, they are most likely to be physically aggressive. Growing older, some torture animals as well as being belligerent and combative. Fear and anger, carried into the teen years, block learning and boil over as school disruptions and bullying. With alcohol and drugs a commonality, around 40% of teens get into trouble with the law. Others join violent gangs. Or explosive urges break out later in domestic abuse. Prison populations include a large percentage of violent offenders who, as defenceless children, were treated violently by the adults in their lives.

Individuals who do not act out their hurt and anger on others, project it onto themselves with drugs, alcohol, cutting, or other self-destructive habits. Despair and rage may lie buried deep inside, to be expressed through physical ailments, mental illness, or suicide.

Spanking has been accepted and promoted as a perfectly normal part of our culture for centuries, making it difficult to see as abusive or to examine critically. Spanking has simply been a routine, unquestioned part of life, as automatic as breathing.

---

[51] For the Psychohistory of child-rearing practices and how they affect the development of a society, please investigate the work of Lloyd deMause. His many years of research show a clear link between the way children are treated within a given society and whether or not, as adults, they will pursue wars in unsuccessful attempts to solve problems. Find a list of his books and very interesting articles at www.psychohistory.com.

In his book, <u>Spare the Child: The Religious Roots of Punishment and the Psychological Impact of Physical Abuse</u>,[52] Philip Greven describes our predicament with the lifelong effects of childhood spankings as follows: *"The effects of punishment permeate our lives, our thoughts, our culture, and our world."* Dr. Greven devotes Part 4 of this diligently-researched book to describing adult emotional disorders and mental illnesses traced back to physical punishments.

If you have believed spanking to be a useful and harmless way to make your child cooperate, I encourage you to seriously examine your beliefs.

PLEASE STOP FOR A FEW MOMENTS TO CLOSE YOUR EYES AND THINK ABOUT THIS:

ISN'T THERE SOMETHING STRANGE ABOUT INTENTIONALLY HURTING BABIES AND CHILDREN AS A WAY TO TEACH THEM TO BE GOOD PEOPLE?

If, until now, you have been using spankings to control your child, there is no reason to feel guilty. You have only been doing exactly what the surrounding culture has taught you to do.

You are not a bad parent.

Besides the cultural influences supporting spanking Alice Miller[53] suggests another motivation. After having been hit and spanked as children, we try to convince ourselves it was done for our own good and in this way we preserve favorable visions of our parents. We may spank to prove our parents loved us no matter how much they may have hurt us.

---

[52] <u>Spare the Child: The Religious Roots of Punishment and the Psychological Impact of Physical Abuse</u> by Philip Greven, Copyright 1990, Published in the United States by Vintage Books, a division of Random House, Inc., New York, NY.

[53] To see the work of one of the world's most respected researchers on the subject of physical punishment, go to www.alice-miller.com where you will find many informative articles, a list of the books she has written, and a summary of her most famous book, For Your Own Good: Hidden Cruelty in Child-Rearing and the Roots of Violence.

The most common reason we spank is because it was done to us and we are following the examples set for us in our homes. **We learned it.** Our application of this parenting style is reinforced when we believe we deserved to be yelled at, spanked, or banished from sight.

"I was spanked plenty when I was a kid and I deserved it" is a common response to the question of spanking. Believing we deserved to be treated this way demonstrates the mind control we were subjected to and the hold it still has on us. Convincing a little child he did anything to deserve being hit by a grownup three or four times his size and strength is an ancient and widely used form of brainwashing. This is effective mind control, inculcated by the propaganda promoting it: *"I'm doing this for your own good." "This will teach you a lesson." "All you need is a good spanking."*

And it works!

This level of mind control opens the door to sexual violation as well as the physical abuse children are trained to believe grownups have the right to inflict upon them. The adult assumes ownership of the child, who has been conditioned to accept whatever is done to him, becoming too submissive and/or terrified to protest or ask for help. In her book, <u>Miss America By Day</u>: <u>Lessons Learned from Ultimate Betrayals and Unconditional Love</u>,[54] Marilyn Van Derbur describes her mind-shattering terror, living under this level of control from the age of five until she was eighteen, as the victim of her father's incestuous abuse.

When we spank, there may also be an element of, *"Now I get my turn to be boss."* Deeply buried hurt and anger boil up to be directed at our own children and the cycle of violence continues into another generation.

I mention, again, the neurological links researchers are finding between the punitive treatment of infants and children and lifelong health problems. Of course, when you are frantically trying to get your child out the door in the morning,

---

[54] <u>Miss America By Day: Lessons Learned from Ultimate Betrayals and Unconditional Love</u> by Marilyn Van Derbur, Copyright 2003, Published by Oak Hill Ridge Press, Boulder, CO.

and spanking him seems to be the only way to do it, you are not worrying about whether or not he's going to develop hypertension when he's thirty. This new knowledge is, however, forcing us to take a critical look at our long-held beliefs about what we have been doing to children in the name of discipline.

If you have reason to believe spanking is helpful in teaching your child to "be good," I urge you to explore the website www.nospank.net where you will find research reports and a wide variety of articles on the subject. This website offers, free of charge, Jordan Riak's booklet, <u>Plain Talk About Spanking.</u>

While recommending a website for your investigation, I want you to know my earliest beliefs about spanking were the same as 99% of all Americans in the1950s. I sincerely believed responsible parents fed their children, kept them clean, let them cry themselves to sleep, and, among many other duties, spanked them. Before my first child was born, I had the good luck to work for a pediatrician who advised against spanking and had decided to omit physical punishment from my disciplinary strategies before becoming a parent. My personal change stopped there, however, and I went on to be the pure embodiment of all the punitive Authoritarian practices I argue against in this book. I do not point a finger at anyone. I have been there!

We can only act upon the reality and information we have been exposed to. When I apologize now to my first son for the way I treated him, he has the perfect answer I now pass on to you:

"YOU DID THE BEST YOU COULD WITH THE INFORMATION YOU HAD AT THE TIME."

Isn't this all any of us can do?

My life was changed by Parent Effectiveness Training. I felt as though I had been transported to another planet! I hope what I offer here can do the same for you and launch you into the heady atmosphere of living with children in supreme contentment!

Eliminating spanking not only relieves a child of pain and suffering, it gives parents a whole new sense of Self by opening up an entirely different perspective. **This is Liberation only possible to understand when it happens to you.**

Note: In November of 2018 the American Academy of Pediatrics publicized a statement recommending the elimination of all forms of physical punish ment to include spanking, hitting, slapping, and anything done to cause pain as a disciplinary measure. They have also spoken out against verbal abuse. The complete statement and their recommendations can be found on the internet.

4

WHAT ABOUT THE BIBLE?

SPARE THE ROD AND SPOIL THE CHILD.

Although the Bible states this advice in eloquent language, it has been condensed to this wording and followed by conscientious parents for generations.[55]

Since King Solomon has been credited with promoting this belief, wouldn't it be a good idea to know how his own children turned out? According to the Bible, he had dozens of wives and many children. He fathered a large group of sons who were half-brothers to each other and to the son, Rehoboam, who ascended the throne after his father died.

Solomon had ruled harshly and repressively and the populous held out hope for Rehoboam to be a more fair and decent ruler. Their hopes were dashed when representatives of the people came to him asking for a kinder and gentler reign. After consulting with and considering the advice of a number of his half-brothers, his response was to say to his subjects, in effect, *"If you think my father was brutal, wait until you see what I can do."*[56]

---

[55] You can find extensive research findings on this subject in the 2011 book by Janet Heimlich, Breaking Their Will: Shedding Light on Religious Child Maltreatment.

[56] Hebrew Bible 1 Kings 12.

He was not only viciously oppressive to his subjects; he was violently aggressive toward members of other governmental factions. The civil war he incited lasted his entire lifetime.

Some opponents to spanking interpret the biblical "rod" as the shepherd's rod wth which he gently guides his flock.

Christian readers will find it helpful to remember Jesus as a leader who never advocated punishing children.

5

OBEDIENCE

When Parent Educators advise us to enforce rules for our children through a system of rewards and punishments, let's ask ourselves what this is doing to and for our children.

The Behaviorist's books and instructors focus on obedience as their goal.

What's wrong with this?

Behaviorist instructions for raising children emerged from experiments with laboratory animals and the belief that humans are born without emotions or feelings.

A newborn baby is a small human being with intrinsic needs, drives, sensitivities, feelings, and aptitudes in a uniquely complex combination. When we treat him like a laboratory animal by manipulating his behavior with bribes, rewards, punishments, and various forms of love withdrawal in our attempts to make him obedient, we deprive him of the cognitive and emotional growth he would otherwise experience by being instrumental in developing his distinctive capabilities for solving his own problems and controlling his own behavior.

Behaviorist techniques disregard his inner being and interfere with or block the emergence of the unique Self.

When following Behaviorist commands, children obey to either avoid punishment: *"I'll probably get grounded if I don't do what she wants me to do,"* or to gain approval and reward: *"If I do what she told me to do, Mama will love me and give me a puppy sticker."*

Nothing from within the child is called upon to evoke heartfelt gratification when sensing the value of his cooperation. He is denied feelings of achievement and fulfillment from an experience of self-motivated involvement in a mutual effort.

Instead of finding pleasure in working together with loved ones, he looks for ways to avoid cooperating unless threatened with a punishment or bribed with a reward, exactly as our manipulative techniques are <u>training</u> him to do.

With parents and schools setting a high priority on obedience, and focusing much of their efforts at enforcing it, we have populations of individuals walking around who will go to absurd lengths to follow orders from anyone they believe to be an authority. For a jarring example of this, look into *Strip Search Prank Call Scam* on the internet. Also, see the 2012 movie, Compliance, written and directed by Craig Zobel, dramatizing the same disturbing incident, and showing just how far typical Americans will go in following orders.

In 1963, a famous Yale University research project revealed a shocking level of blind obedience to authority. Known by the head researcher's name, the Milgram Experiment produced alarming results. The participants set aside their own human feelings of empathy as they administered, what they thought to be, painful electrical shocks of increasing intensity to other adults simply because the person directing them was presented as a scientific authority conducting research on learning. As distressed as they were to see their subjects screaming and writhing in, what appeared to be, intense pain when shocked for giving a wrong answer, they were willing to continue administering jolts when ordered to keep going by the authority figure in charge.

Child-rearing, with an emphasis on obedience, can produce adults who will automatically follow orders from any individual seen as an authority who knows how to exploit and continue their behavioral conditioning.

Jonestown comes to mind.

Jonestown was founded in Guyana by cult leader Jim Jones and was intended to be a Socialist agricultural community for members of all races and ages. The jungle site had been a bad choice, with poor soil for growing crops and intense heat and humidity making working long hours exhausting and debilitating. Jones became overwhelmed and dependent on a variety of drugs. When his plans fell apart, he orchestrated a mass suicide. About 900 community members were ordered to squirt poison from a syringe into the mouths of babies and children before drinking the cyanide and Flavor-Aid mixture themselves. The term "Drinking the Kool Aid" stems from this incident and has come to mean blindly following orders and an unquestioning submission to authority. Although there were armed guards overseeing the suicides to prevent escapes, many participants cooperated willingly.

Historically, parents have imposed their designs on children with complete disregard for a child's inborn agenda. Response to objections has been to force him into compliance and to tell him they are doing this for his own good.

Morton Schatzman calls this SOUL MURDER and has written about an extreme manifestation of it in his book by the same name. He tells the story of Dr. Daniel Gottlieb Moritz Schreber, a highly respected medical doctor who became the leading German authority for raising children in the early 1800s.

His two sons became insane and one, Daniel Paul Schreber, kept a diary describing his delusions and mental suffering. The book, Soul Murder: Persecution in the Family,[57] establishes a link between the son's mental aberrations and the corresponding control tactics his father used on him.

---

[57] Soul Murder: Persecution in the Family by Morton Schatzman, Copyright 1973, Published by Random House, New York, NY.

Although Dr. Schreber's measures were extreme—with the inclusion of various combinations of straps and braces for controlling a child's posture and movement—his beliefs about human nature and the goal to control a child's behavior, underpinning his teachings, were the same as John Watson's and B. F. Skinner's who later devised their Behaviorist formulas for raising obedient children.

Dr. Schreber's Parenting instructions fostered a collective consciousness leading to the emergence of such a person as Adolph Hitler and the millions of good Germans who followed his orders without question. Good little boys and girls, as well as good citizens, did not question authority in Nazi Germany. They were perfectly obedient.

Tradition has had us trampling on the personal agendas of our children without regard for their inner selves. After the missed childhood opportunities for developmental expression, the Self may lie dormant throughout life or be destroyed completely.

In his book, The Betrayal of the Self: The Fear of Autonomy in Men and in Women, Arno Gruen explains *"how obedience replaces autonomy and leads to dehumanization."*[58]

We can only guess at the number of grownups walking around, never knowing who or what they might have been if only they had been free agents in the individuation of their unique Selves. Writing this reminds me of folks who say, *"I was hit plenty when I was a kid and it didn't hurt me."*

One wonders: *"How do you know? How do you know how different you or your life might have been?"*

---

[58] Page 24, The Betrayal of the Self: The Fear of Autonomy in Men and Women by Arno Gruen.

6

AM I PROMOTING PERMISSIVENESS?

With the P.E.T. philosophy advocating against punishment, am I promoting permissiveness?

No!

Permissiveness is a form of neglect. It is neglect of a child's need for counsel and information. We are letting children down when we fail to provide the direction and dependable support they need for finding their place in the family and in society.

The critical ingredient is in how we go about providing this support and direction.

P.E.T. fosters self-control and self-confidence while preventing unwanted behaviors, creating a home environment where the thought of punishment never comes up.

Contrary to reward-punishment control, which positions the parent in the role of adversary and enforcer inside the home, the P.E.T. model establishes the parent as a friendly guide, allied firmly on the side of the child.

> Once a cooperative relationship has been established, by about the age of two and a half or three, the thought of punishment becomes downright silly. A P.E.T. child has important learning to do. Getting into mischief is not on his agenda.

When parents have not sidetracked him into power struggles or confused him with unsteady, unclear expectations, a child's energy goes into expanding and pursuing his own compelling interests while becoming a contributing member of his family and, eventually, his community.

The Traditionalists are, in fact, the permissive ones. Because they have not learned how to work with a child to prevent problems, they can only react after problems occur. This means they generate an environment producing difficulties and conflict followed by various punishments or they hold out bribes and issue threats hoping for positive results.

This is a bleak and stressful way to live!

With P.E.T., we never get into all of this. We live together and enjoy each other's company without the time-consuming and energy-draining monitoring of Time-Outs, enforcements of Punishments, or Sticker Chart maintenance. No energy is expended in the complications of Behaviorist methods of control or the conflict, hurt feelings, and alienation such antagonistic relationships propagate. Giving up our position as family police officer frees us to enjoy life. Relieved of the time, effort, and stress of policing our child's activities, we find ourselves out from under a big tiresome job. The entire hassle simply vanishes!

Note: Folks who intuitively sense the authoritarian path to be a hazardous one, or are repelled by the heavy-handed parents next door, may see permissiveness as the only alternative way for being with children and find themselves living as joylessly and with as much work and stress as their strict neighbors. Children need our involvement and dependable guidance for finding their direction in a complicated world. Directionless kids are unhappy kids who, in their confusion, generate problems for themselves and the adults around them.

7

LIMITS

Don't kids need limits?

Yes, they do!

They need limits to keep them safe, and we certainly don't want children hurting other people or damaging property.

All through this book, without using the word "limits," I give detailed advice about establishing and maintaining necessary limits.

As a P.E.T. parent with all the additional Neufeld and Maté Parenting information under my belt, I had completely forgotten about the whole idea of limits. I thought I had finished writing when a friend asked me what I had said about setting limits.

And now, I am adding this bit about limits, hoping I can help you forget about them, too.

Remember! We are getting rid of the burdensome adversarial job of Enforcer in our home. We don't need to police our children's behavior in accordance with a list of limits. Through the strength of Relationship, we are creating a sanctuary of peace and harmony for our children and ourselves. Where the heck would a family cop fit into this picture?

Everything I have said about Toddlers addresses the limits we impose on them. If we install a gate at the top and bottom of a flight of stairs, we have established a limit. When we cover electrical outlets, we limit access to them. When we create a daily routine, we limit when and where certain daily happenings will take place in our home. A designated time for going to bed is a limit to staying up. When we lovingly remove our child from jumping on the sofa and give him a big pillow to jump on, we have established a limit for protecting our furniture. Being buckled into a car seat limits movement inside a vehicle.

When speaking to parent groups about new ways to be with children, I almost always hear this question:

"How will I teach my three-year-old boy to stay out of the street if I don't spank him?"

Using my answer to this question as an example, I hope to relieve all concerns about limits.

First, we must assume full responsibility for keeping our young child safe from the dangers of traffic. We do this by ALWAYS being with him when he has any way to go into the street. If he is not in the house or in a fenced yard, we are right there beside him, close enough to pick him up or turn him in another direction if he starts moving toward the street. Nothing needs to be said at this point. We are doing our job keeping him safe without drawing his attention to a "forbidden" possibility. Remember! Counterwill is always ready to take over if we awaken it.

If unusual circumstances have him darting into the street, we rescue him from danger with swift action, grabbing him with an exclamation of fear: *"You could get hurt out there. I was really scared!"*

When we decide to cross the street with him, we take his hand into ours and tell him what's happening: *"I am holding your hand because we are getting ready to cross the street."* Enough said for now. The next several times we cross a street together, we automatically take his hand. After many times crossing the street holding his hand we will one day say, as we stand at the curb, *"I hold your hand to keep you safe from the cars."* This new information is both instructive and reassuring to him. As he gets a little older and will understand our comments about safety, we describe HOW we are keeping him safe from the cars by looking both ways: *"I'm looking both ways to see if cars are coming before we cross the street."*

Soon we add additional information about walking when we cross a street: *"If we think we need to run to stay safe from the cars, they are too close for us to cross. Walking is the only safe way to cross the street."*

Eventually, we add to our teaching: *"I have looked in both directions and, see? There are no cars in sight. So here we go, across the street!"* The next step in his learning experience will be when we invite him to do the looking: *"I'll bet you can look both ways for us and tell when we can cross the street."*

The last step will be letting go of his hand as he takes charge of looking both ways before we cross.

Our engaged street-crossing continues until we are convinced he can get safely to the other side on his own. Many things enter into this decision: the volume and speed of traffic where he will be crossing, the age and personality of the individual child, whether or not an ongoing power struggle may have him needing to defy our instructions, and observing when his looking both ways becomes a habit.

Once you have turned this responsibility over to him, reminders to look both ways every time he'll be crossing a street are not appreciated and can stir up Counterwill instead of helping him to remember.

Hitting is another one of many behaviors parents want to set a limit about. Please read the chapter on FIGHTING, HITTING, BITING to help with questions about aggression

MEAN WHAT YOU SAY in section 4 of this book is all about limits.

Your children, including babies and toddlers, will learn which behaviors are acceptable and which are not by watching your behavior, with intervention, information, and through observation of the folks they spend time with.

Everyone wants to BELONG. Toddlers and children of all ages are no exception.

One of our most important responsibilities is in providing information compatible with their level of development and helping them apply their new knowledge, as described in the street-crossing scenario above. They do not need to hear about limits to understand them, and we do not need to worry about limits in order to plant them firmly in place.

8

WHERE'S THE MAGIC?

There are various Parent Training programs telling us a more carefully designed system of rewards or more consistent application of punishments will be the right trick to get a child to comply.

Moms and dads are driven to wit's end, searching for the magic formula to end their problems.

The following true scenarios illustrate how completely parents have been persuaded to believe in the magic of punishment. The fathers in both cases believed in the magic of spanking.

The first illustration is of a father pacing the floor of a hospital waiting room as doctors try to save the life of his three-year-old daughter. An ambulance brought her here after she was hit by a car in the street in front of her home. The father is distraught, as any father would be, and filled with self-blame when he makes the following statement: *"I don't know how this could have happened. We always spanked her when she ran in the street."*

The other father, a well-known media celebrity, was similarly baffled when his twenty-year-old daughter jumped to her death from her apartment window. Told the girl had been experimenting with LSD, which had probably precipitated her suicide, referring to her drug use, her father said this to reporters: *"I don't know how this could have happened. When she was little, we always spanked her whenever she did anything wrong."*

Each father believed hitting a little girl on her bottom should have prevented the tragedy he was now facing.

Working with parents over the years, I have found most to be delighted and amazed when engaging in new ways to build relationships with their children. They find great relief in being free of the complications of punishment-reward conflicts and stress.

However, there have been a few who, finding P.E.T. not to be offering new tricks for making a child "behave," continue searching after finishing the course.

There are no magic tricks.

Six minutes in Time-Out will be as useless as four minutes were.

Taking away the car keys or grounding will only serve to breed alienation.

We find the peace we are looking for by learning to work with our children instead of doing things to them. When our focus is on Attachment and Needs, instead of Behavior and Control, we step out of the Illusionary World of Magic into the Real World of Relationship and happily living with children.

9

MOMMIE DEAREST

You may know Mommie Dearest[59] to be the title of a book by Christina Crawford, daughter of Joan Crawford, once famous Oscar-winning Hollywood movie star. After her death, the glamorous actress became famous all over again—this time, for her physical and emotional abuse of Christina. All her fame and fortune had been ineffective in mitigating whatever abuses the actress, herself, had suffered early in life, dooming her to leaving behind an angry daughter and an ugly legacy.

Parents from all walks of life and at every income and educational level hurt children in many different ways. Year after year, the number of children neglected and physically maltreated in the United States remains high: from around 700,000 to over a million, according to various reporting agencies. The reported count only offers a clue to another number; the incidents no one knows about.

After centuries of seeing babies as naturally bad and in need of adult training and control, followed by legions of Behaviorist "experts" giving instructions and license to manipulate children through their widely-accepted and promoted systems of punishments and rewards, the scene is set for the consequential ongoing abuse of power by today's parents.

---

[59] Mommie Dearest by Christina Crawford, Copyright 1978, Published by William Morrow and Company, New York, NY.

> It will take a totally different way of thinking about children, our responsibilities toward them and relationships with them, to make any real difference in how we move forward as a culture.

The first comprehensive study of child abuse in the United States was conducted by Dr. David Gil at Brandeis University in the late1960s. Before the term Battered Child Syndrome was coined in 1962, not much thought had been given to what was happening to children behind closed doors. Like Wife Abuse, it was a "family matter" and people looked the other way. If neighbors were beating their children, it wasn't anyone's business. The term **sanctity of the family** was tossed around a lot.

In 1970, Dr. Gil's findings were published in his book, <u>Violence Against Children: Physical Child Abuse in the United States</u>.[60] His exhaustive research painted a dismal picture. This was a time when 98% of American parents believed spanking to be necessary and helpful in bringing up children. All the interviews with medical professionals, parents, social workers, and psychologists culminated in one clear conclusion: the general societal disregard for the welfare of children and the ingrained belief in controlling them with physical force, positioned breaking their bones and bruising their flesh on a continuum with the fully-accepted practice of spanking.

In the last paragraph on page 11 of Dr. Gil's book, we read: *"Some measure of violence against children is patterned into the child-rearing philosophies and practices of nearly all Americans."*

We have not made much progress since 1970 when such a large majority of American parents viewed spanking as a routine duty. Various research studies today find us anywhere from seventy to ninety percent in favor of hitting children.

---

[60] <u>Violence Against Children: Physical Child Abuse in the United States</u> by David G. Gil, Copyright 1970 and 1973 by the President and Fellows of Harvard College, Harvard University Press, Cambridge, MA, and London, England.

With many, or possibly most, incidents going unreported, statistics on sexual abuse are unclear. According to the National Center for Victims of Crime, one in five girls and one in twenty boys will be sexually molested before reaching their eighteenth birthdays. Whatever the number, after suffering under this humiliating control by the adults in their lives, a large population of our fellow humans enters society psychologically maimed from this widespread form of abuse along with all the other physical and emotional pain adults mete out to infants and children.

As wise observers of human nature have warned, the ripple effect of the dehumanization and objectification of children hurts every member of a society and, along with the misguided obsession with power and control, constitutes a genuine obstacle to the progress of our species. The consequences of disrespect for the young resonate into all facets of a culture. Serious thinkers have been telling us this for hundreds of years.

Psychohistorian Lloyd deMause wrote about all manner of child-rearing customs practiced throughout the world and their effects on human development and culture over the centuries: *"As nations evolve their less abusive child rearing practices they can create adults who are not time bombs, and rates of war and social violence decrease."*[61]

Psychologist Carl Rogers revealed our inherent abilities for living together without the need for control and the conflict it generates.

Marshall Rosenberg developed a communication process for resolving conflicts and living together cooperatively.

For a psychoanalytical view of the physical and emotional abuse of one little German boy in the late eighteen-nineties, culminating in the annihilation of an estimated 11 million fellow humans when he reached adulthood, please read

---

[61] This quote was taken from the www.lloyddemause.com website which has been replaced by a new site, www.psychohistory.com, where you can find many interesting articles and a book list for anyone wanting to know how we have come to where we are today in our treatment of children.

about Adolph Hitler in Alice Miller's book, <u>For Your Own Good: Hidden Cruelty in Child-Rearing and the Roots of Violence</u>.

Thoughtful, dedicated Parenting researchers and writers offer us their wisdom, advice, and conclusive reasons for giving up the control mentality. Can we finally hear what they have been saying and embrace the revolution Traditional Parenting calls for?

10

PUNISHMENT JUNKIES

We live in a society unable to solve problems because of our addictive reliance on punishment and blame.

This dependence begins within the autocratic family where the customary culturally-implanted physical punishment of children, along with a wide variety of other punishments, takes the place of and interferes with the development of creative thinking, conflict resolution, and the ability to solve problems.

It has become the American Way to turn to Punishment when facing problems, much like an addict turns to alcohol and drugs.

Problems only multiply, and as they do, the alcoholic increases consumption, the drug addict escalates usage, and the punisher intensifies punishments. Jail sentences are lengthened, schools enforce stricter penalties, and parents grasp at harsher chastisements.

In recent years, various advocacy groups, such as The American Civil Liberties Union, The New York Civil Liberties Union, and the Attorney General of the United States have called for an end to what they term:

THE-SCHOOL-TO-PRISON-PIPELINE.

In the penal atmosphere of schools where police officers patrol the halls and unwanted behaviors are seen as crimes, youthful rule-breakers are treated like criminals and can slip into the pipeline.

Young lives are forever changed. Many forever ruined.

Isn't it odd? When punishments fail, punishers impose more severe punishing and more of it. We have now reached the stage when kids are going to jail instead of being sent to the Principal's office.

There are elementary schools where children are locked in closet-size rooms, some with padded walls, to contain the rage and despair such treatment of humans generates.

Five-year-olds have been written up for pointing a finger, gun-like, at other kids, with reports going into their permanent records. We have elementary schools where overwrought children are handcuffed and jailed, sometimes overnight, for hitting or kicking their inadequately prepared teachers. Other young children have been arrested and jailed for throwing tantrums in school.

In the United States of America, at last count, the physical punishment of children in nineteen K-12 public school districts is supported by law. This means grown men and women are allowed to strike children with thick wooden boards, euphemistically referred to as "paddles."

Note: In November of 2016, the United States Secretary of Education sent a letter to all school districts urging them to ban the physical punishment of children. You can read his letter and reactions to it on the internet. In December of this same year, France became the 52nd country in the world to ban all spanking of children. In October, 2017 a similar law was passed in South Africa.

Without identifying and examining the sources of conflicts and arriving at mutually-agreeable ways of resolving them, Authoritarian parents, school personnel, and public officials habitually rely on punishment, and more of it, as the answer to difficulties.

Self-confidence, strength of character, empathy, and responsibility are obstructed from development in an atmosphere of punishment, blame, criticism, fear, and suppression.

Most Americans grow up impaired to some degree by typical repressive childhood environments and enter adult society carrying a load of anger, fear, and psychic pain, while at the same time, being unequipped for solving problems.

The most severely emotionally wounded join the community as psychopaths.[62]

Risk is heightened for the development of psychopathology, addiction, criminality, and violence when a child is born into circumstances lacking the existence of at least one caring adult who is firmly ON HIS SIDE.

Unless such a child has the good fortune to, somehow, connect with an empathic grownup— teacher, social worker, mentor, neighbor, parent of a friend, anyone— to hear him out and lend support, he can sink into a "Me Against Them" mentality, primed for creating havoc.

He now becomes easy prey for child molesters and any of the other world's users: cult organizers, gang leaders, drug dealers, terrorist recruiters, and others.

As damaging as it is to the fabric of a society to have a large proportion of the population emotionally crippled by early experiences, far-reaching harm occurs when such damaged individuals gain political and economic power, with thousands or millions of others falling victim to their suppressed anger and rage.

Exploding feelings of insignificance and rage are manifested in murder, shootings, wife-battering, gang violence, road-rage, child abuse, armed conflict, war-mongering, and terrorism.

---

[62] Pages 1 through 26 in the book, High Risk: Children Without a Conscience by Dr. Ken Magid and Carole A. McKelvey.

You can learn about the early childhood roots of the terrorist phenomenon by reading, THE WELLSPRINGS of HORROR in the CRADLE by Alice Miller, written after the 9-11 terrorist attacks and available on the internet, where we also find articles by Lloyd deMause explaining how particular life circumstances prepare a person for the beheadings of fellow humans.

In addition to structuring the brain for adult violence, physical and emotional pain suffered in infancy and childhood can emerge as addictions to harmful substances, sometimes as early as a person's teen years, ruining an entire life. In his book, In the Realm of Hungry Ghosts: Close Encounters with Addiction,[63] Gabor Maté describes the adverse effects of childhood mistreatment and neglect on the structuring of the brain, culminating in addictions.

Our huge prison population of adults and juveniles is stark evidence of failure to address and solve problems, while habitually relying on counterproductive punishments. America, with only 5% of the world's population, can claim 25% of the world's prison inmates.

The focus of efforts toward reducing violent crime must shift from punishments and lengths of prison sentences to ways for providing optimal nurturing support for healthy brain development during the first years of life.

The violence and misery all around us will be reduced only by extensive child development education for families, in schools, and throughout our communities, along with a serious commitment to facing and solving problems, abandonment of faulty patterns of interpersonal communication, and the habitual dependence on punishments.

---

[63] In the Realm of Hungry Ghosts: Close Encounters with Addiction by Gabor Maté, Copyright 2008, 2009, 2010, Published by North Atlantic Books, Berkeley, CA.

VI

No social problem is as universal
as oppression of the child.

~ Maria Montessori

1

TERRIFIC TODDLERS

FACTS ABOUT TODDLERS:

- They want to fit in.
- They are born with a drive to cooperate.
- They have a strong capacity to resist outside influence.
- They are quick learners.
- Play is their important work.
- They are curious and interested in everything.
- They imitate what they see and hear.

MISUNDERSTANDINGS ABOUT TODDLERS:

- They are difficult and troublesome.
- The Terrible Twos is a natural stage of development.
- They need our control.
- They need praise and rewards for learning to behave well.
- They should learn to obey.

When we reach an understanding of the inborn resistance to outside influences and pressures, we are on our way to some of the happiest days of our lives as we live them with one of nature's most delightful creatures: a human toddler.

Committed to interacting with our little child as a loving guide, avoiding pressure and coercion, we experience the delight of being present at the fascinating unfolding of a new person.

When living with a toddler, it is essential to always keep in mind the power of the brain's Counterwill.[64] This inborn drive, beyond a child's control, is directing him to be his own person and to do it his way.

Punishments and rewards draw his attention to what the adult wants him to do and exposes our agenda, thereby stimulating the powerful force of Counterwill.

Your two-year-old entered this world with his own agenda: a design rooted in his unique combination of strengths, aptitudes, sensitivities, feelings, and needs.

The less interference he is subjected to, the more he can attend to learning about his world and his place in it. This is his important work, and conflicts occurring when the adults in his life activate Counterwill are avoidable obstacles to his progress.

> When we consistently demonstrate being on our child's side as an ally in his learning adventure, we have the privilege of enjoying the companionship of one of the happiest and most fascinating beings on earth.

The strength of our Attachment bond will determine how much influence we can have on his behavior and his level of cooperation. The more firm his Attachment, the more he will look to us for direction.

How we give this direction will either strengthen or weaken the bond.

It is important to create an environment in which he can play and explore without constant interference. Harsh orders, insistent demands, angry tones of voice, and

---

[64] Please read about COUNTERWILL in the book, Hold On to Your Kids: Why Parents Need to Matter More Than Peers for a full understanding of this powerful instinct.

slapped exploring hands will weaken the bond while stimulating and intensifying Counterwill.

The language we have used to control children for hundreds of years combined with punishments, rewards, and today's disordered culture make being a parent difficult, discouraging work, while making being a child unnecessarily frustrating and stressful.

Thomas Gordon identified this perilous language as The Twelve Communication Roadblocks.[65] Parents create their own misery when they speak to a child with divisive words and fight against an impulse over which this little person has no control. Nature directs him to stand up for himself.

> If we fall into the desolate trap of believing we possess some automatic power because we carry the magic title: PARENT, we entangle ourselves in a destructive battle with our own innocent child.

Without knowing what's happening, we diminish our NATURAL POWER of INFLUENCE while undermining our own personal happiness.

Certainly there will be things he must learn are not to be played with and adjust to our physical boundaries for keeping him safe.

When he starts exploring some object or some place we want him to understand as being out-of-bounds he will accept our direction when we connect with affectionate touch, eye contact, and a smile before offering an enticing alternative along with a clear statement of fact in a friendly tone of voice, *"The TV is not for playing. Let's find something more fun for you to do."* And off we go with him in loving arms to engage his interest in a very appealing substitute for the TV controls.

Or if he is climbing onto a high tippy stool, we present him with a safe place to climb. When we make it our responsibility to always stay close and are right there

---

[65] See the chapter listing the twelve ROADBLOCKS in section 1 of this book.

when and if he starts to climb onto the stool again, supported by our friendly teaching, he will soon come to feel the satisfaction of understanding his place in the scheme of things. We are providing the fertile soil in which his inborn drive to cooperate will flower.

To preserve intrinsic motivation, we refrain from rewarding or praising his compliance. Praise and rewards draw his attention away from the natural pleasures of collaboration and direct his focus to our goals, igniting Counterwill and blocking cooperation.

His inner feelings of reward will heighten with his awareness of being an active participant in the family group. We must resist the temptation to chime in with the usual, *"Good Boy"*[66] distracting him from his first glimpses into seeing his place in the family. His early stirrings of natural pleasure from exercising his drive to cooperate are Nature's rewards and are exactly what he needs to keep him happily moving forward in his personal growth.

If we are preoccupied the next time he becomes interested in the TV and are "too busy" to offer calm and loving reinforcement of the lesson, he becomes confused and unsettled. His inborn drive to become a cooperating member of the household is left unsupported.

Now we may find him going back again and again to the forbidden object. Parents call this "testing." And they are correct. He is looking for clear dependable information.

He is looking for the security in knowing we mean what we say so he can settle down and get on with his important work. He is testing to find out if he can believe us.

Directed by his inner needs, he is not consciously aware of his motivations and is not "trying to be bad," as some parents will believe. You may hear them say, *"He knows how to push my buttons."*

---

[66] Alfie Kohn's essay titled, Five Reasons to Stop Saying "Good Job" describes the negative effects of verbal rewards for manipulating behavior. It can be found at www.alfiekohn.org.

He knows absolutely nothing about our buttons or how to push them. He is confused and uncertain. Our unwavering trust in his natural inclinations toward positive growth will sustain his way forward.

I can hear some readers asking, *"This all sounds like a lot of effort. How many times do I have to redirect him?"* Yes, for the moment, sitting across the room and yelling, *"No"* takes little effort. Slapping his hands is quick and easy, too.

THE DIFFERENCE IS IN THE RESULTS. REMEMBER, YOU ARE SETTING THE TONE OF THE RELATIONSHIP AND WHETHER IT WILL BE ONE OF COMPATIBILITY OR OF ANTAGONISM. THE TIME YOU SPEND IN DEVELOPING A HELPING RELATIONSHIP IS ONLY A TINY FRACTION OF THE TIME YOU WILL SPEND IN TROUBLE AND STRIFE LATER ON IF YOU DON'T BUILD GOODWILL NOW!

When we work with him instead of against him, he finds his way in his world and his confidence rapidly grows. How many times a lesson will need to be taught will depend on how vigilant we are in making certain we hold up our teaching end of the process by always being there to reinforce the restriction and in maintaining a friendly, helping attitude. If we have failed to make our requirements clear by sometimes interrupting an activity and sometimes not, and if we ignite his Counterwill by being harshly punitive and coercive, the interaction is changed from a happy learning occasion to one of frustration and sorrow for parent and child.

By "WORKING WITH" instead of "DOING TO", many children reach contented compliance with a restriction after only one instructive intervention.

There will be situations when his safety is at risk and action will be needed to avert disaster. If, in the tippy stool example above, you have become involved in a power struggle and your child has grown defiant, he may keep going back to climb on the stool or he may just simply love climbing.

This is an occasion for MODIFYING THE ENVIRONMENT to eliminate an unwanted behavior. In this case, at a time when he is asleep or away from the house, it will be your responsibility to remove the threat to his safety by storing the stool completely out of sight. Doing this when he's not around avoids any suggestion of a contest—not as though you are showing him you are "winning" by taking away the stool. If he asks about the missing stool, a brief honest answer, said without emotion, will suffice: *"It was dangerous and has been put in storage."*

At a time like this, old Traditional thinking could sneak up on you and your automatic response might be something like, *"You wouldn't stop climbing on it so I put it away."* There are limitless combative remarks a parent could make and keep a struggle for power alive.

If you had been punishing or yelling at him when he climbed on the stool, Attachment was weakened and Counterwill aroused by the coercion. Remember! You are in charge of the situation. The stool has been removed and you are now free to walk away from whatever clash revolved around it.

To give you a break from watching everything he is doing every minute he is up and about, I strongly suggest arranging a gated room or area in the home supplied with a few age-appropriate and interesting playthings where he can follow his own initiative without interference, as described in the chapter, PLAY.

By honoring your child's needs, working with, not against him, you will find yourself enjoying the best years of your life, sharing them with a Terrific Toddler.

A common obstacle to this happy outcome is unrealistic parental expectations. Some of the things parents expect are simply beyond a child's developmental capabilities. When a neighbor tells you her two-year-old is using the potty or eating everything put before him, beware of the comparison pitfall. What another child is doing has nothing to do with your child's development. The accomplishments parents are tempted to pressure a child to achieve will be realized without hassles and "right on time" when adults get out of the way and allow this little person to advance at his own pace, following his unique genetic blueprint. Parents can help by providing the environmental components for allowing each advancement to take place.

> Your child will walk when he is ready.
> Your child will talk when he is ready.
> Your child will use the potty when he is ready.
> Your child will eat a variety of foods when he is ready.

Putting a child in some sort of a "walker" to hurry his ambulation is unnecessary. Holding him up by his arms and pulling him into stepping forward is disrespectful of his internal timetable.

The natural way you talk to your child, describing what you are doing and giving names to the things he sees, models our speaking language for him to imitate when the speech centers in his brain are ready. Reading to children every day from infancy onward facilitates brain development for language acquisition and literacy.

Please do not waste your money and your child's time on Educational DVDs. Research shows DVDs marketed to build early vocabulary or boost learning actually do the opposite. They impede word acquisition and interfere with natural cognitive growth.[67]

With a little potty chair placed on the floor in the bathroom and your clear statement of why it was put there, you have done your part in providing what he needs for following his internal cues: *"This little toilet, like Mommy's and Daddy's big one, is for you to use when you are ready."* Beyond this, allowing him to observe other family members using the big toilet, dressing him in clothing he can easily handle, and making yourself unobtrusively available to help if needed, will take care of toilet learning. Putting him in cotton training pants so he can feel the wetness will help him along toward using his potty and staying dry.

---

[67] For a PDF and video about this research, look for Dr. Andrew L. Meltzoff on the internet.

Note: One mother keeps a little set of story picture books to place alongside the potty chair. They are known as The Toilet Books in this family of several children.

As for eating a variety of foods, please read the chapter, HOW CAN I GET MY CHILD TO EAT?

Modeling plays a huge part in every stage of a child's growth. Manners come to mind. Very young children are sometimes punished for failing to say *"Please"* or *"Thank You."* This is terribly unfair. Etiquette for easing us through social interactions is far beyond the comprehension of a toddler or any child until around the ages of five or six. Some children do, however, arrive at the habitual use of such niceties at an early age simply through Modeling. When they are firmly attached to the adults around them and this is the language they hear, with such courtesies being extended to them day in and day out, you may hear standard polite responses coming from three-year-olds.

The same holds true concerning table etiquette. Trying to enforce table manners at any age, from toddler to teen, is divisive. A well-respected, firmly-attached child will want to be like his parents and will imitate the table manners he observes in his home. Criticizing table manners, like all criticism, harms relationships and weakens Attachment. Always keeping the fundamental importance of Attachment and Respect in mind, you can relax and enjoy your delightful toddler.

TREASURE EVERY MOMENT!

Time flies. Next week he'll be leaving for college!

2

TANTRUMS

Preventing or minimizing tantrums begins with mindful consideration to the quality of life in a baby's earliest days, weeks, and months. The first nine months are particularly critical as being the period when the brain's basic wiring is being put in place in response to the infant's experiences with his caretakers and his physical environment.

Maximum efficiency in this process depends on continual contact between the baby and one aware, responsive adult. Each additional month and year of this one-on-one attuned interaction adds to healthy neurological development.

This should be a period of peace and quiet enhanced by a daily routine. Taking infants and babies shopping and into other public places can be over-stimulating and jarring to the delicate developing nervous system.

If there are two parents in the home, it is in the infant's best interest for one parent to stay home with the baby while the other runs errands, goes shopping, or engages in other outside activities. This is a time for bringing home favorite take-out foods instead of subjecting a baby to the sensory input in a restaurant.

A single parent may be able to exchange sitting time with another parent or find help from a trusted neighbor or friend.

For the future welfare of our child, every effort should be made to keep his early months as sheltered, orderly, and peaceful as possible.

Although this degree of sheltering may seem like too much effort or too restricting, we save ourselves countless hours of difficulties and future turmoil by getting our baby off to a stable start.

A well-respected, well-Attached child, living with routine and order, free from exhausting demands and exposure to over-stimulating situations, may sail along through childhood without ever having a tantrum.

Or a sensitive child may explode when just being a little kid in a big confusing adult world becomes too much to bear.

A tantrum can also be a desperate reaction to the need to be really seen, understood, and heard.

However, children are frequently "taught" to have tantrums.

This happens when a child cries spontaneously after being told he may not have a particular item or do a particular thing. We're in the checkout line at the grocery store; our child has spotted the candy display and wants a candy bar. We say we are not buying candy and now he's crying. If we are not routinely arbitrary, exercising our power with unnecessary *NO* responses, he will learn to accept disappointments and grow toward maturity through the natural process of adaptation, unless the tears bring him a positive result— today in the form of a candy bar.

If embarrassment about our child's noisy upset prompts us to grab the candy and give it to him, a young child will very quickly see crying as a way to get what he wants.

If your child cries when disappointed, remember it is not within your power to prevent all disappointments. Nor would it be in his best interest if you could. Your helpful response is to acknowledge his distress by Active Listening with sincere understanding while allowing him the right to express his feelings through crying or raging. If his crying followed your *"No"* to something he wanted, you invite future tantrums if you give him what he wants to get him to quiet down.

Other tantrums are the boiling over of overwhelming frustration and unbearable pressures.

A young child's days are filled with frustrating experiences as he learns through trial and error, faces physical challenges, and is forced to adjust his needs to the requirements of adults. When it all becomes too much for his nervous system to accommodate, he explodes into a tantrum.

Whatever the source of the upset, ignoring a tantrum and walking away is not recommended. It is in no way helpful to leave him as some Parenting advisers advocate. He is not "taught a lesson" by being abandoned while in this highly volatile state. Whether a learned get-my-way behavior or a sudden explosion of pent-up emotional stress, his fury is real and beyond reason.

It will make matters worse, both in the short term and in the long run, if you lose control and rage back at him. At a time like this he needs your calm strength. He needs to know you can control yourself no matter how out of control he may become. Joining him in chaos is damaging to your position as the strong competent adult and frightening to your child.

Stay in close as the solidly assured grownup while being calmly supportive and communicating empathy by Active Listening to what he may say. Asking questions about what's wrong would add to his overload. Hold him closely if he will allow it. If he resists being held or touched, one quiet comment in an Active Listening way will let him know you feel for his distress. *"You're having a terrible time. I'll be right here if you need me."* If just hearing your voice makes matters worse, sit quietly nearby without further comment.

In his rage, he may say he hates you and call you names. Active Listen to his anger, *"You are hating me so much you just have to scream."* Allow his tears to come without trying to stifle them. He may scream at you to go away and leave him alone. You may feel like attacking back at his rejection. Please stay cool. If he needs to be alone, respect his need and go about your business elsewhere with an unemotional comment like, *"I'll be in the kitchen."*

When he has vented whatever needed venting and the storm has passed, move on in a calm and friendly way. If he was resisting being touched or held during the explosion, he may welcome your affection now with a comment from you, such as *"Here's a big hug before I start getting dinner ready."* If he isn't ready for a hug, your friendly attitude keeps you in position as the sturdy adult in charge of yourself and the situation without ever having tried to control your child's emotions or stifle their fierce eruption. You understand. He exploded because he needed to explode. After the storm has passed, a refreshing drink of water may help bring his system into equilibrium. Without asking if he wants a drink, hold out a glass or cup of water. *"If you're thirsty, here's a drink of water."* He may not want a drink and you can feel perfectly fine, without getting your feelings hurt, if he rejects your offer. Give him a few minutes of your involvement settling into play before you get on with whatever you had planned to do.

Never punish, threaten to punish, or hold out a bribe to stop a tantrum. Do not try to talk him out of or distract him from his upset by diverting his attention, making jokes or tickling him. We want to prevent the accumulation of stress fueling tantrums with an informed approach to his daily life, not stifle his emotional expression; no matter how noisy or unpleasant it happens to be. If he loses control in a public place, try moving him to an inconspicuous location where you can help him through his distress.

Many tantrums are combinations of the two types described above. A child may blow up over not getting his way and once the explosion has begun it becomes further fueled by an accumulation of stored stress.

Finding ways to reduce pressure and frustration from your child's daily life will diminish or eliminate emotional outbursts. A small child may fall apart from hunger or exhaustion. He may not be aware enough of his body's signals to put into words what's going on. Pushing a tired or hungry child past his limits of endurance is a common cause of meltdowns.

Whatever lies beneath your child's explosive outbursts, be careful not to talk about his tantrums with another person within his hearing. His difficulties with life should not become the subject of conversations he could overhear.

When and if tantrums occur, your calm strength and your own ability to maintain self-control serve as a dependable support system.

Once again, I ask you to visualize a situation involving adults.

You are sitting with a friend at a picnic table, when she suddenly bursts into tears and throws her head down on the table sobbing and crying loudly. Would you say any of the following to her?

"Stop it immediately!"

"This is awful. You're making a scene."

"Shut up! You're embarrassing me."

"If you don't stop this right now, I'm leaving."

Now can you imagine how you really would respond to your friend's upset?

I expect it would be nothing like Traditional reactions to an overwrought child.

When we extend the same level of respect and sympathy to our children as we offer adults, our world improves dramatically.

Question asked by a four-year-old: *"Mama, why is it when a grownup is upset, other grownups try to help him and when a little kid is upset, grownups get mad at him?"*

3

I HATE YOU!

Hearing words like this coming from our child can knock us off our feet. Depending on our way of thinking regarding our position as parents, there exists a variety of thoughts to automatically pop into our heads.

"What's happened to my sweet little boy?"

"What a terrible thing to say."

"This kid is out of control." "He has no respect!"

"No child of mine can get away with this."

"I'm a failure as a mother."

"My own child hates me."

"He didn't really mean he hates me."

"I'll tell him I know he didn't mean it."

The first thing to think about if and when our child says he hates us, is the importance of allowing feelings to be voiced. And, yes, at the moment he said it, he meant it and is probably as frightened at having said it as we are in hearing it.

Feelings are real. They can also be fleeting.

Let's get back to basics. Remember! Attachment is every child's most compelling need and so our first response, as in all difficult encounters, is to protect and secure Attachment. Somewhere deep inside, our child knows he has stepped out onto relationship thin ice and it is up to us to throw him a line.

Our first move is to acknowledge his hateful feelings. They are real and will not go away by being denied or called unacceptable, only to be shoved down inside until they come out, possibly in a dangerous form, sometime in the future.

Our initial response must be one of awareness. If we know what triggered the outburst, such as denial of something he wanted, a clear statement of understanding is needed: *"You are super mad at me for keeping you out of the snow today."* WE DO NOT ADD, *"because you still have a cold."* This is not about defending our side of the story. This is only about showing we grasp the intensity of his feelings.

We may not know of a specific frustration when the word *hate* is shouted at us. A three-year-old may call us a "dirty poo-poo." An older child may hurl a string of the nastiest names he can come up with. A child may be expressing his anger toward us personally or blowing off an uncontainable buildup of frustration and directing it at us as the most convenient and, he would hope, safest target.

Whatever may be going on, he is helped, and the relationship endures when we show understanding by Active Listening and not allowing any of the Roadblocks to interfere with the restoration process.[68]

He may recover from his outburst feeling uneasy or guilty. To relieve him of fearing our alienation, we can take a few moments at an opportune time to reassure him, *"There's something I want you to know. There is nothing you can say or do to ever make me stop loving you."*

Facial expressions sometimes show derision or hatred toward a parent when smirks or eye-rolling take the place of words. Adults can get completely bent

---

[68] The ROADBLOCKS are described in section one.

out of shape when what they see on their child's face looks like gross disrespect and the old bugaboo of Control slips in with thoughts of, *how dare he?* No need for alarm. When we see what's written on a child's face as another form of communication, we can make an Active Listening response as effectively as if words had been hurled at us: *"You think my ideas about a neat home are ridiculous."*

Dorothy Baruch talks about the healing power in a child's freedom to verbalize his angry feelings to a caring adult, and sees most behavior difficulties as being rooted in denied, stifled, unexpressed feelings of fear and anger. Her 1949 book, New Ways in Discipline: You and Your Child Today,[69] is available through most libraries and for a few cents from Amazon.com used books. Dr. Baruch gives us a clear look at the way fear and anger affect a child's behavior and what parents can do about buried feelings distorting his world and theirs.

So let's hear the words *I hate you* as a call to our empathy and a signal alerting us to being there for our child as a therapeutic agent when he faces life's challenges and overwhelming frustrations.

Note: If you know or suspect a child of any age to be feeling hatred toward you, some other person, or toward the world in general, this is a time for reaching out beyond any defenses of your own to extend caring support. Active listening will be critical to healing and professional help may be needed.

---

[69] New Ways in Discipline: You and Your Child Today by Dorothy Walter Baruch, Copyright 1949, Whittlesey House Publishers, New York, NY.

4

NO REASON TO CRY

A baby's crying is irritating to us.

Nature designed us this way to stimulate us into responding quickly to the need behind the crying. This works well for a baby—and for us—when we know why he is crying, are able to satisfy his need, and the crying stops.

Trouble begins when no matter what we do, our baby continues to cry. The longer this goes on, the more helpless we feel and the more frustrated we become. When the irritating sound goes on and on or causes us to lose sleep, our nerves become raw.

Children die each day for this very reason. Frustration turns to anger and frantic parents become violent trying to get a baby to "shut up!" Crying babies are slapped, spanked, thrown down and against walls, yelled at, and shaken.

We can sympathize with irrational responses to the crying of a helpless infant when we see them as being rooted in old mythology and beliefs about our superiority over children. After all, we are the boss and this baby should stop crying because we want it to. Traditional thinking has conditioned us to believe being a parent automatically positions us to control our baby. Implicit in such expectations is believing total control over another human being is possible or desirable.

So let's start by knowing a baby is going to cry and may possibly cry at times when we do not know how to "make him shut up."

When a baby cries and screams and all attempts at comforting him fail, an acute medical problem must be ruled out immediately. Ear infections are extremely painful and respond well to treatment by a qualified physician. Teething hurts and is particularly difficult for some babies. A baby with a bowel impaction will be in great pain, his crying having parents walking the floor with him.

Modern diagnostic tools disclose the source of pain, whatever it is, and provide a medical doctor with the information needed to intervene on a baby's behalf.

Again, addressing the idea of demons or the devil, as believed by some to be the source of crying, I want this book to help readers accept and tolerate crying as the natural response to distress without recourse to extreme measures, such as exorcisms or beating the devil out of infants and children.

Babies have many real-world things to cry about. Before they learn to communicate with words, crying is the only way they can tell us they need help. Becoming angry, seeing a baby as "bad" or blaming supernatural forces gets in the way of finding the need behind the crying.

Our first step toward a solution will start with our baby's physical surroundings. Please see my chapter on STRUCTURE AND ROUTINE for ways to make the environment conducive to a baby's serenity. And yours, too!

Emotional turmoil and violence in his surroundings will transmit to him and may translate into crying for no reason apparent to us.

When every immediate reason for crying has been addressed—the baby has been fed, his diaper changed, he is not suffering from an acute illness, such as a painful ear infection or feeling the pain of a new tooth—we look for other possible sources of the crying:

1. Is there a still-undiagnosed physical reason for his crying?
2. Is his nervous system jangled by exposure to excessive sensory input from television, loud music, and/or public environments?
3. Do his days follow a regular routine for providing rhythm and predictability to his life?
4. Is he exposed to adult discord, angry voices, or violence?
5. Is his mother suffering from depression, overwhelmed, or acutely anxious about her new responsibilities?
6. Is response to his needs delayed to fit him into an imposed schedule?
7. Is he deprived of physical closeness and affection?
8. Has he become fearful and agitated from rough handling or angry responses to his needs?
9. Has he undergone an Attachment loss, such as a parent's return to work, requiring adjustments to a new caretaker or to unfamiliar surroundings?
10. Is his caretaker focused on him when they are together or distracted by other demands or interests? Very possibly a phone.

Episodes of crying can, many times, be reduced or eliminated by finding a time of at least thirty minutes every day to take your baby in your arms and settle into a relaxed frame of mind in a rocking chair. This can become a treat you give yourself as well as providing a stabilizing physiological effect and emotional nourishment for your baby.

I do not suggest rocking to stop a crying spell. I am recommending a daily intimate interlude of pure pleasure for you and your baby at a time when he is not crying. This could be immediately after he wakes up when, during the transition from sleeping to full wakefulness, you share this lovely rocking chair time with him.

Rocking is therapeutic whether or not your baby has crying spells. Besides being wonderfully relaxing and enjoyable for both you and your baby, rocking provides stimulation to an infant's developing internal balance system.

However, rocking, bouncing, and swinging are not mentally or physically healthful ways to stop fussing or crying.[70]

A daily walk of about thirty to forty-five minutes or an hour should be part of his routine, providing a change of scenery and fresh air as a tonic to his nervous system. This walk in his stroller is not for putting him to sleep. We want him wide awake, enjoying the outdoors, and the pleasures of being pushed along by his engaged companion.

If a baby continues to have extended crying spells after all possible physical problems have been ruled out and other suggestions have brought about no change, we may assume he has an accumulation of stress needing to be relieved.

Damaging toxins from an accumulation of stress are discharged from the body with the shedding of tears.[71]

Babies and infants live through frustrations we can never hope to become fully aware of or prevent, no matter how devoted and diligent we may be. Developmental hurtles in mastering their physical bodies and communication capabilities can tip sensitive babies over into crying episodes.

When babies or children of any age release stress through crying, we interfere with healing when we look for some way to stop the crying. Bouncing, rocking, nursing, a pacifier, waving toys in their faces, are methods of control we impose upon them hoping to relieve us of the abrasive noise and our escalating frustration.

It is never a good idea to leave a baby alone to "cry it out" until he's exhausted and falls asleep. Old false beliefs about babies gave rise to instructions for abandoning

---

[70] On page 70 in <u>Tears and Tantrums: What to Do When Babies and Children Cry,</u> Aletha <u>Solter explains the difference between beneficial rocking and bouncing when babies are awake and alert and the harmful effects of using rocking and bouncing to quiet their fussing or crying.</u>

[71] We learn about the physiology of crying and the harmful effects of suppressing it in <u>Tears and Tantrums: What to Do When Babies and Children Cry</u>. Much of what I have written here comes from what this book has taught me about crying.

a baby in this way to avoid "spoiling" him. This is bad advice and not supported by the last sixty years of research on brain development, behavior, and Attachment.

With older children, various tactics, such as telling them there's nothing to cry about, tickling, distracting, calling them a cry-baby, making them laugh, ignoring them, shunning, and walking away, are common disrespectful and harmful methods for stifling emotional expression.

A crying baby needs to know you are there for him. Instead of telling him to "hush," he is helped by your sympathetic tone. Holding him close, using a simple form of Active Listening and talking softly as you try to put his feelings into words, will let him know you are paying attention to his distress and offering your loving support. Although he may be too young to understand your words, he will pick up on a caring sympathetic tone of voice and be comforted as you provide acceptance for his free expression of emotion.

Holding a crying baby until he becomes settled can be hard to do and requires commitment with mental preparation on the part of the adult. As trying as it may be, it is well worth the effort for the well-being of a baby and the eventual peace of the family.

When a toddler or an older child cries, our most helpful response is to hold him while Active Listening, without minimizing what he is going through or trying to talk him out of his distress. We want to avoid cutting off his emotional expression with attempts to stop the crying. Boys need the freedom to release feelings through crying and shedding tears as much as girls do.

There is always a reason why babies and children cry, whether we know what it is or not. Believing and telling children they have no reason to cry is an example of our customary disrespect toward them and our casual dismissal of their feelings and needs. Telling a crying child he has nothing to cry about invalidates his experience and tells him he is wrong to feel what he is feeling, undermining his confidence and his self-esteem.

5

SHARING

Whenever parents bring children together for play, you are likely to hear a lot of talk about sharing. If you happen to be the parent of the child who refuses to give up a toy when another child is tugging on it, you find yourself in an awkward position. Should you force your child to hand over a toy he's been enjoying because another child wants it? If you do, are you a mean parent? If you don't, will the other adults see you as a bad parent because you are not teaching your child to share?

Let's stop for a moment and picture a different scene:

It is 8 PM and you finally have time to catch up on email. Your neighbor, Carol, knocks on the door and asks to borrow your computer for a few hours. You tell her, as much as you would like to help, you are using it and she leaves without it. Your spouse comes into the room and says something like this: *"What's wrong with you? Carol is your friend. You should share with her. Shame on you for being so selfish. Take the computer over to her right now and apologize for not giving it to her when she asked for it."*

Would you drop everything and run next door to deliver the computer? How would you feel toward your spouse? Toward Carol? Would you now embrace the idea of sharing?

Perhaps you would feel better about giving up your computer if approached like this: *"Sweetheart, you should have given the computer to Carol. She's one of your best friends and you don't want her to be sad, do you? Good friends share. She may not want to be your friend if you don't share with her. How about being a good neighbor and running on over there right now. Wouldn't you be proud of yourself if you took her the computer and apologized for refusing to share?"*

Although either scenario is outright ridiculous when the imagined participants are adults, they are common happenings when children are the main characters.

Looking at sharing from a developmental viewpoint, we know why we will eventually see our child become a generous human being without our intrusive efforts at convincing him to share.

To bring us to this understanding, I give you this quote from Eleanor Reynolds:

"Children are, by nature, possessive, territorial, and egocentric. All this is a natural part of development. They must first be established and feel secure in their own identities before being able to take the great leap toward empathy, consideration and generosity toward others. This is why insisting toddlers share their precious toys with friends is unrealistic and seems cruel to them. Sharing is a concept totally foreign and perplexing to infants and toddlers. Somewhere between three and four years of age, however, children who have been allowed total control of their belongings will begin to enjoy a limited amount of sharing. Again, this must be their own decision. If children have always had the right to say no to sharing, they will acquire the maturity and desire to say yes."[72]

How can this knowledge help the parent on a playground watching her child struggling over a toy with another youngster? Should she let them fight it out on their own? Or should she "save face" with the other parents, take the toy away from her own child and give it to the playmate?

---

[72] From the very important book, <u>Guiding Young Children: A Problem-Solving Approach</u> by Eleanor Reynolds, Third Edition, Copyright 2001, Published by Mayfield Publishing Company, Mountain View, CA, page 136.

Although both options will be seen in action on every playground, we can follow a different approach and take the opportunity to give our child an experience with Problem-Solving.

We go to the children, get down to their level, look into their eyes, smile and offer our support by saying something like, *"It looks like two kids both want the same toy. Let's see if there's some other great toy here so you will both have something you like."* Finding an equally appealing toy may solve their problem. Or you may help them take turns. If there appears to be no solution to this particular conflict with this particular toy, moving them on to a different and enjoyable joint activity could be the answer. Maintaining a friendly helpful approach, using Active Listening, without placing blame or asking questions about who did what and why, you can help facilitate a favorable outcome without forcing your own child to succumb to adult pressure and unrealistic demands.

If anyone, adult or child, pressures your unwilling little kid to share, you can take charge with a non-confrontational statement: *"Connor isn't ready to share his toys just now. He plans to play with them himself today."*

When children are treated with respect, growing up in an environment in which sharing is free to emerge according to Nature's timetable, generosity will bloom without prodding or coaching.

6

SAY YOU'RE SORRY!

How many times do we hear this when adults are supervising children at play? Coaching a small child to say he is sorry seems to be a major part of raising kids. What we are actually doing is teaching children to lie by making them say the words *"I'm sorry"* when they are neither sorry nor do they have any concept of what we are demanding of them.

Meaningless words. Lessons in dishonesty.

When a child grabs a toy from another child, pushes or hits, we do not teach empathy and responsibility by demanding the utterance of two little words.

Our culture has come to use apologizing as a quick fix when dealing with ethical issues. We do well to help our children understand the effects of their actions on other people and give them conflict resolution skills to serve them through life without making them mutter, *"I'm sorry."*

If a youngster has accidentally or purposely smashed another child's block tower, we can allay the resulting upset by Active Listening to both children and facilitating an amenable outcome to their difficulties. We resist asking what happened, placing blame, or taking sides. Active Listening to each child's feelings about the smashed structure will provide both children with an opportunity to see a situation from the other person's perspective.

We take the same approach when a child has physically hurt a playmate. Resolution can include involving the offending child in administering first aid, an excellent way to arouse empathy while we Active Listen to everything each child may say about their encounter.

As for teaching your children to say the word *Sorry*, this is best learned through imitation from the examples you set for them. When you have made a blunder or accidentally inflicted physical harm, your sincere speaking of the word *Sorry*—along with describing your mistake, how you happened to do something careless or harmful and repairing the damage—will teach your child the true meaning of the word. It will be important to guard against making this same mistake again, to uphold your honest use of the word.

"Oh, look what I did. I wasn't being careful. I knocked over your fort and bumped your knee with the vacuum cleaner. I am so sorry. I'll rub some lotion on your knee and help put the fort back together."

As in all learning through modeling, the better your relationship with your child, the more he wants to be like you and to emulate your social habits. We are back again to Attachment and a dependable blueprint for eliciting desirable behavior:

1. Preserve and protect the relationship.
2. Be the kind of person you want your child to be.

When our children do say they are sorry, we want them to grasp the word they are using and why they are saying it.

Note: Trouble lurks when the word, *Sorry*, is used by us as a crutch when, instead of controlling our abusive behavior toward a child, we let loose with a slap or a cruel diatribe and later, knowing what a mistake we made, go back to the child and apologize to fix things. Yes, we all lose control sometimes and when we do, we must tell our child how wrong we were. *"I don't like what I said to you. I was way off base to act the way I did."*

Relying on the word Sorry to relieve us of responsibility for the hurts we cause, sets a bad example and hinders our own growth in self-discipline.

7

RUN, JUMP, SKIP, TUMBLE!

. . . and dig, splash, squish, splatter, climb, scramble, crawl, bounce, roll, touch, feel, enjoy!

Nature's sensory input is indispensable to the healthy growth of young bodies and young minds in the FEEL, SCENT and SOUNDS of rocks, sand, mud, grass, flowers, leaves, pebbles, shells, flowing water, warm earth, cold earth, wind, rain, sunshine . . . all nature offers to the awakening senses.

Growing bodies need to move, to climb, leap, crawl, and tumble. They need to reach and stretch, testing themselves against nature's challenges.

A child may protest a requirement placed upon him by the adults in his life, hoping they will give in to his arguments. Nature teaches lessons unequivocally, this being the one circumstance where natural consequences come into reality and allow no room for argument.

Modern youngsters spend hours glued to phones or passively watching television. Many are confined indoors for long periods of time at home, in daycare or in various schoolrooms. Playground equipment, though necessary and healthful, will not meet their needs for the types of physical and emotional nourishment only accessible through regular engagement with the natural world.

Fresh air and sunshine are vital ingredients to your child's physical health and emotional well-being.

By the time a healthy baby weighs ten pounds, he benefits substantially from being outside for two to three hours every day. If he is in daycare, we have little control over this possibility except for whatever outdoor excursions we can fit into early evenings and weekends. If we are at home with him or are paying someone to care for him in our absence, this becomes an important responsibility in fortifying the wellness of our child.

Daily outings with a baby in a stroller or walks with an older child are part of a routine both physiologically and neurologically healthful. If you have a covered padded stroller, fold back the top and settle your baby into a sitting-up position. In cold or windy weather, dress him accordingly; bundled up and always with a hat covering his ears. Let's get him out of the depths of the stroller's upholstered interior where he may as well be in the house. We want him wide awake, sitting up, seeing the world, feeling the wind and the sun on his skin, inhaling nature's fragrances, taking in the blue of the sky, colors of foliage, and absorbing all the sensations stirring his senses. Your place accompanying him in his communion with nature is contaminated if you are talking on a phone or engaging with some other form of electronic connection. Please save this type of activity for times when you are away from your child. Be firm in your requirement for a caretaker to exercise the same restraint.

Seeing an outdoor walk as a daily necessity to a child's well-being instead of an occasional luxury immeasurably enriches the life you share with him. If you live in a place like Seattle, where it rains nearly every day for weeks or months at a time, the daily walk remains a significant feature in your child's developmental nourishment. In strollers, bundled up and protected by waterproof outerwear and an umbrella, babies learn to savor this side of Nature. Out of the stroller, older children in sturdy raingear find special delight walking and splashing in the rain.

Wherever you live, in a house or an apartment, try to find a spot where your young child can dig in the dirt and poke around in the earth with spoons, small shovels and sticks. Provide a sandbox, where possible, and safe water play when you can.

Look for interesting places to explore, such as streams, dry creek beds, hills, woods, sea shores, nature trails, open fields, and parks. All offer new delights and new sensations for the sensitive developing brain to record and integrate. Allow as much freedom as possible without warnings of, *"Be careful"* or *"Watch out!"* A skinned knee or a bumped elbow is nature's lesson and is not forgotten.

Besides nourishing your child physically and mentally, providing abundant opportunity for outdoor physical exertion will cut down on restlessness and behavior difficulties caused by unspent energy.

Japanese scientists are reporting on the significant physiological benefits of what they are calling *Forest Bathing*. I urge you to read the internet articles describing the very real physical and emotional boost you will afford your child and yourself by getting out into the elements. An article on the New York State Dept. of Environmental Conservation website cites improvements in health from immersion in nature along with over three pages listing the many research projects supporting the following claims:

- Boosts immune system
- Lowers blood pressure
- Improves mood
- Increases ability to focus*
- Accelerates recovery from illness or surgery
- Increases energy level
- Improves sleep

*Research results include decreased levels of the stress hormones cortisol and adrenaline in children and adults as well as finding a reduction of ADHD symptoms.

Sharing experiences in nature with your child is one more very satisfying way of strengthening the Attachment Bond. Sniffing pretty blossoms, watching a hill of busy ants or a crawling fuzzy caterpillar, finding an unusual rock to add to a growing collection of treasures, exploring the natural world together, will add to the fun of being a parent and, for your child, the fun of having a parent like you!

8

HAPPY BEDTIMES FOR TODDLERS
AND PRESCHOOLERS

With bedtime coming around every 24 hours, let's arrange a pleasurable experience for parents and children alike.

There are many reasons why a child may balk at going to bed.

Bedtime resistance is frequently an extension of an ongoing power struggle. Separation anxiety can make going to bed a grim ordeal. Bad dreams and fears sometimes make bedtime truly terrifying. Feeling lonely and left out may make going to bed looking like a dreary proposition. Agitation from stresses outside the home in daycare or preschool can interfere with sleep.

I'll list for you some basic considerations to keep in mind for orchestrating an inviting day's-end interlude.

- PROTECT AND STRENGTHEN ATTACHMENT.

  Attachment insecurities will surface as resistance to separation at bedtime. Look for any and all possible threats to your child's feelings of unconditional acceptance. Anything you do to secure the Attachment bond will support bedtime cooperation while anything you do to weaken it, such as punishments and angry responses, will undermine it.

- MAKE BEDTIME PART OF ESTABLISHED ROUTINE.

A daily routine, with children knowing what to expect, is one of the most important components to harmonious living and happy bedtimes.

- DO NOT THINK IN TERMS OF "GETTING RID OF THE KIDS."

Children are super sensitive to cues and clues from adults. If we want to get rid of them, they will know it and Attachment will be threatened. They will cling, balk, delay, whine, cry, beg, ask for water, ask for food, complain about the darkness, be too hot, be too cold, as they grasp for any possible tactics to hold off unbearable feelings of insecurity.

- SEE BEDTIME AS A WINDING DOWN, RELAXING INTERLUDE FOR PARENT AND CHILD TO RELISH TOGETHER.

We set the tone. No matter what sorts of bedtime struggles we are now experiencing, this is one big step to end them. When we become fully conscious of the closeness, which we have the power to create, and we genuinely look forward to sharing this end-of-the-day intimacy with our children, they will reflect our attitude.

- AVOID WRESTLING, ROUGHHOUSING OR EXCITING GAMES BETWEEN THE EVENING MEAL AND BEDTIME.

We do not want to stir up adrenaline and overcome the natural sleepiness accompanying digestion.

- UNDERSTAND THE IMPORTANCE OF SLEEP.

  Children need daytime naps until age four. Some children can go without naps as young as age three, although they still need them and would benefit from a daily nap if it were part of the regular order of things.[73]

- DO NOT MAKE IT A "TREAT" TO STAY UP PAST BEDTIME.

  Looking at going to bed as something to "get out of" makes it undesirable and to be avoided. We are creating something comforting and inviting. Do not make exceptions because Grandma is visiting or there's a new puppy. Staying up to see Fourth of July fireworks would be an exception.

- IT IS NEVER ADVISABLE TO TELL A CHILD TO "GO TO BED."

  Bedtime is particularly open to the arousal of Counterwill. Also, with our understanding of the Communication Roadblocks we know about the problems associated with giving direct orders. Don't you think the words, "Go to bed" have a strikingly lonely sound to them? Peaceful bedtimes are among the warmest, most satisfying and companionable shared moments we can create for our children when we fully engage with them at the end of each day, maintaining some level of ritual on through the pre-teen years instead of trying to send them off to bed with words.

- LEAVE PHONE OR ANY OTHER ELECTRONIC DEVICE OUT OF THE ROOM WHILE YOU ARE SETTLING YOUR CHILD FOR SLEEP.

  Think of this as a common courtesy and a necessary ingredient in showing respect, besides knowing any phone call will come as a sharp disruption to the mood you are setting.

---

[73] The internet offers several websites providing information about sleep requirements for each age group.

- HONOR THE IMPORTANCE OF A REGULAR BEDTIME.

  A predictable and pleasant end to a child's day affords physical and emotional benefits beyond measure. It is never worth it to forgo this routine for a matter of convenience. You may come across websites and books—as devoted to children's freedom and self-direction as I am—advising us to extend their freedom to going to sleep when and where they happen to drop off. Sleep is so consequential to physical health and neurological development that allowing this option for today's frazzled kids, living in their highly over-stimulating environment, would put them at risk. There's too much going on in their lives to give Nature responsibility for fulfilling a child's sleep requirements. Sleep shortage impairs balanced hormone production and brain development. Our children need us to set the stage for their turning off and shutting down.

- STAY ALERT TO THE SUBTLEST CLUES AND HINTS ABOUT BEDTIME FEARS.

  Anxieties and misconceptions regarding sleeping and worries about bad dreams can generate a strong resistance to falling asleep, as in the example about Danny in the Active Listening chapter of this book. Such fears need to be voiced and talked through, never ignored, made fun of, belittled or discounted.

- REGULATE TV AND COMPUTER INVOLVEMENT.

  Be carefully selective about what your child is exposed to. Violence, including cartoon violence, and high levels of action as well as rapidly changing visuals are known to be unsettling influences on immature brains and are confirmed causes of bedtime resistance, restless sleep, and nightmares.

If bedtime at your house is now in a state of chaos or involves a prolonged nightly struggle, here's a sample plan to get you started into better days and nights ahead. This is only a sample, adjustable to your unique needs. The steps I suggest are ways for preparing a child for a smooth transition from wakefulness to deliciously inviting sleep. As I write this, I will be picturing a three-year-old little boy.

You will be able to make suitable changes for a younger or older child and for your own situation.

(To begin moving toward bed, go to your child, touch him gently or take his hand in yours, smile, look into his eyes and say something like, *"I've picked out a book to read before you go to sleep tonight. Let's bring the little horse with us to get ready for bed."* If he's small enough to carry, pick him up. Otherwise, guide him gently by putting a hand on his shoulder or holding his hand. If he objects, struggles, or cries, keep moving toward bed or bathtub, again make eye contact, and Active Listen intently: *"Wow! You were really busy there with your blocks and animals. You hated having to stop when you were having such a good time."* Keep moving forward and Active Listening all through getting into pajamas or into the bathtub. If you are bathing him, have fun with tub toys and soap bubbles[74] before pulling the plug and drying him with loving pats and a big hug. Maintain a calm steady pace, leaving no room for dawdling as you help him into his pajamas. Remain easygoing and relaxed while he uses the toilet before heading to bed. Attempting to hurry him will work against you and slow things down. To prevent a common hassle with brushing teeth, it can work well for a parent to join in brushing teeth immediately after eating or, as one mother found workable, to brush teeth in the bathtub.

---

[74] You can make great soap bubbles by sudsing your hands, making a circle with thumb and forefinger, and blowing through the soap film in the circle. The internet offers several demonstrations. Bar soap works as well as liquid.

(Have the book you picked out or one your child has requested there on the bed and tuck him in.

(Stretch out next to him or sit on the bed to read the book.

(Including back drawings after the story is read is a soothing way to boost Attachment and induce relaxation. With a child lying on his stomach, he tries to identify simple pictures from outlines a parent draws on his bare back with a fingertip. A smiley face is a good starter. Flower petals with stem, a sun, star, or crescent moon work well. To avoid requests for more, make your intentions clear: *"I'm going to draw five pictures on your back before you go to sleep,"* or *"I have four back pictures for you tonight."*

(Tell him what you are going to do next, such as *"I'm going to clean up the kitchen now."*

(Give a big hug and a goodnight kiss. Say goodnight with the same words each night. Always include something about seeing him in the morning to "bridge" the gap in connection between the two of you while you are apart for the night. *"Goodnight, sweetie. I'll see you in the morning."*

(Leave the room. Whether the door stays open or is closed will depend on your personal preference and what your child can tolerate and/or has been accustomed to since infancy.

(If he gets out of bed, do not engage in coaxing, scolding, lecturing, threatening, or explaining why he needs sleep. Calmly carry or lead him back to bed, settle him in again and, with an affectionate pat, voice a positive expectation, *"You will be able to settle down and sleep in a few minutes. Goodnight, sweetie. I'll see you in the morning."* Do not start a power contest by ordering him to stay in bed or telling him to go to sleep. Stick to your ritual goodnight words.

(Maintain your relaxed matter-of-fact attitude no matter what. Do not play with him, tease, try to distract, be talked into reading another story or break the pattern in any way.

(If, after escorting him back to bed several times, you feel exasperation rising, take a few deep breaths and give yourself soothing self-talk along the lines of, *"He's having a hard time settling down. I can do this for him. Years from now I'll look back and think about this sweet time in my life."*

(When a bedtime struggle has been long-standing, it may take many such guided or carried returns to bed. As exhausting and frustrating as this can be, do whatever you can to remain calm and relaxed. Staying in control of yourself and of the situation will get you through with flying colors . . . eventually.

(By keeping the entire ritual the same each night, with no phone calls or other interruptions, you will likely have a happy bedtime established within a week. If not, go back over this chapter for any missing links and persevere. Pay particular attention to getting yourself into a relaxed frame of mind each evening. The inclination to push or rush is a common obstacle to bedtime success. You have the power to create an intimate treat to share with your child each night. I urge you to take advantage of this fleeting opportunity.

(Making time for about thirty minutes of rocking chair intimacy sometime during the day can be exactly what's needed to boost Attachment and completely put an end to a bedtime problem.

(Stay tuned to the quality of your relationship with each child. If you have slipped into disconnecting habits, symptoms are likely to surface at bedtime.

(A bedtime routine of approximately thirty minutes works well.

Note: On pages 201 and 202 of the book, <u>Hold On to Your Kids: Why Parents Need to Matter More Than Peers</u>, the authors explain protecting Attachment and allaying insecurity by always bridging our time apart from a child. Whether at bedtime, leaving for work, dropping a child off at school, or at a friend's to play; we support Attachment by mentioning our next time together.

Researchers are seeing escalating numbers of stress-related medical and emotional problems in children. Planning and following a nightly bedtime ritual greatly reduces stress for both parents and children. Designing pleasurable bedtimes to enjoy at the end of each day has beneficial effects on the entire family and brings the gift of warm memories to last a lifetime.

VII

If we wish to create a lasting peace,
we must begin with the children.

~ Mahatma Gandhi

1

SIBLING RIVALRY

For a first child, a new baby entering his life is a shocking event.

If he is under six years old and has not reached some level of independence, the blow can be devastating.

The following analogy may be familiar to you. I present it here for folks who have never thought of a new baby's impact on their first child quite this way. Here's a scene to ponder:

You, the young wife, are working in the yard. Your darling husband is running errands. You hear his car and run to greet him. There's someone with him. It looks like a young woman and he's helping her out of the car. When you get up close, he turns to you and says, *"Honey, I want you to meet Sandra. I brought her home to live with us. Isn't she cute? I know you will love her and have lots of fun with her."*

You could have any number of responses to this idea your husband has come up with. Whatever your initial reaction, the final outcome would be along the lines of, *"Either she goes or I go."* Being an adult you could make such a choice.

Not so for a child. He's stuck with the situation. While being incapable of automatically "loving" the new baby as his parents do and as they may mistakenly expect him to, he has no way to escape the new reality. When parents say their toddler loves the new baby, this is a warning sign of dangerous wishful thinking. Dangerous because by believing it, they deny what their child is going through.

It makes life easier for our first-born if we tone down our delight with the newcomer when he's around. We make matters worse if we try to "sell" him on the fun and advantages of having a baby in the house. The only thing on his mind is this intruder's interference with his vital Attachment. He's terrified of being replaced in our affections and talk about the advantages of having a new baby only adds to his fears.

Infants sleep a lot and when the newcomer is sleeping the best way we can spend our time is with the bewildered first child. Giving him our focused one-on-one time will help ease him past his anxiety.

We do well to leave out references to or chatter about the baby when we are spending time with the older child. If he has anything to say, there couldn't be a better time for our Active Listening. Some children will be open and blunt about their opinions and feelings. Remember, all feelings are legitimate and do not go away by being shamed or denied. If he says he hates the baby—yes, he hates the baby.

We help him handle his hateful or other negative feelings by acknowledging them and by avoiding telling him he should love the baby or saying he someday will. When we can accept his fearful, angry, sometimes hateful, feelings as normal they will gradually be replaced by good ones. Our Active Listening will facilitate his change of heart.

When faith in his belonging and Attachment remains secure, he can relax and settle down. If his insecurity has brought about regressions, such as bedwetting, sleep disruptions, or thumb sucking, we take them in stride as normal expressions of his anxiety without making an issue of them and Active Listen to anything he may say about what's happening.

Once we are over the New Baby hurtle, chances for rivalry difficulties to pop up are not forever behind us.

Let's stop here to look in on a very frustrated mother, worn down by her children's constant fighting. Seeking solace, she turns to friends and family describing and complaining about the nerve-wracking squabbling. Although this much-needed venting may afford temporary relief, verbalizing to others about her battling children cements this view of them more firmly into her consciousness, making this mental image readily transferable to the kids. Seeing themselves through her eyes, as children will do, positions them to live out her perceptions and continue their young lives in antagonism and unhappiness.

Relief for her and for her children will come when she understands and addresses the source of their conflict, rooted in Attachment insecurities and exacerbated by adult maladaptive responses to their rivalry.

Each time she yells at them to *"stop fighting,"* lectures about *"learning to get along,"* or berates them about their *"terrible behavior,"* she feeds Counterwill, weakens Attachment, corrupts their self-images, and throws fuel on the fire of her own misery.

If you are facing this problem, please read my Addendum to Self-Esteem.

You can find help in solving the problem from Doctors Neufeld and Maté with their guidance on Attachment and from Dorothy Baruch for her advice on uncovering and releasing children's anger and fears. Their books, referred to earlier, can be found on my Recommended Reading list.

Maintaining the P.E.T. approach to the developing relationships between siblings helps children grow to love and enjoy each other. If conflicts occur, we can guide them through the understanding of negotiation skills and Problem-Solving for resolving their differences.

Making comparisons either in our own minds or with comments about their personalities and behavior is particularly damaging: *"I don't know why your room is always such a mess. Look how neat your sister keeps hers,"* or *"I wish your brother would keep his room clean the way you do without my nagging."* Favorable and unfavorable comparisons are equally counterproductive. They function to create rivalry and resentment between children who, at every age, need to feel secure in our acceptance.

It would take another book to cover the complex and sometimes lifelong difficulties with sibling rivalry. One of the best is:

Siblings Without Rivalry: How to Help Your Children to Live Together So You Can Live Too.[75]

Contrary to Traditional thinking about sibling rivalry, ongoing discord and conflict are not inevitable. Continual fighting and bickering are not something families are doomed to live with. Any number of children can live together peacefully when given enough support and understanding from the adults each child is firmly connected to.

If you are regularly reaching wit's end with ongoing fighting and competition, be proactive. See problems coming and intervene before they escalate.

Example:

Seven-year-old Tommy has assembled the pieces for building one of his creations. Three-year-old Sarah wants to be included in the project. Tommy will never stand for this and as she tries to "help" he tells her to go away. ANTICIPATING THIS ENCOUNTER AS HAVING THE MAKINGS OF AN EXPLOSION, THIS IS WHERE YOU STEP IN. You do not call to Sarah from another room and tell her to leave Tommy alone and you do not call from this same distant location and tell Tommy to let her play. Past experience will have told you neither of them will follow your orders and when they don't, your exasperation will quickly follow. To completely avoid the inevitable battle and your irritation, you can stop all this unhappiness before it starts by derailing the squabble at the beginning.

And how do you do this?

---

[75] Siblings Without Rivalry: How to Help Your Children Live Together So You Can Live Too by Adele Faber and Elaine Mazlish, Copyright 1987, 1998, 2012, Published by Avon Books, New York, NY.

1. You appear, in person, at the scene of the developing dispute.
2. You get down to their level and collect each child by smiling, nodding, and looking into their eyes.
3. You take little "left out" Sarah onto your lap and make an Active Listening statement: *"You wanted to help."*
4. Your attention turns to Tommy and his need to pursue his project without his sister's interference and make an Active Listening statement to him: *"You want to do this by yourself and she's really bothering you."*

Now you affectionately carry or guide Sarah out of the room and take a few minutes to get her completely involved in something she enjoys. If you suspect she'll be back to bother Tommy in a few minutes, you bring her with you to observe or "help" with whatever you are doing or otherwise engage her.

Oh, yes. This takes time and effort.

And it will determine how you live: struggling and fighting with struggling and fighting kids or living in peace and happiness for the next ten or fifteen years. Having read this far, I expect you are seeing **the power you possess to determine the direction your family will take.**

2

FIGHTING, HITTING, BITING

Like all other unwanted behaviors, aggression will not stop through our becoming aggressive ourselves with punishments and reprimands. We must remove the cause and in this case we know where to look.

"Aggression is motivated by frustration," as explained by Ashley Montagu in chapter 10 of the book, <u>The Direction of Human Development: Biological and Social Bases</u>.[76]

Now, today, with computer brain studies informing their findings, Dr. Neufeld and Dr. Maté tell us the same thing and cite frustration with faulty or missing Attachments as a primary source of children's aggression.

Our first efforts in the prevention of aggression and violence are in the ways we respond to an infant in his early weeks and months. The quality and tone of our responses to his needs will determine the structuring of our infant's brain. Unmet needs and lack of warmth and patience in daily interactions with adults will interfere with development of brain circuits for regulating emotion.

Traditional Parenting, with emphasis on control taking precedence over our children's needs, has resulted in the frustration and detachment of many growing

---

[76] I highly recommend this very interesting book.

children, creating a large population of aggressive toddlers, children, and teenagers.[77]

Please understand! I do not recommend pampering, doting on and "spoiling" children to protect them from frustration by giving them whatever they want or letting them do whatever they want.

We must keep in mind the importance of allowing youngsters the lived reality of facing unchangeable facts of life and developing the adaptability to move on. Instead of catering to their wants or trying to protect them from all sadness and frustrations, we further their growth with our understanding and empathic listening when they face disappointment and unhappiness.

Our goal is to establish the emotional and physical environments in which our children learn to control their own behavior. What I refer to here is respecting and responding to a child's legitimate needs with kindness and understanding.

The most devoted and conscientious parents will not be able to prevent all frustrations in their child's life. We would be over-protective if we tried. However, it is important to read the signs of an intolerable load of frustration and take serious steps to reduce it.

Knowing frustration, generated by unmet Attachment needs, is a fundamental cause of aggression, we can address this deficiency by finding some way to schedule regular, focused one-on-one time with our children and by giving our full attention during our day-to-day interactions with them. We must, also, be resolute in eliminating negative responses to perfectly harmless childish activity. Is a little kid really causing a problem by rolling a tennis ball around on the floor, or is Mom just being bossy when she yells at him to stop?

---

[77] You can gain a full understanding of this early brain-building process by reading the book, Ghosts from the Nursery: Tracing the Roots of Violence. Pages 199-202 explain the formation of the very earliest roots of aggression.

We remember how important it is to always CONNECT BEFORE WE DIRECT by establishing eye contact with a smile and a nod when making a request or intervening in a problematic situation and remaining alert to recognizing adversarial habits we may be falling into.

Are we showing respect?

A child regularly treated disrespectfully will gradually disconnect and build up a reservoir of anger. When frustrations build, such stored anger will eventually find an outlet in hitting, fighting and other aggressive behaviors or it may turn inward and appear in the form of illness or depression. In schoolchildren, it may show up in poor schoolwork or disruptive behaviors in the classroom.

For toddlers and young children, unbearable frustration can be a strong spontaneous reaction to an immediate impasse with a playmate or the inability to accomplish a physical goal or master a skill. Some young children will express this type of irritation in tantrums or exhibit both tantrums and aggression with fighting, hitting, and biting as common outcomes.

Biting is particularly upsetting to the victim and to parents because it is so painful and seems so "over the line." For the biter, it carries with it a uniquely satisfying oral sensation and gives power to an otherwise powerless little person, making biting one of the most difficult behaviors to eliminate. Parents and care providers report a connection between biting and fatigue. The general approach to all aggression offers hope for releasing a biter from this urge. Like all aggressive behaviors, biting is a response to frustration; either an immediate frustration or a systemic buildup of it. Once again, we must not see biting as "the problem" and instead focus our attention on identifying and reducing frustrations and overstimulation in our young child's life.

Biting becomes most challenging when it has turned into a modus operandi and a child reacts to difficulties by chomping down on the nearest flesh. The best protection is in learning to see it coming and getting out of the way. Making a big issue of it will not help. Lecturing, punishing, and scolding increase frustration and make matters worse. Carefully paying attention to reducing frustrations and unsettling occurrences of all kinds will speed up recovery from this behavioral symptom.

Never bite a child back as one writer has suggested.

We sometimes see a completely different type of bite from a baby. This usually happens during the first year when he's busy taking in the world through all his senses and biting everything in sight. Your arm may be the most convenient target the moment when he feels the urge to sink his teeth into something. Reacting excitedly or with an angry NO may change his spontaneous impulse into an event and start a game or initiate a conflict. Your best move is to get out of range immediately without comment. If you are holding him in your arms, turn him facing away from you or put him down to play in a casual natural move. For the next few months be alert to keeping exposed flesh a safe distance from his teeth. A nice big teething ring may satisfy his urges.

At about this same life-stage, a baby may pull your hair or knock off your glasses while you are holding him. Like excited reactions to biting, making an issue of this can get a contest going. Laughing and playfully letting him do it, or swatting at him in annoyance, as at a pesky insect, would undermine your Alpha position. Being the adult in charge, you casually—without comment—take your hair out of his hand or place your glasses back on as you put him down to play. Staying out of range and always in charge of the situation will ease him past this phase.

Some children express unbearable frustration with kicking and may go so far as to kick a parent. Being kicked by a little kid is an outrage to our dignity. *"How dare he? This kid has to be put in his place."* I've got news for you. He's already in his place and it is not a pretty one.

A throbbing shin and rising indignation will put any adult's self-discipline to the test. This is a time for taking a deep breath and finding the humanity within us for **shifting focus from the behavior to the child**. Retaliation or measured responses, such as *"It hurts Mommy to be kicked"* or *"Remember to use your words,"* completely miss the point. Admonishments of any kind will be counterproductive and he already knows kicking hurts. As for using his words, he has no way to verbalize his desperation. Pain and outrage from the kick are nothing compared to the helplessness and emotional suffering the kick represents.

What can we do?

We comfort him. We Active Listen with real heart. And we get busy tightening-up Attachment; keeping it in mind as our number one, ongoing responsibility. We, also, take immediate measures to reduce his sensory input, minimize frustrations, and simplify his daily life.

Making certain a child enjoys a happy regular bedtime routine and is getting enough sleep can help reduce aggressive behaviors, including biting and kicking.

Overstimulating TV shows and videos are known to excite young children into violence. The influence of television on behavior is no longer in question. A show needn't be violent in content to stimulate violence in the child viewer. The frenetic activity and rapidly changing bright images of most shows aimed at children assault their nervous systems and can translate into violent behavior.

Most TV shows for children display a brand of humor based on sarcasm and put-downs, both a form of what's called Relational Aggression. Researchers are finding it imitated in peer interactions, as would be expected, and are also seeing it TRANSLATED INTO PHYSICAL VIOLENCE by young viewers.[78] This modeling of sarcasm and insults serves effectively as early training in bullying, both physical and verbal.

What can you do when your two-year-old has hit a playmate over the head with a toy truck?

---

[78] Find reports of this research by looking up Dr. Jamie M. Ostrov on the internet.

In a "WORKING WITH" move, you take him onto your lap, while responding to the distress of the victim and providing comfort to both children. Your unexcited demeanor—without questions about who did what—is basic to reaching a favorable outcome. Active Listening along the lines of, *"Things aren't happening the way you want them to,"* will let your child know he has your understanding.

Nothing is accomplished by telling him to say he's sorry.

You have this opportunity to model empathy as you put an arm around and soothe the other child, making an apologetic statement of your own: *"Are you all right now? I'm so sorry you were hurt."*

At times like this, your own self-talk can make a big difference. If you are thinking, *"What's wrong with my kid? He's always causing problems,"* you communicate this thinking to him in subtle ways and diminish your effectiveness. If you think, *"Now is a time when my calm support will help my child learn to handle his frustrations without hitting,"* although you are not speaking out loud, your body language, tone of voice, and the look in your eyes will communicate understanding and influence his feelings about himself.

When conflict occurs, the old recommendation to let children fight it out between themselves is bad advice. Adults can facilitate experiences in Problem-Solving and practice in negotiation. With such learning opportunities, children become Problem-Solvers themselves.

In the excellent book, <u>Guiding Young Children: A Problem-Solving Approach,</u>[79] Eleanor Reynolds provides several examples of common conflicts between children and the Problem-Solving way of approaching them. Here I copy her words for this one example from a preschool setting.

---

[79] <u>Third Edition, Guiding Young Children: A Problem-Solving Approach</u>. Although written as a textbook for daycare professionals and teachers, this book is invaluable for parents in learning how to create a Problem-Solving lifestyle.

Jonny and Nick are tugging on the red trike and trying to push each other away. They scream at each other.

Nick: *"Mine!"*

Jonny: *"I want it!"*

Kneeling down to eye level with the children, the teacher facilitates.

Teacher: *"Looks like there's a problem. You both want the same trike."*

Nick: *"I had it first!"*

Jonny: *"No, mine."*

Teacher: *"I hear you both saying you want the same trike. Nick says he wants it and Jonny says he wants it, too. What can you do when two people want the same toy? Do you have an idea, Nick? How about you, Jonny?"*

Nick and Jonny continue to push and scream.

Teacher: *"Is it OK for each of you to get pushed? If you don't want to be pushed, you can say, 'Stop.'"*

Both children yell, *"Stop"* at each other and stop pushing. They continue to tug on the trike and scream.

Teacher: *"Looks like you've stopped pushing each other. Are you ready to solve the problem now?"*

The boys are slowing down now and starting to think.

Nick: *"Jonny could have the green trike."*

Jonny: *"No, I want this one! Nick can ride the green trike."*

Teacher:	*"You each had an idea about riding a different trike. Both of you still want this one. Any other ideas?"*
Nick:	*"I can ride the red one first."*
Teacher:	*"Nick has an idea about taking turns."*
Jonny:	*"I want to be first."*
Teacher:	*"Sounds like Jonny agrees to taking turns and he wants to be first."*
Nick:	*"OK, you can be first for just one minute."*
Teacher:	*"Is this OK with you, Jonny?"*
Jonny:	*"No. I want five minutes."*
Teacher:	*"Will a turn of five minutes be OK for both of you?"*
Nick and Jonny:	*"OK"*
Teacher:	*"Great! You solved the problem. I'll let you know when five minutes are up."*

In this real-life incident, Jonny hops on the red trike and Nick gets on the green one. They go off riding, still friends, proud of their solution. By the end of five minutes, they are in the sandbox and have forgotten about the trikes. Chapter five in this book offers many more examples of negotiation and engaging young children in Problem-Solving, a skill to serve them well throughout life.

When we approach conflicts without asking questions or trying to place blame we find Problem-Solving effective in reducing or eliminating aggressive behavior. The earlier in life a child is exposed to and learns Problem-Solving the less likely he will be to become violent as a reaction to frustration.

Here are some suggestions for reducing frustration in the lives of toddlers and young children.

- Protect and strengthen Attachment.
- Establish a daily routine.
- Be certain your child is getting enough sleep.
- Do not make unnecessary requests.
- Do not flood your child with verbal directions.
- When seeking cooperation, connect with eye contact, a smile, and a nod.
- Schedule regular intimate one-on-one involvement doing what your child wants to do.
- Put away forbidden household objects.
- Don't take babies and toddlers to places where they are required to sit still and be quiet.
- Leave young children home when going shopping whenever possible.
- Give full attention when engaged with your child. Electronics out of sight!
- Active Listen.
- Provide DAILY vigorous physical activity. Preferably outdoors.
- Take long walks together.
- Regulate access to, or eliminate, TV and videos.
- Remove child from a kindergarten requiring homework, a preschool teaching the three Rs, a punitive atmosphere, and/or one in which kids are kept in from recess as a disciplinary measure.

Our habitual ways of treating children create countless frustrations and make unreasonable demands on their immature nervous systems. They have landed in a nerve-jangling, disordered culture. It falls to us to make their days as uncomplicated as possible.

Note: If you can possibly manage it, spend a few days in any facility where your child will be staying, whether a daycare, a preschool, or a private elementary school. Glowing brochures and costly tuitions do not guarantee a safe emotional environment. A preschool where children are reprimanded or deprived of outdoor play for something the adults see as "misbehavior," is a toxic place to be and not worth your hard-earned money. A Montessori school where children are scolded, deprived of recess, or sent to Time-Out is Montessori in name only. However, when you find your choice has been a good one, time you can spend there observing folks who respect children and are skilled in working with them, will be a wonderful learning opportunity for you.

PREFACE TO THE NEXT CHAPTER

The advice I am going to give you about the relationship between you, your child, and food has very personal meaning to me.

I confessed earlier in this book to having been a perfect example of the Traditional Authoritarian parent. One of the ways I tried to control my first son was in attempting to control his eating.

As I coaxed, pressured, threatened, and withheld dessert, he ate less and less and became thinner and thinner. Folks commented on his thinness. One time a perfect stranger, a grandmotherly woman passing our table on leaving a restaurant, stopped and gently urged him to eat. Friends asked why he was so skinny and if he was eating enough. Well no, he wasn't and it was my fault! With a pantry and refrigerator full of food and conscientiously trying to be a good mother, my four-year-old child was seriously undernourished.

I can thank Dr. Benjamin Spock for fixing this problem. He knew about parents like me and underfed little kids like my son. Citing research begun in 1928 by Dr. Clara Davis, he made a strong case for child-directed eating and convinced me to withdraw.

I wonder now how I was able to wholeheartedly follow his advice. This was at least four years before I took the P.E.T. training and I was still trapped in my Controlling mindset. I did it, though. I managed to remove myself completely from any involvement in my son's meals, beyond preparing and serving. I don't remember how many days or weeks it took his appetite to emerge. I can tell you this: Emerge it did! Before long, he was eating everything on his plate and sometimes asking for more! He grew up with a hardy appetite for every kind of food and thoroughly enjoying mealtimes.

And so, dear reader, if you are caught up in an eating struggle with a child of any age, take heart. Help is at hand.

FREEDOM BECKONS!

3

HOW CAN I GET MY CHILD TO EAT?

All healthy animals, including our own human babies, are born with an appetite-regulating system perfectly tuned to their nutritional needs.

This inborn mechanism can be thrown off balance and into a state of dysfunction when the adults around a child attempt to take charge of his food consumption.

Poor associations with food can begin early in life. Pressuring or forcing an infant to take the last ounce of milk, hoping to make him sleep all night, can derail the natural appetite. Eating may start to go off track when solid foods are introduced too early, are fed from a nursing bottle, or adults coax a baby to take a few more spoonfuls after he turns away or closes his mouth to the offered food. Adult theatrics, such as waving a spoonful of food in the air and zooming it in like an airplane are never a good idea.

Typical eating problems spring up during the toddler years when appetite slows down as it synchronizes perfectly with a slowing growth rate.

An average newborn weighs seven pounds. Average weight at one year is 21 pounds. We humans triple our weight in our first year of life. Imagine how gigantic we would be if our growth continued at this rate! Because our growth slows dramatically after our first birthdays, our caloric requirements drop off just as dramatically. This big change comes at a time when the human impulse toward autonomy is in full bloom and Counterwill is at a peak.

If you opened this book to information about eating problems before reading the first sections, please go now to the chapter titled MY CHILD DEFIES ME to read about Counterwill. This instinct, deeply etched into our human brains, is an element of eating resistance in healthy children of all ages. Knowing about Counterwill is basic to unleashing a repressed appetite.

To keep their appetites functioning properly, babies need the opportunity to begin feeding themselves all of their food at about eight to twelve months of age, starting with finger foods and progressing to using utensils when they are ready. Your cue to withdraw from feeding your baby will be his ability to feed himself finger foods.

One fine day, place a nutritionally balanced variety of his favorite finger foods in front of him along with his Tippy Cup® of milk or water and get out of the way, making room for him to take over completely. Allow him this opportunity without praising or coaching. Relax into easy interacting and busying yourself with your own meal. Resist any temptation to "help" by picking up and offering something he seems to be missing. He'll know what's there.

After he's been on his own for a few weeks, give him a spoon along with his finger foods to practice raising tidbits into his mouth. Pick up a piece of food from in front of him, place it on the spoon and make a brief comment, *"Here sweetheart, looks like you're ready for a spoon,"* as you put it down before him or place it in his hand if he reaches for it. Say no more. From having watched adults using spoons he'll know what to do with it. You will see when he's ready to handle a bowl of an easy-to-scoop food, such as mashed potatoes or oatmeal. Give him his first bowl of a favorite cooked cereal with a spoon in it one day at breakfast. Place his bowl in front of him and serve a bowl of the same or a similar food with a spoon in it to each other family member. If you are alone with him, sit down and eat with your spoon making no special comment. If older children are eating with you, coach them ahead of time to pay no attention to baby with his spoon. This is just another ordinary day as the two of you and any other family members enjoy breakfast together. In a few minutes, after he's had time to focus on spooning food into his mouth, bring in any other items usually served for breakfast, such as toast and fruit. If having something soft and mushy in front of him prompts smearing it around and squeezing it through his fingers, maintain your composure. This is a common way some babies become acquainted with their own first bowl of cereal. If no one makes an issue of it and the food is something they really like, they move on from playing with it to only eating it in a day or so. As funny a show as this may be, please don't laugh or give attention to it. We do not want to encourage development of a smearing and squishing comedy routine. In a few days, add spoonable foods, such as mashed potatoes, squash, and applesauce, to his lunch and dinner menus. As he becomes skilled in handling a spoon, you will see when he's ready for a small fork.

Resistance to food begins when parents continue feeding past this developmental stage. Once you have turned his eating over to him, curb any urge to hand-feed just a bit to help move things along or to remind him to eat something he's ignoring. Your way to help is in creating an easy relaxed mealtime atmosphere and leaving his eating up to him, totally!

> When adults respond to changing eating patterns— by urging, bribing, threatening, playing little games, distracting, or trying to force a child to eat—a contest begins. Interference with his eating becomes an assault on his physical as well as his psychological personhood and may come close to totally shutting down the natural appetite.

Only the child knows when he is hungry and what tastes good to him. As parents talk about food, talk about what he eats and how much he eats, urge him to join the clean plate club, or distract him while sneaking in a spoonful, food becomes repulsive to him. When children gag under this pressure, they are not "putting on an act," and we are wrong when we say they refuse to eat. **In reality, they are blocked from eating.**

The problem is compounded when dessert is held out as a reward for eating other foods, making dessert more tantalizing and other foods more offensive. Frequently a child enduring such pressure will settle on one or two foods he can tolerate to sustain himself. Plain white toast and bananas are common choices and parents feel lucky to see this much nourishment getting into him.

The struggle will end when the adults come to recognize and have faith in normal bodily functions and can learn to stay completely out of what should be a child's own business. It is his body and his appetite. He deserves the right to enjoy the foods his taste buds tempt him to eat from a well-balanced variety of wholesome products served to him.

Since the research by Dr. Clara Davis, mentioned earlier,[80] subsequent studies in the United States and Europe have continued to show babies and young children maintaining a balanced diet when they are completely free to choose from a variety of healthful products. THE LAST WORD ON NOTHING website gives us a list of the 34 foods in the Clara Davis study. Reading about babies with no exposure to sweets or junk foods, contentedly thriving on self-selected unprocessed offerings, jolts us into seeing the bizarre nature of a "Picky Eater" phenomenon.

When allowed to determine what they eat, their choices will not necessarily comprise a day-to-day balanced intake. There may come a day when, after you had decided to follow my advice, there you are with a little kid who hasn't eaten anything except cooked carrots for the past three days. What about meat? What about fruit? What about his good whole wheat bread? All are ignored as he sits there eating carrots. You want to scream or at least want to find some way to make him eat the other foods you took the time to prepare for him.

---

[80] From <u>The Common Sense Book of Baby and Child Care</u> by Benjamin Spock, M.D., Copyright 1946, Published by Duell, Sloan and Pearce, New York, NY. All editions of this book give extensive information and guidance on diet and nutrition.

Parents are thrown off balance, too, when they serve a child one of his favorite foods only to have him say, *"Yucky"* and push it away. His body's chemical balance on this day could be affecting his sense of taste and smell, making it truly yucky to him, or he may have seized upon this way for asserting himself. Whatever is going on, I expect you will know by now to restrain yourself from saying, *"What do you mean, yucky? You always love chicken casserole."* On another day, he may like it again. Or he may not. Either way, you remain unperturbed. With Mother Nature in charge of all this unpredictability, our best course of action is to think happy thoughts and enjoy the ride!

Studies consistently prove, when groups of young children are offered a varied selection of healthful foods to freely choose from, they will all eat well-balanced diets. One child may like a certain food today and hate it next week while another eats only one particular food for several days and switches to some other one for another stretch of time. Yet, when recording every bite eaten, researchers find the total combination of foods consumed within approximately six weeks to be nutritionally balanced and meeting the unique physiological requirements for each individual child.

Quantities of food intake fluctuate, also. Some days it may seem as though your child has eaten almost nothing. This is natural, too, as changes in appetite coincide with normal fluctuations in growth and physiology along with other common factors affecting hunger, such as stress, illness, teething, mood, and physical activity.

The biological appetite regulator adjusts consumption perfectly if not interfered with by well-meaning adults.

Note: The babies in the Clara Davis research study were newly weaned and without experience with solid foods when they entered the study. One little boy had a severe case of rickets from his vitamin D deficiency. When Dr. Davis added cod liver oil to the foods placed before him each day, he drank the vitamin D rich offering in varying amounts, off and on, until he was healed of his rickets.

Today's brain studies are revealing early coercion around food and meals to be a precursor to seriously unhealthy eating habits, including overeating leading to obesity. The body's internal system for regulating appetite can be permanently impaired by adult interference during childhood, leaving a person's relationship with food distorted for life.

Completely distracting a child with an electronic screen, while shoveling in food, is definitely a bad idea. I couldn't begin to imagine where this way of taking over a child's food intake could end up. I do know it represents a frightful trend toward depersonalization and disconnection.

Recent studies at the University of North Carolina point to genetic predispositions for liking or disliking certain foods. Research by the Monell Chemical Senses Center in Philadelphia shows a connection between a pregnant woman's diet and the development of food preferences in her unborn baby.

All the more reason to stop prodding children to eat. If our daughter was born to hate celery and to love tomatoes, what business do we have trying to control her choices?

Although an eating problem can develop at any age, adolescence is the other life-stage besides toddlerhood when children become most vulnerable to disruptions in healthful eating habits. Hormonal and emotional changes along with the strong surge toward independence can bring on unusual food choices, fluctuations in appetite and harmful associations with food. Free access to sweets and junk foods, with their addictive qualities and constant media promotion, increases the threat to good nutrition.

Once again, this is not a time for parents to step in and become coercive.

If you are asking, *"How can I get my child to eat?"* you are already in trouble. By "trying to get him to eat" you are preventing him from eating! If this is your dilemma, I give you a new question to ask. *"What must happen to unleash my child's healthy appetite and free him to enjoy food and mealtimes?"*

And now, I give you the answer:

If an eating problem has developed in your home, it is important to approach mealtimes with a relaxed attitude of respect for a child's right to decide what he will put into his body. Adults and food have become his natural appetite's enemies and it will take your firm commitment to a new attitude before the intimidated appetite can come out of hiding and take over the job of keeping your child healthy. This is as true for a teen as for a toddler or a six-year-old.

> Here's what has happened: You have turned your problem—concern for your child's well-being—into his problem, aversion to food.

To bring about change, at each meal put before your child very small portions of the foods prepared for the family along with some of whatever foods he has been accepting. If he comments about not liking something, tell him to leave it on his plate, *"Only eat what you want, sweetie."* Place a serving dish of bread or crackers and one of sliced fruit within his reach at every meal for all family members to eat by helping themselves.

Drop any rule you may have established for "taking one bite" or "one little taste." Just don't mention it anymore.

Do not ask children what they want to eat. You are in charge of meal planning as the nurturing adult they can depend on to fulfill their need for food.

If you have been serving desserts, now begin placing them alongside each plate when setting the table; and if dessert has been an element in mealtime struggles, your child will ask about this. Tell him you are not going to bother him about eating anymore. You have decided to serve dessert this way from now on and he may eat it when he wants to. He will almost certainly indulge himself at the beginning of meals.

This is fine. Don't let it bother you.

Serving dessert right along with all other foods reduces the exalted status parents have assigned to it by using it as a control tool and a reward. We can help our child come to regard sweets as only one inviting component of a meal.

Some of your anxiety can be relieved by buying or making low sugar desserts. The internet offers recipes for low sugar nutritious goodies. Look out for artificial sweeteners in recipes or foods you buy. All brands are reported as being bad for the health of both children and adults.

While you are placing a custard, fruit cobbler, or peanut butter cookie beside his plate, talk to yourself about why you are doing this strange thing. Tell yourself you are showing the intimidated appetite it can come out of hiding to take over.

And it will!

As pressure is withdrawn, your child will gradually expand the variety of foods he can eat and may ask for another helping of something he wouldn't have touched in the past. MAKE NO COMMENT! DO NOT SHOW EXCITEMENT OR PRAISE HIM IN ANY WAY. Bite your tongue to keep from saying things like: *"I always said you would like meatloaf if you would only taste it,"* or *"Daddy, look! Your big boy is eating his broccoli!"*

This must not be about you. If he sees eating as satisfying your wishes, Counterwill can click in and send the appetite back into dysfunction.

When he begins eating foods he'd been refusing, you will be tempted to try hurrying things up by encouraging him to try other new things. Please resist the temptation. His body systems will come into balance and his biological signals will take perfect care of his food intake when the grownups around him can remain completely unconcerned.

Although we are ignoring what and how much he is eating, we do not want to ignore him. At every age from highchair days on up, children should be included in the socializing around the family table. We do not want them feeling left out.

When people of any age feel unnoticed, they may indulge in provocative behaviors to draw attention to themselves. Mealtimes offer a variety of ways for a left-out little person to get noticed. It will be necessary to educate grandparents, nannies or others involved in the feeding of your child or sharing meals with your family.

If grandparents are reluctant to go along with your new approach and they are not sharing your home, arrange his visits with them for times when meals will not be included.

Various folks are advising parents to set up sticker charts for rewarding veggie consumption and inducing good eating habits. As with all sticker charts, this is a form of coercion, a bad idea, and direct interference with Nature. The internet offers several such charts, all to be bypassed.

If your child is entering daycare or preschool where food is served, do not warn the personnel about his "eating problems." Seeing the other children enjoying food may prompt him to join in with gusto. Whatever the case, we wouldn't want his caretakers starting out with negative expectations about him.

Commenting on the yumminess of a food hoping to entice a reluctant eater is not recommended. **Any and all comments and suggestions about food or eating will interfere with the natural full blooming of an appetite coming out from under adult coercion.**

Do not use sweets as bribes or rewards at mealtimes or any other times, as in *"If you eat all your potatoes, you can have some chocolate pudding,"* or *"If you behave yourself while we shop for groceries, I'll buy you a candy bar when we leave."* Using sweets or any food for bargaining purposes bestows on them significance unrelated to the togetherness of mealtimes and food's natural function for sustaining life and health.

Refrain from talking about food at mealtime or any other time. When you can stop thinking about and talking with family, friends, and neighbors about your child's eating, relief from the distress it has been causing you will be reflected in your mealtime demeanor and in your child's emerging appetite.

Besides helping your child, your new attitude becomes a step in giving up the Old Job of Parenting. You reach a new level of personal Freedom when you quit the job of running a child's life around his eating. This whole source of stress and worry now disappears from your world!

Continue serving him small portions of whatever the family is eating, always with some foods he enjoys on his plate and on the table. If he rejects everything, say this is what's been prepared and you hope he can fill up from what he sees here.

Do not get up and make something special for him or offer alternative foods. If he still rejects everything, invite him to stay at the table to socialize until the others are finished or until he has reached his limit to remain pleasantly involved, at which point you will kindly excuse him. He is not excused to watch television because, *"We don't have the TV on during meals, sweetheart."*

The food your child leaves on his plate is not wasted. Seeing it there makes the look and smell of it familiar to him. Some children need to see, smell, and take tiny tastes of a food on many occasions before gradually learning to enjoy it. This may require putting food into the mouth and taking it out. Repulsive as this may seem, it is a natural taste-testing technique and should be given no attention.

A highly sensitive child with a delicate system may grow up with a limited appetite. Most of us have a few foods we never eat and would be offended if anyone tried to force us to eat them. Everyone deserves the right to eat what tastes good to them and to pass up the things they don't like.

As with learning through modeling in all other areas of life, and with familiarity, children eventually come to enjoy most, if not all, the foods they see their parents eating.

Forget about table manners. As mentioned in an earlier chapter, etiquette and all socially-conforming behaviors are learned through imitation of the adults a child is attached to, admires, and wants to be like.

Honor meals as relaxing, companionable times for family members to enjoy being together. As an adult in charge of your home, you can set a pleasant conversational tone and steer away from criticisms, arguments, or disturbing topics such as homework. Social media and television have no place in the ambience of warm togetherness you can design for your family.

Stock only wholesome foods with no access to junk foods, sugared cereals, or soft drinks.

Keep fast food restaurants outside your children's awareness as long as possible. Instead of making it a treat to go to McDonald's, make it a treat to pack a lunch from home and enjoy a picnic in a park. Eat lunch at a public pond and take bread for feeding the ducks. Don't allow fast food marketing ploys to seduce your young child and give him something to beg for. Children can grow up happily without the Golden Arches beckoning every time you drive past,

Place a step stool or sturdy box at the kitchen sink and a cup for a small child to get his own drinks of water, allowing him another opportunity for regulating his intake.

Maintain a supply of nutritious snack foods, such as whole grain crackers, fruit strips, packets of popcorn, banana chips and other dried fruits, low sugar granola bars, and sesame sticks. If you have time and the inclination, search the internet for wholesome snack items to make at home. Be alert to times when a depressed mood or irritability signal hunger and serve a snack. Without worrying about spoiling the appetite before the next meal, think of it as a mini-meal. Most children benefit from a snack halfway between regular mealtimes. **They do not benefit from snack foods being available for continuous munching.**

Withholding food from a hungry child, hoping to get him to eat at mealtime, supports a power contest around the issue of food and intensifies resistance to eating at the table. If dinner will be ready in five minutes and he says he's hungry, give him something to eat! Without saying, *"Dinner is almost ready,"* be the generous, nurturing adult in his life and give him food. See it as an appetizer or a first course.

If your child has left the table without eating, and says he's hungry at bedtime, resist the temptation to say, *"If you had eaten your dinner you wouldn't be hungry now."* He wasn't hungry at dinnertime. Now he is. The helpful response will be to offer a serving of fruit, toast with nut butter, a cheese stick, a cup of yogurt; something he likes. If the request is for sweets, be prepared to honestly say you don't have any or, *"We don't eat sweets at bedtime."* Give a snack at bedtime only if a child complains about being hungry or asks for something to eat. Do not suggest a snack yourself because you're worried about the missed meal. Leave it up to him.

This is an ideal occasion for comparing our treatment of children to the way we respond to adult friends. Ask yourself what you would do if a house guest said he was hungry before going to bed and act accordingly.

Above all, respect this little person's right to eat what he wants and how much he wants as you do your part by serving a wholesome, well-balanced variety of foods. Your child will do his part when you stick to only doing yours. We are asking for trouble when we violate our children's rights in this most personal sphere of choice.

Nearly everything outlined above can be applied, with adjustments for age, in helping preadolescents and adolescents. When a child of any age gradually eats less and less or suddenly refuses food, physical illness must be ruled out. Schedule a physical exam, presented to your child as a routine checkup. **Make no mention of eating difficulties and coach the doctor to do the same.** Special attention or drama, swirling around an eating dysfunction, intensifies the dysfunction. If no medical problem is found, we know there's something going on at the emotional level. Increasingly common teen depression and anxieties can squelch appetite. Peer pressure, worries about academic or athletic achievement and body image are known precursors to a dangerous association with food. A lot remains to be learned and understood about anorexia, bulimia, and binge eating.

One thing we do know: We are not up against deliberate behavior. Reasoning, insisting, pleading, bribing, lecturing about nutrition and health are useless and counterproductive. Adult pressure, however gentle and caring it may be, only serves to intensify whatever part Counterwill is playing in blocking the appetite. When eating habits become a threat to health, and possibly to life, professional help is needed from someone trained in this field. Beginning on page 89 in his book, <u>For Parents and Teenagers: Dissolving the Barrier Between You and Your Teen</u>, William Glasser explores the power element motivating anorexic behavior, sometimes leading to death.

We come up against the other side of this problem when overeating, overweight, and obesity become our concerns. Here, again, we are faced with complicated tangles of emotions and control when good-intentioned helpful advice or nagging will only make matters worse.

4

STOP FIDGETING!

Do you remember hearing this when you were a child?

I wrote about Dr. Moritz Schreber in the chapter on Obedience. He was the leading German Parent Educator in the 1800s who advocated total control of children. His teachings included control of their physical bodies. To achieve this, he designed a collection of metal clamps, straps, and harnesses for keeping children in recommended positions. He devised a harness to keep the head in proper alignment, a metal clamp with attached straps to hold the back straight when sitting at a table, a shoulder brace to maintain erect posture, and a contraption of metal rings and straps to force a child to sleep on his back in one position all night.

Drawings of his devices display a disturbing component of the Authoritarian Parenting he promoted.[81]

For the past several years, researchers have been studying the causes and effects of fidgeting. Their findings have been reported in recent news stories. Scientific evidence is revealing fidgeting to be physiologically and neurologically necessary and beneficial. Parents and teachers are advised to stop interfering with a child's fidgeting.

---

[81] To see pictures of his inventions, look up Daniel Moritz Gottlieb Schreber on the internet.

Since it has been mostly schoolteachers who have been ordering children to stop fidgeting, let's think about their demands.

In expecting children to sit still and be quiet for hours at a time, isn't this little movement the least we could allow, when young bodies actually need to be outdoors running, jumping, and climbing all through the day?

While pondering recent news stories about fidgeting and thinking how common and automatic it has been for adults to order kids to stop fidgeting, Dr. Schreber's inventions popped into my mind. I am wondering how far removed is the mind-set behind the order to stop fidgeting from the philosophy behind his body clamps? In our role of Parent with a capital P we think nothing of giving orders concerning a child's bodily movements. With the new findings on fidgeting, I am contemplating how far "off base" we have been in believing we have the right to tell a child how to move, or not move, his body.

If he's fidgeting, he NEEDS to fidget. Can anyone have the right to tell him to stop? Isn't this a simple matter of respect? Think of all the other insulting orders we throw at children; things we would never say to a friend, such as sit up, stop slouching, take your hands out of your pockets, or stand up straight. All are forms of criticism; a very efficient destroyer of self-confidence and relationships.

I'm going to bring up another spontaneous quirk some parents find shattering to their nerves. I am thinking about a three-year-old girl who runs through the house, screaming at the top of her lungs, or a six-year-old boy charging around yelling at full volume. By now you know all behaviors are emotionally-driven attempts to fill needs. I'll list just a few possibilities, any one of which may lie beneath one particular child's outbursts:

- An overload of unspent energy due to physical inactivity
- Bursting agitation from screen violence or over-stimulating visuals
- An unbearable accumulation of stress in reaction to overwhelming adult demands

- Frustration of unmet Attachment needs
- Reaction to suppression of emotional expression
- Perfectly natural, healthy childish exuberance

What should you do about this? First of all, try to adjust your attitude. Is it really breaking your eardrums? Can you see this as your delightful kid doing what he needs to do at the moment and take it in stride? If it happens a lot and you're worried about what your neighbors are thinking, let them know what's going on and ask for their understanding.

Make adjustments according to the above list, if needed. Instead of showing irritation or alarm, acknowledge the outburst with an Active Listening statement: *"Wowee, a kid just has to yell sometimes!"* or *"It feels terrific to run and scream and let it all out."*

You might suggest going outside and possibly joining in with yelling, screaming, and letting it all out together.

Once again, I am asking you to be thoughtful in how you go about sharing your life with a child who just happens to have found himself in your care.

The internet lists several articles about research on fidgeting. The one from the National Education Association is particularly relevant to our concerns.

5

CREATIVITY

In the 1980s Teresa Amabile[82] and her colleagues at Brandeis University conducted a series of studies on thousands of young children to learn about creativity.

Seeing creativity as an enhancement to anyone's life, as well as an important facet of problem-solving, we can look upon it as a significant element in human development. A particularly consequential finding in the Brandeis studies was the identification of four Creativity Killers. Our American culture with the help of the Public Education System is very repressive toward and hard on Creativity.

Teresa Amabile and her colleagues were able to identify the following Creativity Killers. I've added suggestions for avoiding them.

1. SURVEILLANCE:

    Provide a good assortment of supplies for creative endeavors without supervising or becoming involved yourself.

---

[82] Dr. Teresa Amabile is director of research at Harvard Business School where her studies on creativity continue. The research findings here are taken from the book, Guiding Young Children: A Problem-Solving Approach, Third Edition, by Eleanor Reynolds.

2. EVALUATION:

Avoid making evaluative statements, such as *"Your picture is beautiful,"* or *"You are a terrific artist!"* To show interest and respond in a supportive way, it is best to comment on the process and elements of the work: *"It must have been fun putting all the colors together,"* or *"You came up with some new colors when you mixed them."*

3. COMPETITION:

Do not make comparisons with another child's creations. *"I think you could do better if you really tried. Look at the pretty flower Amy made."* Equally unhelpful: *"Yours is the best drawing in the class."*

4. REWARDS:

"You win the prize for the best drawing!" or *"Your picture gets a gold star!"* Praise and rewards squelch creativity.

Knowing ways to stifle creativity, how do we encourage it?

Here are some starters:

- Make a changing variety of supplies available. When felt tip markers have lost their charm, bring in finger paints or water colors.
- An easel with an assortment of tempera paints can stir the creativity in any child.
- If you have space for it, set up a place with supplies of paper, old magazines, scissors, glue, modeling clay, pieces of fabric, bits of yarn, crayons, markers, small cardboard boxes.
- Arrange an environment where spills and messes don't bring on a crisis by spreading plastic or newspapers on the floor or setting up a space in a

garage or basement where anxiety about a mess will not interfere with the exuberance of creativity.

- Don't let worries about soiled clothing squelch the creative spirit. Provide aprons, smocks, or old garments for working with messy substances. Mixing a small amount of dish detergent with tempera paints makes them easy to remove from fabric.

As with play, a child's growth in creativity flourishes in an atmosphere of freedom and lack of interference, directions, suggestions or praise from adults.

Being around creative people and exposure to their creative endeavors will enrich and release a child's own creative expression. Visits to museums, gardens, galleries, hobby and craft shows will feed the creative spirit.

Creative instincts can be nourished by seeing live shows of all kinds. Most high schools give dramatic, musical, and dance performances throughout the school year at affordable admission prices.

Turn off the TV and turn on the music! Include some sort of audio device with the playthings available to your child and a collection of everything from classical to jazz. Pick up your baby or young child and waltz around the room. Sing, dance, and have fun!

And this may be the most important tip of all! Allow time. Give your child unpressured, unhurried chunks of free personal time to daydream, imagine, and savor his own unique flow of creativity.

6

PRAISE

In terms of advancing the growth of our child's self-esteem and development of his self-control, the role of praise demands re-thinking.

When we can see the common use of praise as a verbal reward in response to a desirable behavior, our eyes open to a new perspective. Attuned to furthering our child's autonomy and strength of Self, we begin to see the negative side of praise.

A child setting out to accomplish a physical task or to create a product of his imagination, such as a drawing or a construction of blocks, starts with his vision for meeting the new challenge. During the course of the endeavor, he may revise and add to his unique plan. Finally, there will come a point when his brain's neurological alignment signals his success.

THIS IS HIS REWARD.

Nothing we can say is so gratifying as this intrinsic thrill of achievement. When an adult jumps in with expressions of praise, a child's attention is drawn away from his personal delight to now become concerned with the adult's reaction to and evaluation of what he has done. A bit of his autonomy is chipped away.

In families where praise is used routinely to encourage behaviors valued by the adults, you may hear a child ask, *"Did I do a good job, Daddy?" "Do you like my picture,*

Mommy?" Such a child has become dependent on outside evaluations. He has lost interest or confidence in his ability to evaluate his own progress. With his self-esteem sabotaged, he looks to others for validation.

If you are wondering, *"When my child has finished painting a pretty picture, what should I say?"* you can relax in knowing there is really no need to comment. If you feel compelled to say something, show interest in the picture and his satisfaction in making it: *"I see you worked the blue paint in with the white to create the clouds and the sky,"* or *"It must have been fun to mix colors for the brick buildings."* Such feedback not only steers clear of evaluations and praise, it invites meaningful dialogue with a youngster of any age about his creations. Displaying products of his creativity throughout your home and framing pictures to hang and be enjoyed by all family members will assign value and recognition to his work.

Praise is a form of judgment. When we place ourselves in a judgmental position, our child recognizes himself as being open to our negative judgments as well as our praise.

Giving up praise is difficult to do. Using it as a control strategy has been integral to our way of life. When we can restrain ourselves from indulging this old habit, we see how doing without it makes perfect sense for protecting our child's self-worth.

Affirmative I-Messages are the ideal replacement for praise:

"I'm glad you got ready so fast. We're leaving early enough to get really good seats at the play."

"Thank you for cleaning up the kitchen. Now I have all evening to work on my project."

"I have so much fun playing Scrabble® with you!"

Such comments must be an honest expression of appreciation and feelings, not to be used for manipulating a child's behavior. Like Active Listening, the more we communicate this way, the more our thinking follows into affirmative habits of relating.

7

PROMISES

A LOT OF FAMILY STRIFE CAN BE AVOIDED WHEN WE DO NOT MAKE PROMISES.

We want our children to believe and trust us. If something unexpected comes up or we don't feel like following through, we may break a promise and strike a blow to trust. Or, because of a promise, we may keep a commitment when we really don't want to and end up communicating reluctance or resentment.

The hurt and erosion of trust caused by a broken promise can be completely prevented by not asking for or making promises in the first place. Our word should be good without adding a promise.

Whether or not we use the word Promise, we risk ending up with an unfortunate outcome when we tell a child we are going to do something together at a future time.

Picture this: Three-year-old Emily's mother told her they would bake cookies together on Saturday. Going to bed Saturday night, Emily is sobbing because the day has come and gone and Mommy had so many things to do, their baking did not happen. This caring mother hugs her little girl and tells her they will make cookies another day. Emily stops crying, settles down, falls asleep, and everything seems fine.

Everything is not fine. Deep down inside, beyond verbalization, Emily feels insignificant to the mother who could not find time for her today. This feeling has registered in her Attachment brain. Next week, her resulting Attachment frustration will erupt in aggression when she pulls the cat's tail at home and explodes in a tantrum at daycare.

I want you to stop with me for a moment to think about little Emily. Try to feel with her as we put ourselves into her shoes. She's hurting deep down inside without knowing what's bothering her. Out-of-sorts and with an urge to be mean, she pulls the cat's tail. At daycare, some little disappointment flips her over into a screaming meltdown. Now, in her shoes, how do you feel when Mommy sends you to Time-Out for hurting the cat and, at daycare, you are kept in from outdoor play to teach you not to have tantrums?

Moving on . . . We invite dissent when we ask kids to make promises. The concept is beyond comprehension for a young child and for children of any age, it asks them to look ahead and predict what they will be able to do under future unknown conditions, setting them up for possible failure and the antagonism surrounding a broken promise.

Above all, we want to communicate positive expectations. When we say, *"If I take you to the park, will you promise to leave without making a fuss?"* we are announcing our expectation of difficult behavior. Because children have an uncanny way of living up to our expectations, let's assume there will be no problem on leaving the park.

If there is, we address it in an empathic way. This is a time when we stay in charge of the situation. **We do not change our mind about leaving the park to prevent a scene.** We show our understanding by Active Listening as we support our child through an unwelcomed transition, all the while remaining the kind, self-assured adult to be depended upon. The "old way" would be to get mad at him for not wanting to leave, thereby discounting his feelings and intimidating him into compliance by scaring him with our anger. If we had extracted a promise from him to leave the park without a fuss, he now experiences failure. A Traditional response would be a reminder of his promise with a lecture about the importance of keeping his word, adding a dose of guilt to his unhappiness. None of which would have come up if we had not asked for a promise.

When we are respectful and reliable in our interactions with children, promises do not fit in with the essence of the relationship.

8

EMPATHY AND CONSCIENCE

There has been a lot of talk about Emotional Intelligence in recent years.

In 2010, I attended a lecture on Emotional Intelligence by a famous author on the subject. Following an engaging talk about the need to be aware of the emotional needs and emotional education of our children, a mother in the audience asked if she should continue to use Time-Out to address the unwanted behaviors of her three-year-old boy.

The respected researcher answered "*Yes*" to the mother's question.

I was shocked and dismayed to hear this eminent educator give a mother the go-ahead to subject her little boy to the old Behaviorist technique of love withdrawal.

A 2010 book by a respected Developmental Molecular Biologist, researching and teaching at a major university, gives us a jarring example of the challenges we face in extricating ourselves from deeply entrenched Behaviorist views. Following interesting descriptions of the effects of the emotional environment on an infant's brain, the last chapters—consisting of parenting advice—find this writer falling back into reliance on Behaviorist control. He prescribes and uses the term Operant Conditioning when he describes how the Behaviorist method of shaping could be used to manipulate a three-year-old boy into going outside to play.

His Behaviorist instructions are void of empathy. The child is simply treated as a rat in a maze. Without getting to know her own little boy, why he resists going outside, what fears or anxieties are undermining his ability to enjoy the outdoors; a mother is directed to treat her child the way we would treat a rodent, or in this example, a chicken.

NO EMPATHY IS BEING CALLED FORTH FROM THE MOTHER TO FURTHER HER GROWTH AS AN UNDERSTANDING, FEELING HUMAN BEING OF A PARENT AND, AT THE SAME TIME, SHE MISSES AN OPPORTUNITY TO MODEL EMPATHY FOR HER CHILD.

Books flood the market suggesting novel ways to control children. Although some writers are moving away from punishment, most are still advocating control through some form of manipulation.

One such book tells us to correct a child's hitting with hard toys by having him punish the toy, banishing it to the Time-Out box for bad toys. The author—in looking for kinder, gentler control tricks—fails to direct a parent's attention to finding the source of the hitting behavior and, instead, advises misleading the young child into transferring responsibility to a toy. Intended as a fun little game a child may actually enjoy, it misses what is really happening. The needs behind the little boy's aggression remain unmet and will continue to trouble him and be acted out in one form or another. Hitting and other acts of aggression are outward symptoms of frustrations and bottled-up anger. When we fail to identify and respond to his needs, while diverting him with games and other distracting and controlling tactics, we trample on his inner Self and thwart his drive for autonomy.

I bring all this up here to emphasize the obstacles confronting us as we work toward the humanization of parenting and the importance of HONESTY, RESPECT, and EMPATHY in our interactions with children.

All humans are born with a capacity for empathy. However, having grown up in a culture in which power and control are the major driving forces, much of our empathy lies latent within us as an underdeveloped emotional resource.

Our culturally-driven, habitual punishing reactions of yelling, hitting, and sending children away from us have overridden our natural predisposition for Empathy. By treating children as little machines without feelings or needs, look what has happened to us!

> We have been turned into machines ourselves. Automatic delivery systems of Punishments and Rewards.

When we are able to overcome our conditioning and learn to treat children with kindness and respect, empathy becomes our automatic response to difficulties. With adult examples and nurturing, we see a child grow into an emotionally intelligent empathic individual.

We stimulate development of empathy when we express our own feelings and needs to our children. However, most of us have grown up unable to recognize and communicate our needs. Parents and teachers trained us to repress our feelings, leaving us with never having learned to identify them for ourselves.

Marshall Rosenberg's Nonviolent Communication teachings highlight the importance of being able to identify our own feelings to ourselves and to others. Great help in this regard is available on the internet page titled Marshall Rosenberg's Feelings Inventory. There we find two lists. One gives names to our feelings when needs are met and the other identifies feelings when our needs are not met.

Adults have traditionally squelched self-disclosure and personal awareness by dismissing and denying a child's feelings. Do you remember sobbing with disappointment or sadness and being told you had nothing to cry about?

By learning to communicate our true feelings to our children they learn by our example to recognize, define, and express theirs. Our non-judgmental recognition of their everyday emotions put into words models and facilitates the development of empathy. Our own personal growth and finding parenthood to be fascinating and enjoyable are the great pleasures we discover by making this fundamental change in what we do and who we are.

The folks at Echo Parenting in Los Angeles have created an effective way to teach and demonstrate empathy with what they call Empathy Books. They make little "books" in response to a child's experiences. Here's an example:

Three-year-old Julie skinned her knee and is crying. After administering first-aid, Mom says, *"We're going to make a book about this skinned knee of yours."*

She grabs a piece of paper, folds it in half, and starts drawing. A stick figure of Julie with the noticeably bruised knee decorates the cover and Mommy starts an Active Listening dialogue, *"A skinned knee hurts a lot,"* as she draws the stick figure with tears running down. Opening the folded paper, she adds drawings according to whatever Julie is saying. They finish the book with a figure and words on the back surface of the paper. Now this little girl has an illustrated record to keep and go back to for helping her assimilate the painful experience.

Empathy Books record happy experiences as well as disturbing events in a child's life, all the while putting words and pictures to feelings and helping to make sense of daily happenings. This way of being with children is described in detail and with a video on the Echo Parenting website.

At this point, I must say something about teenage boys and empathy:

From time to time we hear a report telling us teenage boys are incapable of empathy. We are told that something in the structure of their brains makes it impossible for them to feel empathy and they grow past this stage of arrested brain development by the time they reach their twenties.

This is what we are told. Sort of a modern version of inborn evil and the creation of a new dangerous myth.

The **intrinsic capability** for empathy is right there in the teen boy's brain. What we sometimes see as unempathic behavior is his instinctive reaction to the way the adults in his life are treating him. Coercion, disrespect and hostile reactions to Counterwill, combine to stifle empathy.

Being treated with respect and living within the context of relationship to at least one caring, attuned adult to whom he is securely attached keeps his natural empathy alive and well.

The defiant disrespect exhibited by some teenage boys is a clear reflection of the way they themselves are treated. If you look around you, "out there" in society, you will see teenagers being severely disrespected in all sorts of situations. Instead of approaching a teen courteously, many adults—total strangers to a boy—will approach him with stern demands and blatant animosity, quite effectively stirring up his Counterwill.

The well-meaning researchers telling us teen boys are incapable of empathy are lacking in awareness and understanding of Attachment and the Counterwill instinct.

This is the same level of ignorance generating the misunderstandings and reactionary punitive approach to the widespread problem of Bullying.

Here we are again.

THERE IS NOTHING WRONG WITH OUR KIDS. WHAT IS WRONG IS WHAT WE ARE DOING TO THEM.

VIII

What's done to the child is done to society.
~ The Buddha

1

ELECTRONIC INTERFERENCE

Day by day, personal electronics, computer games, social media, and television are taking up more and more time in the lives of children when their optimum physical and emotional development depends on other types of activities. At the same time, electronic devices are drawing parents away from their children and into the digital world.

Although it has become common protocol for friends to ignore each other as they engage with electronic devices, this is not advisable behavior when a parent is with a child. The younger the child, the greater the impact when we tune out from him in this way. For the first six years, and most essentially during the first three, our level of engagement when we are with our child is arranging his brain circuits to serve him for life. When we are with him and not really there because we've connected with an object, his developing brain is responding accordingly.

Robin Karr-Morse and Meredith S. Wiley give us a full scientific description of this process in <u>Scared Sick: The Role of Childhood Trauma in Adult Disease.</u>[83] You can find a discussion of this particular problem on pages 113 and 114 of this important book.

---

[83] The research cited in this book leaves no doubt about the damage done by our antiquated Parenting practices, including the resulting poor health of our general population.

As for the children, they need vigorous physical activity. They need emersion in the natural world. They need meaningful communication and engaging enjoyable activities with adults and other children, all unavailable and left out when watching television, playing video games, talking on, texting on, or otherwise engrossed with electronic devices.

The question of whether to give iPads to babies and toddlers has fueled a new debate. I expect you can predict what I think about this trend.

I readily understand the strong temptation to find relief from the continuous demands of parenthood. An iPad can seem like a fine solution for silencing a fussy baby or a screaming three-year-old.

Electronics are here to stay and children must be prepared for a future of change none of us can imagine.

However, some things do not change! What babies and toddlers need has not changed in thousands of years and will not change in our future with unimaginable electronic wonders.

Growing bodies and growing brains need physical activity and intimate involvement with other humans.

Crawlers and toddlers need floor time. They need to hold objects in their hands, feel them, manipulate them, do things with them. They need wheeled toys, things to build with, to stack, to push, to roll, bounce, and throw.

Little children need to feel the earth under their feet, the sun and wind in their faces, to dig in sand, mush around in mud, splash in water.

THEY NEED AS MUCH FREE INDEPENDENT PLAY AS THEY FIND PLEASURE IN.

My recommendation? Please hold off on introducing electronic screens into your child's life. When and if you do, treat it the way Pediatricians and researchers have been recommending monitoring children's TV viewing for years. Limit the time a young child spends with electronics to an hour or so per day and be alert to signs of an addiction.

The internet is full of opinions about this subject. Some parents are all excited about their baby's ability to operate an iPad. As adorable as a baby may look, operating and enjoying an electronic device, it will not give him what he really needs for development in full accordance with his genetic endowment. Doctors and teachers are beginning to see signs of developmental deficiencies in children who have been spending time with iPads.

British Psychologist Dr. Richard House[84] sees giving iPads to infants and toddlers as *"Tantamount to abuse. Unnecessary, inappropriate, and harmful. Like playing Russian roulette with their development."*

A good approach to media encroachment is through parental control of the environment instead of trying to control a child.

Keep electronics out of your baby's and young child's world while providing one-on-one time with you, daily opportunities for free play, and physical activity indoors and out. Parents who are at home with children can construct a daily routine to get outside regularly and arrange for indoor play to be free of electronics.

If you have a caretaker for your baby or child, be certain this person is committed enough to his welfare to provide the same quality of daily life for him as you would. If your child will be entering preschool or daycare, be deliberate in your search for a setting free of electronics.

When we are engaged with our children it becomes a matter of courtesy to keep devices turned off whether at home, in the park, or taking a walk. Texting or talking on a phone while in the company of our child is outright disrespectful, damaging to our connection to him and to his sense of his importance to us.

---

[84] You can read this September 2015 article on the Daily Mail website.

Talking on a phone while we are with our child leaves him dangling in a state of hurtful disconnection.

For school-age children surrounded by all media forms, Problem-Solving sessions can engage family members in setting boundaries on usage. It is important to avoid contributing to the problem by slipping into the tempting habit of using TV and videos as babysitters.

In controlling the environment instead of the child, some parents find it functional to store video games in a cabinet or closet only to be brought out at agreed-upon times. It can become a part of an established lifestyle for television to be turned off in the home during the day. The ideal solution to the TV dilemma is to not own one.

There is no perfect answer to this growing problem. Each family must work toward the best ways to address it without creating antagonisms, while not allowing media to take the place of real-life and face-to-face involvement.

I have never heard a parent say anything like, *"I am so glad we bought video games for our son."* I only hear complaints about ongoing disputes over the amount of time spent on them, neglected homework, lack of physical activity and long hours of isolation submerged in the world of games. When I think about such complaints, my mind goes back to my opposition to pacifiers for babies. Like plastic nipples, solo video games become barriers to healthy interaction between children and parents. Both replace intimacy and create distance between children and the adults responsible for them. Time spent playing electronic games is time lost to meaningful interaction with family, time without healthful physical activity or engagement with nature, hobbies or creative pursuits. Video games are not something children "need" and are always a waiting source of antagonism. My advice? Don't introduce them into your family environment to begin with, leaving you completely free from this source of conflict and threat to Attachment.

If you love video games yourself and want to bring them into your child's life, think of them as an activity your child engages in only when he also has plenty of outdoor fun, spends time involved in creative activities or hobbies, and is involved in ongoing meaningful Attachment-fulfilling interactions with you.

Try to think about video games and television this way: They are indulgences we make time for after the real business of living has been taken care of. We do not let them take the place of robust involvement in life and enjoyable engagement with friends and family.

Our human brains undergo significant changes during the teen years and on into our early twenties. Long before the advent of today's media boom, motion pictures were rated to keep a certain level of violence and sexual imagery unavailable to children. We said such fare was a "Bad Influence" on kids and protected them from it.

Today, previously unimaginable degrees of violence and sexual activity are at the fingertips of most teenagers. Scientists are just beginning to see how their brains are being impacted and/or permanently changed in negative ways by this exposure.

I have this mental image of kids being sucked into a stew of social media and electronics where, untethered, the Self floats about in a state of disconnection from nurturing adults.

Don't let your kids be sucked away from you!

Like any behavior we want to influence, we know "laying down the law" is not the way to go. You may find it helpful to share, with your teenager, informative books and websites on the subject of adolescent brain development. so you can work together on reaching sensible guidelines.

Dr. Neufeld gives us his perspective on this turn in our culture with his YouTube presentation on Raising Children in a Digital World. The 2013 and 2014 editions of <u>Hold On to Your Kids: Why Parents Need to Matter More Than Peers,</u> include a section titled A POSTSCRIPT FOR THE DIGITAL AGE offering invaluable advice for parents trying to figure out what to do about this burgeoning complication to living with children.

I feel secure in trusting Bill Gates on this subject. His children were fourteen before they had Smartphones.

2

SCHOOLCHILDREN AND SLEEP

The National Sleep Institute tells us children ages five to ten years old need ten to eleven hours of sleep each night. Maintaining a regular sleep schedule on weekends as well as school nights is recommended.

One of our important responsibilities as parents is orchestrating the fulfillment of our children's sleep needs. Continuing with some form of bedtime routine, as established when they were toddlers and during their preschool years, we now adjust our level of involvement as children in this age group take over more responsibility for getting themselves into bed.

Setting the time for lights-out to accommodate sleep requirements is our starting point.

When a child has taken over bedtime preparations, it remains supportive to the relationship for a parent to stay somewhat involved. This may require connecting and making eye contact with a non-coercive statement, *"I'm going to get your bath ready. We have 40 minutes until lights-out."*

It may be workable for you to finish up in the kitchen or attend to your own interests during this time. Or bedtime may run more smoothly when you stay nearby folding down the bed covers, checking on the next day's outfit, just being there.

Children in this age group enjoy chapter books, looking forward to what comes next in the story each night. When they become readers themselves, they may like reading awhile on their own before you return for a goodnight kiss and lights-out.

Many parents find that stretching out to wind down while their youngster prepares for bed is a perfect setting for Active Listening and ending the day well connected. However bedtimes evolve in your family, keeping Attachment in mind remains a priority.

If a youngster balks at going to bed or has trouble falling asleep, a Problem-Solving session could bring a solution. He may be able to offer ideas on exactly what's needed to help him get the sleep he needs for healthy development.

As always, we remain tuned in to all possible ways to reduce stress and the weight of demands being made on our child. If chronic anxiety has produced insomnia, we will need to look over the recommendations for preschoolers and toddlers and apply this knowledge to the older child. A soft furry pet as a sleeping companion may be the answer. A carefully selected dog can be the perfect "medicine" to cure the inability to let go into sleep.

Bedtime for teens becomes much more complicated and open to difficulties. From ages ten to seventeen the sleep requirements are 8.5 to 9.25 hours per night and accomplishing this can become tricky. When sports and other extracurricular activities take up big chunks of time, trying to fit in enough hours for sleep may not be easy.

By now, we know nagging and pressuring teens about anything gets us nowhere. Our best contribution will be in maintaining the stability of home life. The evening meal takes on added significance as an anchoring point for a busy teenager. Serving dinner at an established time or as near to it as possible provides predictability in his hectic world. Dinner should be respected and honored as a getting-together time for a family whether it consists of two parents and one or more children, a single mom with one child, or any combination of family members.

Nutrition enters into the picture, too. Teen bodies are growing and changing rapidly. With junk foods readily available in the outside world, it is up to us to serve wholesome well-balanced meals without the availability of junk foods in our home.

Besides tight schedules of after school activities, teens are flooded with homework; another obstacle to healthful sleep habits. At this age, their internal clocks have shifted to 11 PM for going to sleep, putting their sleep requirements for optimal mental and physical development out of sync with most school schedules. For this reason, some United States school districts are starting classes later in the morning.

With all the pressures they are under, some teens are developing difficulties with getting to sleep and staying asleep. Insomnia may be brought on or made worse by the consumption of caffeine for staying awake to do homework. Eliminating caffeine after late afternoon and substituting it with fruit juice or chocolate milk may provide a needed boost for completing homework without keeping your child awake. The National Sleep Institute's website on Teens and Sleep is filled with information and advice for teenagers and their parents.

Sleep medications are not recommended. In the long run, homework, school system demands, sports, and extracurricular activities are not worth messing up your teen's body chemistry and inviting dependence on drugs.

Some teenagers find reading in bed, before dropping off to sleep, to be conducive to a good night's rest. A parent's contribution can come in the form of a good reading lamp.

An accumulation of stress is a common cause of teen insomnia. We can help by eliminating any stresses we may be creating. Thinking about the sort of emotional climate our home offers and going over the Communication Roadblocks will be a good place to start. High action video games and television shows jangle nerves and are a common cause of nightmares and restless sleep for all age groups.

If your teen is seeking relief from insomnia, you may find a solution with a Six-Step Problem-Solving session to identify and reduce or get rid of contributing factors.

This big teen-of-a-kid still needs the security of Attachment, dependable support, and unconditional acceptance. Providing them is our best way of helping with sleep challenges and all the other hurdles confronting young people at this stage of life.

3

HOMEWORK

I will start by saying I am opposed to homework and find it particularly problematic in middle school and the elementary grades.

Homework for kindergarten children is nothing short of abuse. Demanding homework from five-year-olds is counterproductive and oppressive. It goes against everything research has taught us about child development. Real learning in young children comes about through independent play and free interaction with people and the environment.

Homework has gradually been introduced into middle and elementary schools for a variety of reasons.

- Parents who worry about "achievement" want evidence of something important going on in the classroom. They see homework as this evidence.
- Teachers are tired of being blamed for the poor performance of some students and want to shift part of the responsibility for learning onto parents.
- Poor school performance is primarily a child's reaction to and rejection of boring hours of being forced to memorize masses of irrelevant information for the purpose of passing tests. People in power are causing great harm

by demanding high-stakes testing and believing homework will improve learning.

- Schools use the assignment of homework to get uninvolved parents involved. Some are aggressive about this by providing worksheets for parents and children to do together and checklists to record production; extending the schoolroom and long school day into the evening hours.
- Parents view homework as necessary to a good education; a belief not supported by research. I refer you to Alfie Kohn's articles about homework on his website and his excellent book on the subject.[85]

Most modern parents have far too little time to share bonding intimacy with their kids. Homework, particularly for young children, robs them of this precious time.

Homework creates conflict between parents and children and has become an agitating invasion into the home.

Children need physical activity and free interaction with each other throughout the day. Long hours sitting passive and silent while expected to absorb information for passing tests disregards their natural needs and individual capabilities. Enduring this all day in a schoolroom is hard work. To add schoolwork to their hours at home is abusive, unfair, and an intrusion into what should be their own personal time.

In many homes, battles over homework generate an ongoing undercurrent of animosity and unhappiness.

The politicians who dictate what goes on in public schools are not educated in child development, are not qualified to make decisions about education, and are motivated by political ambitions and monetary interests having nothing to do with the welfare of children.

---

[85] The Homework Myth: Why Our Kids Get Too Much of a Bad Thing by Alfie Kohn, Copyright 2006, Published by Da Capo Press, a member of the Perseus Book Group, Philadelphia, PA.

The testing industry reaps multi-billion-dollar profits and, along with the drug corporations, have found a gold mine in our public education system. Children are cogs in the wheels of their vast enterprises.

In addressing homework challenges, we start with an unemotional approach by arranging a mutually-agreeable time to sit down for a Problem-Solving session:

1. Let your child define his needs. Active Listen as he thinks out loud about meeting the school's requirements.
2. Brainstorm together for ideas about where and when to do homework. Immediately after school? After an hour of play? After dinner? In the dining room? In the kitchen?
3. Talk about the where, when, and what each of you will do to arrange a work area.
4. When the two of you have come to full agreement, write down the plan and post it in plain sight.
5. Implement the plan.
6. Check with each other in a week or so to see if your ideas are working. Are changes needed or is sticking to any plan a useless endeavor?

Note: I have not included your child's bedroom as a good homework area because we want to make the room where a child of any age sleeps an inviting haven for winding down at the end of each day. Associating it with homework may interfere with this goal. Some children do, however, find their own private room their choice as the ideal homework environment.

Beyond your willingness to help when he asks, leave responsibility with your child by saying something like, *"I'm always here to help if you need me and to look over your work if you want me to. I'm not going to bug you about homework or try to make you do it. I'm leaving it up to you to take care of yourself."*

MAKE THIS ANNOUNCEMENT AND STICK TO IT! SAY NOTHING AT ALL ABOUT HOMEWORK. DON'T ASK IF HE HAS ANY TO DO. DO NOT ASK IF HE HAS DONE IT. DON'T ASK TO SEE IT.

If he complains and moans and groans about homework, put your Active Listening skills to work. Homework is his problem and you can help him figure out how to cope with it by Active Listening to his frustrations **without advising or lecturing**.

Think of homework as your child's business. Leave it up to the teachers to monitor his production. You may want to inform them of the position you are taking.

TURNING HOMEWORK OVER TO YOUR CHILD WILL RESULT IN SIGNIFICANT BENEFITS TO HIM AND TO YOU.

1. It tells him you trust him to handle it.
2. He will learn not to depend on you to get him to do the assignments.
3. His inborn untapped strengths and abilities are free to emerge when outside pressure is removed.
4. With you out of the picture, Counterwill fades.[86]
5. A major source of conflict is banished.
6. His sense of responsibility broadens.
7. His self-esteem grows when he discovers he can do this on his own.
8. Space is opened up in your relationship for mutual good feelings.
9. You have one less thing to think about and feel responsible for, taking a big chunk out of the Old Parenting Job.
10. The unpleasantness of your prodding and his delaying disappears from the relationship.
11. Threat to Attachment is eliminated.
12. The stress level in your home is substantially reduced.

---

[86] Please see my pages on Counterwill in the chapter entitled MY CHILD DEFIES ME or read about it in <u>Hold On to Your Kids: Why Parents Need to Matter More Than Peers.</u>

As important as a homework assignment may seem in the here and now, in the long run it is never worth the fighting and Attachment damage it can cause.

Beware of allowing the demands of a School System to turn you and your child into adversaries. Homework and whether or not it gets done can never take priority over relationship.

Grades are another common source of conflict and unnecessary stress for parents and children. **The less importance you can place on report cards the better!**

Beware, also, of school demands undermining your child's love of learning. It is particularly problematic to require new readers to read for a prescribed length of time at home each night. We could not design a better way to turn off a young child's excitement about learning to read. I highly recommend circumventing this requirement, if at all possible, as you continue with the pleasures of reading to your child until he gradually finds his own enjoyment in books.

If you have been struggling with the academic and behavioral fallout from an Atypical Learning Style, you will need a specific kind of guidance in addition to what I am offering. Dyslexia, or any of the other known Learning Differences, need to be addressed by someone your research finds to be a reliable expert in the field. When a correct diagnosis has been made, and your child is settled into a teaching environment geared to his distinctive capabilities, this chapter, along with all the others, can brighten your days.

And, Mom or Dad, if you are worrying about whether your child will be prepared for college if he isn't doing his homework, stop worrying! Never allow fights about homework or grades to come between you and your precious child, diverting you from enjoying and appreciating him in the here and now. TODAY IS WHAT MATTERS!

Folks who care about children and understand their developmental and emotional needs have been trying to change the American system of compulsory education for many years. Constructive innovations developed by John Dewey in the 1920s were mostly undone under the force of political demands when old-fashioned ideologies and economic priorities stopped Progressive Education before it could gain momentum.

In 1968, The Carnegie Institute commissioned Charles Silberman and his wife to conduct a two-year on-site evaluation of American schools, resulting in his eye-opening book, <u>Crisis in the Classroom: the Remaking of American Education</u>.[87] During this time, a crop of dedicated young educators, sickened by what they saw in the schools, wrote penetrating books about what was happening to children, forced by law, to spend their childhood days in destructive environments. A few innovative schools popped up and some survived until the last huge onslaught when President George W. Bush introduced No Child Left Behind. Under the pressures of government-mandated Standardized Testing, the piling on of homework, zero tolerance, heightened competition, and—in 19 states—children under threat of being struck with a wooden paddle if an adult judges their behavior to be inappropriate, American public schools are in a state of CRISIS far beyond anything Charles Silberman could have imagined! Government bureaucrats ignored his findings. The innovations he and other reform advocates called for exist in only a small number of private schools throughout the country.

Academic pressures have now crept into preschools where teachers are being patted on the back for getting little four-year-olds to write sentences; an absurd goal good only for pleasing politicians who know absolutely nothing about the emotional and cognitive needs of young children. Their push for "higher standards" satisfies their misguided notions of the meaning and purpose of something they call education. Instead of abating when President Bush left the scene, the call for Higher Standards continues to steamroll over children and teachers under different names with new mandates.

---

[87] <u>Crisis in the Classroom: The Remaking of American Education</u> by Charles E. Silberman, Copyright 1970, Published by Random House, New York, NY.

Some level of individualized instruction has become more and more difficult to maintain within the requirements of various experimental programs. As schools become less about the real needs of children and more about meeting government demands, publicized letters of resignation from disheartened teachers are popping up on the internet, giving us a glimpse into the reality of life in today's schools. One such letter hit the internet in 2014 when Susan Sluyter, a Massachusetts kindergarten teacher, resigned in despair over what today's public schools are doing to our children and wrote, *"Children are screaming out for help. They are under too much pressure and it is just no longer possible to meet the social and emotional needs of our youngest children."* I urge you to read her complete letter on the Washington Post website. A similar letter from retiring teacher Wendy Bradshaw can also be found on the internet.

There are, of course, wonderful exceptions to harmful school environments. Dedicated principals and teachers, who love and understand children, work their hearts out as they manage to perform their magic going against the tide. They are worth whatever effort it takes to find them!

4

ASKING QUESTIONS

The habit of asking children questions brings me around to how differently we relate to them compared to how we treat adult friends when it comes to matters of respect.

Example: Your friend has dropped in for coffee. After serving her, you leave the room for a few minutes. When you return, you find her with a broken cup and spilled coffee on the floor.

What do you do? You grab a towel and help clean up the mess, all the while comforting her in her distress. I don't think you ask any of the following questions:

"What did you do?"

"How did this happen?"

"Why weren't you careful?"

"Were you playing around?"

When a child spills or breaks something, he learns a lesson all on his own. As soon as it has happened, his brain is recording the entire incident as a learning experience. When we adults intrude with questions and admonishments, we distract him from this learning opportunity, drawing his attention to our reaction and stirring his feelings of embarrassment and guilt.

Rule of thumb: Avoid asking questions and never, never ask a question when you already know the answer; a form of dishonesty and entrapment, permanently damaging to your child's trust when he sees through it.

Interrogations put children on the spot and direct their attention away from the problem at hand to focus on protecting themselves.

One more example:

Your two children are playing in another room and one lets out a scream. As you enter the room, you get the whole picture. Johnny has hit Susie with a toy.

There is no reason to ask, *"Did you hit your sister?"* This is an excellent way to teach children to lie!

"Why did you hit your sister?" would be equally unproductive.

So why do we do this?

Old Traditional habits have us acting as detective, judge, and juror; gathering evidence so we can place blame and administer punishment. **In a Problem-Solving household we work with children instead of punishing them.** Addressing the above incident, we comfort both children by Active Listening to their distress and helping them resolve their violent dispute in a Problem-Solving way. We empathize with the older child and put his frustration into words, *"Little sisters are a big bother sometimes. You wish she would leave your things alone."* Little sister can be consoled, too, while we are showing him we understand his frustration with a troublesome sibling. If hitting is becoming brother's usual reaction to difficulties, this is our signal to identify the underlying frustrations fueling his aggression. In this case, competing with his sister for parental love and recognition is a powerful ongoing source of frustration.

Asking questions puts children on the defensive and makes them feel uneasy. In trying to tell us what they think we want to hear or to avoid difficulties, their natural response is to lie. Research by Kang Lee of The Institute of Child Study at the University of Toronto reveals that a large percentage of children of all ages and all social groups will lie regularly to avoid conflict, social discomfort, or embarrassment.

Probing and questioning are on the P.E.T. list of Communication Roadblocks. The simple question, *"What did you do in school today?"* can get an evening off to a bad start. Many children answer by saying, *"Nothing."* Whatever happened, they don't feel like talking about it. Parents say how annoyed they are with this answer: *"I'm only trying to show I'm interested."* Like any question, this one makes a child feel uneasy or anxious, wondering, *"What is she trying to find out?"* or *"What can I say to satisfy her?"* When children do answer this sort of question, they usually make up something to get out from under the questioning. No meaningful communication takes place.

It works best in support of the relationship to limit questions to impersonal queries, such as "I'm going shopping. Do you need any school supplies?"

Parents who follow this advice are pleasantly surprised when children open up and begin sharing all sorts of information with no prompting. Without the pressure of trying to find the "right" answer, a child is free to ruminate on his private thoughts and ideas about situations he encounters in daily life. With this freedom he becomes eager to share and make sense of his inner thoughts with a good listener. You!

No matter how well-meaning, children are intimidated by adult questioning. We improve communication and strengthen the Attachment bond when we stop asking questions. If our twelve-year-old daughter comes home from school obviously upset, she will probably answer, *"Nothing"* if we ask her what's wrong. Instead of probing, we can offer our support with an Active Listening opening, *"You seem really unhappy, honey."* Now she knows we are there for her if she wants to confide in us or vent with an accepting listener.

A common and particularly disturbing form of questioning comes from divorced parents when their child is put in the middle of ongoing uneasiness or animosity between the two adults. Although the questioning parent may think he or she is being casual and subtle in attempts to elicit information about the new life or relationships of the former mate, the child is put into an impossible position and under avoidable pressure by questions about the other parent.

Divorce places children of any age under a huge emotional burden and maintaining firm Attachments must become the number one priority for each parent. Following closely on the priority scale is reducing stress wherever possible. The adults must be diligent in refraining from all "pumping" of the child for information about the other parent to avoid this source of stress.

As children grow into adolescence, our questions can become a barrier to open communication and a threat to Attachment. The more questions you ask, the fewer meaningful answers you will get. Your teenager or preteen is building an independent life. He's meeting challenges he wants to handle by himself. If your relationship has been strong and steady to this point, he will ask for your help when he needs it. If, on the other hand, he knows that discussing his life or asking for your help will get you going with advice or criticism, most of your questions will be responded to with avoidance or lies.

Active Listening opens the best route into the life of your teen. See yourself in a "need to know" position and guard against worrying and asking a bunch of questions about what's happening when he's out of your sight. If your Attachment is strong, you will know whatever you "need to know." Any influence you have over his behavior out there in the world is in the quality of his relationship to you.

As we replace doing things to children with ways of working with them, we are liberated from the job of detective. Everyone, children and parents alike, can relax, get to really know each other and reap the benefits of unpressured family living.

5

LYING

Parents become particularly upset when they discover their child has lied to them. How much our children lie and what they lie about will depend on how realistic we can be about this behavior and what we may be doing to invite lying.[88]

Why do children lie?

- To protect from criticism.
- To protect from punishment.
- To protect from embarrassment.
- To protect from blame.
- To protect a friendship as in, "Yes, I like your dress."
- To protect from doing something they don't want to do.
- To protect from a lecture.
- To protect from being judged.
- To protect from being scolded.
- To protect their image.
- To protect from conflict.
- To protect from shame.

---

[88] Please read the chapter, ASKING QUESTIONS.

Lying is a child's logical coping mechanism in a home with coercive, controlling adults. Traditional Authoritarian parents may as well accept this as a fact of life. When parents punish with spankings, isolation, removal of privileges, grounding, or whatever other strategies they come up with, their children will lie.

Lecturing about the importance of honesty, emphasizing the shame of dishonesty, fairy tales warning of the pitfalls in lying are all a waste of time. **When children are treated in such ways as to believe acceptance of them depends on their behavior, they will lie. Being punished for lying will turn them into more skilled liars.**

When we establish a Problem-Solving, Non-Punitive family, we automatically eliminate a child's need to lie. Whether or not we prevent all self-protection through lying will depend on the level of emotional safety our children feel with us and the security in their Attachments to us.

If a situation arises when getting at the truth is of real importance, such as a problem at school when various authorities have made accusations about a child, the best approach will be through Active Listening. Being firmly on our child's side and showing sincere empathy, we may get to the bottom of things. Depending on the seriousness of the problem and the age of the child, we make a supportive opening remark to ease his distress and, it is hoped, to facilitate honest communication:

> *"So many people being upset with you is awfully scary."*

> *"You're wishing all this mess had never happened."*

> *"It feels terrible to be getting so much negative attention."*

You will know what to say to match your child's age, sensitivities and the situation. A child has not become some sort of deviant because he has lied to protect himself. Research shows lying to be widespread developmental behavior.[89]

---

[89] Find research results on children's lying at www.kangleelab.com.

6

TROUBLES WITH TEENS

We hear about problems with teenagers every day and from multiple sources. Teachers complain about disrespectful students. A neighbor bemoans her sixteen-year-old son's surly attitude. News stories deplore shocking activities of teen gangs.

People ask, *"What's going on?" "What's wrong with today's kids?"*

I can tell you for certain, there is nothing wrong with them. The behaviors we are asking about are their reactions to a fractured, speeding culture and the ways in which they have been and are being treated by their world of adults who are, themselves, operating the best they can as they see fit within their own set of unique circumstances.

I was one such an adult, when working hard to control my first son through the Traditional system of punishments and rewards I depended on, had me asking, *"What's wrong with him?"*

I was lucky to have stumbled onto Parent Effectiveness Training in time to avoid making the same terrible mistakes with my younger son, and my older son was lucky enough to find his own path to survival and rise above the hurt from my controlling emotional abuse.

If you have picked up this book looking for solutions to problems with a teenager, I can assure you that life will start going better for you when you put the concepts you find here into practice in your own home.

Start by reading all of it. Read about infants and toddlers and things you may think have nothing to do with your teenager. From diapers to high school, it all has meaning as part of the whole, in the same way each piece in a puzzle has a place in completing the picture. Pay particular attention to the elements of P.E.T. when you are reading about Active Listening, I-Messages, The Roadblocks, and Problem-Solving.

The information on COUNTERWILL will give you great hope. This instinctive reaction to control, impels your child to reject your direction as he struggles mightily to become his own person. **Learning how to Work With his push toward autonomy, you will be the friend he turns to for help and understanding during the passage to adulthood.**

P.E.T. Problem-Solving will help you build a mutually enjoyable relationship with your teen by eliminating arguing and anger when values and needs clash about everything from homework to clothing styles and social media.

The sections on teenagers in the P.E.T. book are so helpful and so important, I urge you to read them if you are now having problems. Or better still, long before your children are teenagers, get your hands on this book. You can find it in libraries, in bookstores, order it from the Gordon Training website or from Amazon, either new or used.

When we follow the P.E.T. philosophy and are able to resist trying to control our child, we can expect substantial results very quickly. Sometimes astonishing improvement happens overnight. The more we are able to put this new attitude and the communication skills into practice, the quicker we see dramatic results.

And, as always, the strength of our child's Attachment to us is the chief factor in maintaining the stability of our family and the emotional and physical safety of our teen.

Sometimes an act we call Delinquent is a consequence of home and school environments in which a youngster's creative drive follows the only course apparent to him. A bored, directionless fifteen-year-old with no compelling interests, harboring a simmering combination of anger and stirred-up Counterwill, may find the answer to his creative urge by dreaming up a petty robbery, climbing through a window, and stealing his neighbor's coin collection.

If you find out your teen has done something deliberately hurtful or illegal, a Traditional Punitive state of mind can swing into action, filling your head with ideas for making him pay and suffer. Just as it was when he was a toddler and broke your favorite vase, this is a time when your self-control and determination to STAY ON HIS SIDE are integral to a satisfactory outcome.

No matter how alienated a teenager may become, whether spewing hate from across the room or isolated behind closed doors, he needs you desperately. Your greatest strength for bridging the frightening chasm between the two of you is in your ability to LISTEN. Determination to rise above your own defensiveness and anger can bring you and this floundering kid to a place of hope and peace.

NEVER UNDERESTIMATE THE POWER OF DENIAL!

We enter into dangerous territory when we think we have nothing to offer and see ourselves as outside observers to our child's dysfunctioning. When operating in denial mode, we humans can become blind to the part we are playing in a dire situation. Embracing your child in a big warm hug can be the ideal start for entering into a healing connection.

NEVER UNDERESTIMATE THE POWER OF A HUG!

If you are both so stuck in hurt and bitterness with understanding and connection hopelessly beyond reach, this is a time for seeking professional help. Counselors trained in P.E.T. and/or Attachment offer the best hope for bringing an end to the difficulties. A family must be careful to avoid therapists who follow the Behaviorist model. If someone begins talking about strategies for getting control of a teen, they are promoting the very methods kids fight against. This approach is sometimes called Tough Love and has been known to bring tragic results. Tough Love will typically intensify a teen's peer Attachments, can exacerbate a serious emotional imbalance, trigger running away, or if the teenager is a girl, may send her into the arms of a man. Desperate for connection, her choice is not usually a wise one and can bring with it the complications of an untimely pregnancy.

Military-style boot camps present another counterproductive and hazardous course of action that parents are sometimes advised to take. Although the extreme measures of a boot camp may scare a teen into compliance during the time when he is held captive and keep him "in line" when he is dismissed, the harshly punitive environment will not bring about an emotionally healthy adjustment to living in today's world and, in many cases, will increase a young person's confusion, hostility and rage.

You may find all the help you need in the P.E.T. book, along with Dr. William Glasser's book, <u>For Parents and Teenagers: Dissolving the Barrier Between You and Your Teen.</u> [90]

It is never too late to repair a relationship, no matter how hopeless it may seem. The love and affection you felt for the tiny baby your teenager once was is still there inside you, ready to emerge and open the way for building a mutually satisfying connection.

What an adventure!

---

[90] <u>For Parents and Teenagers: Dissolving the Barrier Between You and Your Teen</u> by William Glasser, M.D. An excellent resource for anyone facing problems with a teenager.

Note: I want to touch briefly on the escalating Bullying Problem. As you will expect by now, it too is an Attachment dysfunction and a very complicated one. Punishment, the usual response to the behavior, adds to what's wrong in this person's life to have created his bullying personality. I now refer you, once again, to the work of Gordon Neufeld and Gabor Maté. Their book explains the bullying maladjustment and how to address it. Dr. Neufeld's DVDs on the subject are available through his website and some public libraries. I urge you to take advantage of both Dr. Maté's and Dr. Neufeld's YouTube presentations on Bullying and other problems, such as ADD and ADHD, which are skyrocketing for children in today's culture.

CAUTION!

The next few paragraphs are so vital to your happiness as a parent, I want you to take a few deep breaths, perhaps pour a cup of coffee, and prepare yourself for what I am about to say.

I'm going to construct a cautionary tale with our characters being a single working mom and her little boy. Everything I describe could apply just as well to a stay-at-home mother or any combination of parents and children in any situation. For this example we will be looking at one mother and one son.

Parenting troubles begin when her little boy is five. Nothing out of the ordinary. Only the usual things parents struggle with: lack of cooperation, angry outbursts, tantrums, and one day saying, "I hate you"

She happens to hear about P.E.T. and takes the course. By implementing the communication skills religiously, eliminating punishment and rewards, and absorbing new knowledge from supplemental reading, before long she's enjoying life with a little kid she and all her friends see as a Model Child.

As she lives the P.E.T lifestyle, mother and son advance happily through the years. When other parents complain about their troublesome kids, she thanks her lucky stars for having escaped from the stress and strain they moan about.

Until something goes wrong. With her son now thirteen and the Parenting books on a shelf somewhere, this caring, conscientious mother has gradually slipped into the control mindset of the surrounding culture:

"Have you done your homework?"

"I told you to take out the trash."

"Hurry up! You're making us late."

And one of the most disconnecting habits of all: trying to exert control from a distance by texting and phoning her orders and instructions.

Just when her "perfect child" entered adolescence, with Counterwill at maximum potency, this mom, who thought nothing could possibly go wrong, forgot about the Relationship skills she had so carefully applied in developing their enviable life together. Now dismayed and worn out from grappling with an angry, uncooperative young man, she finds herself caught in the same desolate world with worried, complaining parents she had always felt sorry for.

Remember what Dr. Gordon teaches us! Relationship is everything! When we lose the relationship, we lose our influence.

Suddenly, it hits her: *"What am I doing?"*

"I would never talk to a friend the way I talk to my son." "When did I stop Active Listening?"

"I don't remember the last time I collected him!"

With commitment and concentration, the mother in my little drama will get life with her son back on track. Brushing up on her understanding of Counterwill, giving herself a refresher course in the P.E.T. communication skills, and paying close attention to avoiding the Roadblocks, she will equip herself for restoring Attachment and rebuilding their relationship. Knowing how pleasurable Parenting can be, she will do what's necessary to bring back the good days.

My advice to a parent reading this?

Remember to Active Listen and avoid the Roadblocks. Keep your Attachment instincts, and your child's, alive and well by Collecting at the start of all interactions, and most particularly when seeking cooperation. Have this book close at hand with any others you are finding helpful. Pick one up from time-to-time, open it to any random page, and just start reading. As the years go by, the words will have new meaning, enrich your Parenting adventure in unexpected ways, and support you in maintaining your smoothly running life.

7

KIDS AND DRUGS

One of each parent's greatest worries is about drugs and what to do to prevent this problem from entering their life. When we consider the element of chance in this common hazard, we see there is no absolute way to prevent a child's encounters or experimentation with drugs.

Not every person, teen or adult, who tries or indulges with drugs, becomes hooked. It is the Individual who has lived through wounding experiences early in life who becomes a victim of substance abuse.

Missing attachments, neglect, physical, emotional or sexual abuse in infancy and childhood prime the neural pathways and hormonal systems as ripe and ready for addictions later in life, sometimes as early as the teen years.[91]

As with all risky activities; scare tactics, threats, and dire warnings do not keep our children safe. Instead, preaching and lecturing will activate Counterwill and may produce exactly the results we had hoped to avoid.

Availability of accurate information helps children make intelligent choices. Keeping a book in the home offering sound non-judgmental information on

---

[91] Gabor Maté describes this process in perfect detail in his book, In the Realm of Hungry Ghosts: Close Encounters with Addiction, Copyright 2008, 2009, 2010, Published by North Atlantic Books, Berkeley, CA.

drugs and their effects on the mind and body is the best way to answer questions when they come up.

All I could say beyond this has already been written by Aletha Solter in <u>Raising Drug-Free Kids: 100 Tips for Parents</u>.[92]

If your child is an infant, it is not too soon to begin absorbing Dr. Solter's recommendations. Although you will find her advice to be fundamentally the same as mine, I believe another writer's perspective on the humane treatment of children and problem prevention is always helpful.

Our best insurance against a child's falling victim to addiction is his own self-esteem, the strength of his Attachments to significant adults, and his security in our unconditional acceptance of him, just as he is, under all circumstances.

---

[92] <u>Raising Drug-Free Kids: 100 Tips for Parents</u> by Aletha Solter, Ph.D., Copyright 2006, Published by Da Capo Press, a member of the Perseus Book Group, Cambridge, MA.

8

RUNAWAYS

According to the National Runaways Switchboard, between 1.6 and 2.8 million children run away from home each year in the United States.

Think about it!

Large numbers of children leave food and shelter for an existence of questionable survival on the streets in order to escape an intolerable life with parents. The three main reasons for taking this drastic step are conflict with parents, physical abuse, and sexual abuse. Of the three, the first two are the direct results of good old Traditional Parenting practices and the kids have had all they can take.

How sad! Sad, too, is finding many Parenting books, where you may go for help, instructing you to do to your children the very things they run away from.

All children suffer in one way or another when the adults in their lives use coercive methods, trying to control them. P.E.T. gives us a sound guide for maintaining a healthy relationship with a child by following an approach with the goal to influence children without the ever-escalating attempts to control them. There is a stark difference in our behavior, and we enjoy a very different way of life, when we work with a child instead of coming up with methods to gain control over him. Our influence is integrated by our child when we function as an involved and caring ally, not as an adversary.

When a child is firmly connected to at least one caring attuned adult who listens to him and accepts him just as he is without trying to control or change him, he finds haven in such a relationship.

As we come to understand and appreciate the quality of life we have the power to create by working with children, not against them, and put this knowledge into practice, we find ourselves automatically building the kind of warm caring connection and home environment no child would want to exchange for life under a bridge.

Punishing an escaped child is a destructive reaction. When we do this, we are responding to him with the very treatment he was fleeing in the first place.

If your child has already run away from home, you must summon the courage to ask yourself this question and to answer it honestly: *"Why would my child, the baby I once held in my arms, prefer the discomforts and dangers of street life to living with me?"*

As hard as this can be to do, your strength to do it will change your life and may save your child.

As you ponder the interpersonal difficulties underlying your child's need to get away, there is no reason to heap blame on yourself. You have only been doing what your own past experience and the surrounding culture have taught you to do. With the information in this book, you can transform the relationship between you and your child into one you will both enjoy and treasure as the two of you move forward into good times together.

9

MAKING THE CHANGE

Has reading this book been the liberating experience I intended it to be? Page-by-page and little-by-little, has your life become less stressful and more enjoyable? Have previous angers and struggles been fading into the past? Here are some final tips to bring you completely into the bright sunlight of blissful parenthood.

With toddlers and preschoolers, the best way to start is by diving right in. When we change from being a DOING TO adversary into a WORKING WITH ally, young children fall into patterns of cooperation automatically.

MEANING WHAT YOU SAY, eliminating the word NO, stating your needs with I-Messages instead of making demands, along with Active Listening and avoiding Communication Roadblocks; will bring about rapid change.

When we adults can simply get out of the way with our ordering and control, children blossom before our eyes. We see youngsters as young as two becomimg self-directed and eagerly cooperative within a few days or weeks.

If you are entangled in a power contest or struggling with an Alpha Child, transformation may take longer. Remember to begin each interaction by Collecting your child with friendly eye contact, a smile, and a nod. A gentle touch feels good, too.

Think:

> Will what I say or do protect Attachment?
>
> Will what I say or do stimulate Counterwill?
>
> Would I say or do this to an adult friend?

For children of about five or six and on into their teens, I suggest telling them about your aspirations for becoming a Problem-Solving family. I recommend arranging a family get-together for making an announcement about your plans. If you have been controlling with Time-Out, grounding, removal of privileges, yelling, or spanking, you can start by telling them there will be no more punishments of any kind from now on. Tell them you will invite their input for solving problems in place of administering punishments. Taking them out to dinner can add significance to your announcement and highlight your commitment to change.

And if you have, indeed, been punishing your children, they will probably not believe you. They may ask what you'll do when they "break the rules." You can say you are not happy with the way you've been treating them. Instead of finding ways to punish them when things go wrong, you want to work together with them to get everyone's needs met.

Along with you, they will have become dependent on punishments and may go somewhat haywire with the punishment rug pulled out from under them. Accustomed to being controlled by adults, they will need practice in self-control and cooperation. How much practice they'll need will depend on how heavily they've been controlled and your level of commitment and support while they are growing toward autonomy and finding satisfaction in taking responsibility for themselves.

The period of transition may require your considerable involvement. With attention to maintaining a strong Attachment and, when necessary, intervening with friendly redirection, they will quickly find inner pride in taking over management of their personal behavior.

Example: Your twelve-year-old son is teasing his younger sister. This has been an ongoing problem and source of conflict. Your usual response has been: *"Ben, if you don't stop bugging Ellie this minute, I'm sending you to your room."*

Now, without a word, you go to Ben and put your arm around his shoulders. Looking into his eyes with a smile and a nod, you say, *"I don't like hearing Ellie being teased. Let's you and I go make some popcorn and check out the stack of books I brought home from the library today."* Or, *"Let's go shoot baskets." "Let's go for a run." "Let's give the dog a bath."* You can come up with a joint activity to interrupt his problematic habit of behavior and, at the same time, extend to him your one-on-one involvement.

Some children need a lot of intervention and help before recovery from coercion and punishments allows their undeveloped talents and abilities for self-direction and self-discipline to blossom and flourish. Others move into change more smoothly and surprise parents with their rapid growth.

Adults need recovery time, too. This is much like joining Alcoholics Anonymous to break away from old dependencies. You may fall off the wagon and without thinking, shout, *"Go to your room!"*

If you experience a personal relapse, damage control comes in the form of your admission of error and immediate repairs to Attachment: "Oops! Wrong move. Forget I just yelled at you. I could use a big hug to get me back on track!" If your child isn't ready to give a hug and there's another adult nearby, he or she can step to the plate with a hug and this change of tone. Now, you and your child can figure out, together, what went wrong. Active Listening may uncover a need behind the behavior triggering your outburst. If you were reacting to an ongoing difficulty, a Problem-Solving session may be what's called for. In place of punishment, you look for solutions in a joint effort with your child, thus providing him with a significant learning experience in solving problems and healthy interpersonal relating.

I highly recommend keeping the P.E.T. book on hand to guide you through the transitional period.

Fundamental change at this depth takes thought, effort, and time. You are escaping to freedom and entering a whole new world.[93]

No small thing!

When you are settled into this new territory, relating to children with respect and equality, the BIG JOB of Parenting will have disappeared. Old worries lie in the past as you participate in the ongoing pleasures of sharing life with delightful, always fascinating, young fellow humans.

---

[93] Please go to the Gordon Training website to read a letter from a Chinese father who made this change and healed an unhappy relationship with his twenty-year-old son. You will find it as the last item in the collection of testimonials at www.gordontraining.com.

10

GUEST ARTICLE

IS IT ANTI FEMINIST TO TALK TO GIRLS ABOUT THE ROLE OF NURTURING?

Written on Friday, 01 February 2013 and posted in Communication by Kesang Menezes who is a facilitator at Parenting Matters in Chennai, India and mother of two girls ages 11 and 15 when this was written.

We live in a society where the majority of women are forced into stereotypical roles and barely given choices about what they would like to do with their lives. But yet there is the emerging middle class which is empowering its girls to go ahead and achieve whatever they would wish for. These girls are doing well academically (and on average far better than boys) and surging into careers like engineering, management, etc. I come from such a family as well, where I was brought up to believe that truly the sky is the limit for my ambitions. I spent my teen years only thinking about what career I wanted and dreaming about all that I would achieve. And then I got married and had a baby . . . all of my own choice.

What happens when you become a mom? Hard choices!

But nothing in my upbringing had prepared me for the wrenching dilemma I faced then. I had thought, like every modern middle-class woman, I would have a maid to look after the house and a daycare for my child, and I could happily carry on with my career. But when the time came I could not go back to work. I think every new mother can identify with the trauma of this choice and whatever decision you take, it's hard to feel completely at peace.

I chose to take a long break (a few years? Would I ever be able to get back?). My peers who were surging ahead in their careers wondered at my decision. Most of my friends and relatives said *"We never expected you to become a housewife. What was the point of studying so much?"* As my daily routine became more mundane, I found my self-esteem plummeting. And when I looked around, I found many others like me - angry, frustrated, or depressed moms who had chosen to stay at home for the sake of their children but were feeling resentful about it. A friend said to me, *"My husband and I met at business school. We were equals. Now look where he is today and where I am."*

Not that the situation is any better for those who choose to go back to work. It tears at their insides, too. Is it fair for a woman to have to make that choice? And for some it isn't even a choice. It is a necessity.

Aren't men and women equal?

All this was all the more disturbing to me as I have always been a die-hard feminist. I started questioning the belief that men and women must be the "SAME." We must be treated as equals, yes, but we are different. After all, nature has created the woman to bear children and breastfeed. The role of nurturing is actually one of the most important tasks we have as a human race. But our patriarchal society has traditionally thrust this role on women and denied them any choice; also, while eulogizing the role of the mother, has in practice placed little value on it. Now in wanting to achieve "equal status" with men, middle-class women like ourselves have started thinking in a similar way: we are dismissive of our role as nurturers and place a very high value on professional achievement. That is why the "stay-at-home" moms feel worthless.

What will happen to a society that does not value nurturing?

Can we imagine what happens to a society that places the least value on the task of rearing children? Having recognized the breakdown of society that is happening from not supporting women in the task of parenting, the most advanced European countries like Sweden and Norway are giving not just women but even men up to a year or two off from work to be with their children. And after that flexi hours and part time jobs. Here I am told that when a professional woman asks if she can work part time she is told that there are countless others ready to work full time and overtime so why should an employer bother with you.

What message do I give my daughters?

Knowing this, I wonder what I want to talk to my teenage daughters about in preparing them for life. Do I prepare them to be career women or "housewives" (as we are still called!)? Do I tell them not to get into fast track corporate careers because that becomes really hard when you have a child?

After much reflection, these are the messages that I now give my daughters who are now in the process of making decisions about their lives and careers. I tell them about how important, joyful and amazing the task of raising a child is, and that they should never consider it to have a lower status than working outside the home. (However, it is very important to be qualified and to be capable of supporting oneself.) I tell them that if they decide to have children, there will come a time when they would be faced with some hard choices between their nurturing and professional roles. If they are not sure about what they want to do, it makes sense to consider careers which give them flexibility.

Maybe I could be accused of limiting my daughters' thinking or being anti-feminist, but I don't want motherhood to hit them in the face like a sudden nightmare. They know that they have all these choices, to get married or not, to have a child or not, to be a career woman or not. But as a parent I would like to prepare them for all the various roles a woman may play, so that they may make these decisions with awareness and joy.

Kesang Menezes has been facilitating parenting groups and workshops since 2004. She believes that small interactive groups are a very powerful tool for learning. She also writes articles for Parent Circle *magazine,* The Hindu, *and other publications, and provides short online videos on Parenting.*

AFTERWORD

In light of January, 2018 news reports about the sexual abuse of child gymnasts by a trusted doctor, I must say something more about the importance of LISTENING to children.

A number of the hundreds of abused girl athletes had told a parent or a coach what was being done to them and were ignored, brushed-off, or told they were wrong about what was happening. Most of them said nothing, and of the few who did speak up, no child possessed a strong enough sense of personal agency to persist until the truth was known.

Our lesson from this?

Although things our children are trying to tell us may seem insignificant, pointless, silly, or not worth our time; whatever they are saying is not insignificant, pointless, or silly to them.

Here's the point:

CHILDREN MUST GROW UP KNOWING THEY HAVE A VOICE AND IT WILL BE HEARD BY ADULTS, NO MATTER HOW OR IF IT IMPACTS THE GROWNUPS THEY TURN TO.

This tragedy is only one isolated example of the relentless suppression children are subjected to in, what we think of as, our advanced culture.

ABOUT THE AUTHOR

I suffered the usual anger, frustration, and distress of Authoritarian Parenting with my first son, all the while believing I was a Perfect Mother. As a stay-at-home mom in the 1950s, surrounded by other parents who shared my lifestyle and Parenting techniques, I didn't know the problems we had with our children were the direct result of our Traditional Authoritarian Parenting practices.

A few months after the birth of another son, when my first boy was eight years old, I was invited to an introductory talk on PARENT EFFECTIVENESS TRAINING and my world was changed forever. P.E.T. lifted me from the dark depths of screaming, punishing control, up into the blissful sunshine of enjoyable, satisfying parenthood.

In 1968, I organized Citizens Against Physical Punishment, a group of Dallas, Texas parents working to stop corporal punishment in the schools.[94] I had read in the Dallas Morning News about a third-grade boy suffering from a ruptured kidney after being beaten with a wooden board, called a paddle, by an assistant school principal.

We were naïve housewives without political backgrounds, standing up to speak at school board meetings, knees shaking, to argue against hitting children as a way to improve learning. We always heard a version of the same answer:

---

[94] Dr. Robert Hagebak was our generous professional consultant and supporter. You can find his article, "Disciplinary Practices in Dallas Contrasted with School Systems with Rules Against Violence Against Children," in the Fall 1972 Journal of Clinical Psychology on the internet.

"We believe physical punishment is useful in disciplining children and in improving the educational environment. Although you believe differently, this is only a matter of opinion and we will continue paddling students."

In 1972, we brought a Federal lawsuit against the Dallas Independent School District with B. F. Skinner and Dr. John Valusek[95] as expert witnesses. We lost the suit after the judge declared he had been hit plenty when he was a kid and it didn't hurt him.

Note: Although Dr. Skinner advocated against punishments, including the paddling of schoolchildren, I have come to view his Behaviorist methods of control to be limitless in the damage they have done to our children and to our society.

I moved from Texas to Seattle in 2004 to be near my eldest son. Soon after settling in, I read the book, <u>Ghosts from the Nursery: Tracing the Roots of Violence</u>. Here it was: the proof we had needed in our confrontations with school boards and school principals! Today's developmental psychologists and physicians can see what goes on inside the brains of infants and children who are hit, yelled at, treated harshly and/or neglected. Computer brain imaging shows we were right after all. What was only our "opinion" is now scientifically verified fact. Energized by this vindication of my long-held beliefs, I was propelled into becoming a certified parent educator teaching Parent Effectiveness Training. Keeping up with the latest research, I continue to learn about child development and how best to support a child's greatest opportunities for growing into a healthy, happy, productive, well-functioning individual. I hope passing what I have learned along to you changes your life as dramatically as it did mine

---

[95] Dr. John Valusek has been a tireless advocate for the humane treatment of children. His response to the defensive old remark. *"I was spanked plenty when I was a kid and I turned out just fine"* was this: *"If you turned out just fine, it was because of the good things your parents did for you between the spankings."* See his article about Spanking on the Natural Child Project website.

RECOMMENDED READING

<u>P.E.T. Parent Effectiveness Training: The Proven Program for Raising Responsible Children</u> by Dr. Thomas Gordon, Nobel Peace Prize Nominee, Copyright 1970, 1975, 2000, Published by Three Rivers Press, New York, NY, a member of The Crown Publishing Group.

Dr. Gordon describes what it takes to create a Problem-Solving family and build healthy relationships with children. His book has helped millions of parents all over the world find a joy in parenthood they never thought possible. I invite you to read what others have to say in their testimonials on the Gordon Training website and recommend owning this book for ongoing coaching and inspiration.

<u>Hold On to Your Kids: Why Parents Need to Matter More Than Peers</u> by Gordon Neufeld, Ph.D. and Gabor Maté, M.D., Copyright 2004, 2005, Ballantine Books, a division of Random House Publishers, New York, NY.

This book is the most important to me, along with the P.E.T book, in my work with parents. I find it absolutely indispensable for the understanding of Attachment and the difficulties we confront when Attachment is weak or missing from adult/child relationships at home as well as in schools or anywhere children and adults interact.

<u>Ghosts from the Nursery: Tracing the Roots of Violence</u> by Robin Karr-Morse and Meredith S. Wiley, Copyright 1997, Atlantic Monthly Press, New York, NY.

This book motivated me into training to become a Parent Educator. During the first years of my child advocacy, there were always detractors who insisted that folks who wanted to change the way children are treated had their beliefs, and others who were satisfied with the status quo had theirs. It was simply a matter of opinion. What I believe and teach can no longer be called "opinion." The authors detail solid scientific brain research to support non-violent empathic parenting. I highly recommend their book for the scientific content and for the compelling story it tells.

Unconditional Parenting: Moving from Rewards and Punishment to Love and Reason by Alfie Kohn, Copyright 2005, Atria Books, New York, NY.

Alfie Kohn offers priceless insight into the sources of our deepening difficulties in relationships with children. This is an excellent book to help us become unconditional in our love for our children. I recommend owning it to refer to regularly and read again and again. Everything Alfie Kohn writes is supported by so much interesting reliable research that his notes are as consequential as each chapter he gives us.

Punished by Rewards: The Trouble with Gold Stars, Incentive Plans, As, Praise and Other Bribes by Alfie Kohn, Copyright 1993, 1999, Houghton Mifflin Publishers, New York, NY.

One would look far and wide to find a book as well-researched as this meticulous analysis of Rewards and their effects on relationships and on our society. Absolutely indispensable reading for parents, teachers, and everyone concerned with child development and our cultural evolution.

Between Parent and Child by Haim Ginott, Copyright 1965, Three Rivers Press, New York, NY.

Haim Ginott, like Thomas Gordon, was a student of Carl Rogers and a Parent Educator. He wrote several groundbreaking books about communication between adults and children to broaden understanding for relating to children in a developmentally sound way.

<u>Siblings Without Rivalry: How to Help Your Children to Live Together So You Can Live Too</u> by Adele Faber and Elaine Mazlish, Copyright 1987, 1998, 2012, Avon Books, Inc., New York, NY.

The authors are mothers who trained with Haim Ginott, established their own parenting groups, and went on to write several excellent books. Drawing from their personal experiences and feedback from the many parents they have worked with, their books give comic book-style illustrated examples of the old ways of relating to children contrasted with the new, making the concepts clear and easy to follow.

<u>Parenting from the Inside Out: How a Deeper Self-Understanding Can Help You Raise Children Who Thrive</u> by Daniel J. Siegel, M.D. and Mary Hartzell, M. Ed., Copyright 2003, Published by Jeremy P. Tarcher/Putnam, a member of Penguin Putnam Inc., New York, NY.

You will find this book to be an affirmation of and valuable expansion on the P.E.T. principals, based on modern brain research. The authors address the anger parents bring with them from their childhoods, how it contaminates relationships with their own children, and what to do about it. This is an important book for all parents and particularly for folks finding Parenting to be a combative and exhausting job.

<u>Scattered: How Attention Deficit Disorder Originates and What You Can Do About It</u> by Gabor Maté, M.D., Published by the Penguin Group, Penguin Putnam Inc., New York, NY.

Although this book is directed at helping adults and children cope with ADD and ADHD at home and at school, I find every word to be of priceless value in living with any and all children. Dr. Maté's understanding offers valuable guidance to anyone interested in the welfare of children and our hopes for their futures.

<u>Guiding Young Children: A Problem-Solving Approach</u> by Eleanor Reynolds, Copyright 2006, 1991, 1990, Mayfield Publishing Company, Mountain View, CA.

The author applied the Gordon Model for building Problem-Solving relationships to her work with children for over thirty-five years. She gives us many examples of the nonauthoritarian way for being with children, from infancy all through the preschool years. Her application of the P.E.T. principles covers the many different dilemmas all parents encounter from day to day. Though written as a textbook for teachers and daycare professionals, it can be equally helpful to parents in the home. In my coaching work with parents, I many times will reach for this book and say, *"Let's see what Eleanor would do."*

Dibs in Search of Self by Virginia M. Axline, Copyright 1964, a Ballantine Book, Published by Random House Publishers, New York, NY.

This is the true story of a severely disturbed little boy who puzzled his parents, teachers, and various professionals with his bizarre anti-social behavior. Through play therapy with the author he emerged as a highly intelligent and perfectly capable child. Encounters with him as a teenager and young adult show him to have grown into an exceptional human being. This is a fascinating and important book for all parents.

Son Rise by Barry Neil Kaufman, Copyright 1964, Warner Books, New York, NY.

Here we have a day-to-day account of the author and his wife bringing their toddler son out of his severe autism. After each expert told them their child was beyond help, the parents refused to give up on their spinning, rocking little boy locked in his own solitary world. They decided to embrace an attitude of unconditional love and, by accepting their child exactly as he was and relating to him at his level of functioning, they succeeded in bringing him into their world. This was not an easy task and required eight or more hours each day of intense interaction between mother and son. Their accomplishment is a testimony to the power of unconditional love and empathy. The Kaufmans have gone on to create an institute for treating autism and other emotional ills through a talking therapy they call Option. Their son is now a fully functioning adult and teaches at the institute. He wrote the introduction to a later expanded edition of the book, titled Son Rise: The Miracle Continues.

<u>New Ways in Discipline: You and Your Child Today</u> by Dorothy Baruch, Copyright 1949, Whittlesey House Publishers, New York, NY.

Although written seventy years ago, this little book is as helpful and relevant as advice being given today, though some of the vocabulary is amusingly quaint and dated. The author draws upon her training as a psychologist, her experience as a therapist, and her work with children in preschool settings. Like Thomas Gordon and Haim Ginott, she was influenced by Carl Rogers and his development of Client-Centered Therapy with Active Listening at the core. Her focus is on the need for children to grow up in an atmosphere of acceptance and trust with the freedom to voice their innermost feelings, including and most particularly their feelings of anger and fear. She identifies most behavior problems as rooted in unexpressed anger and the underlying sources of such anger. This is an important book!

<u>How Children Fail</u> by John Holt, Copyright 1964, Pitman Publishing Company, New York, NY.

As an unusually gifted teacher, John Holt looked deeply into the nature of learning and what is actually happening to children in school, as opposed to what appears to be happening. This book and his other classic, How Children Learn, are compilations of the author's journals. He takes us along through his own personal growth and increasing awareness about the destructive nature of our compulsory education. By 1981, he had given up hope for improving public schools and turned to writing about Home Schooling.

<u>Breaking Their Will: Shedding Light on Religious Child Maltreatment</u> by Janet Heimlich, Copyright 2001, Prometheus Books, Amherst, NY.

In this extensively researched and trailblazing book, Ms. Heimlich gives a detailed account of the many ways children are abused and sometimes killed in alignment with particular religious beliefs. Not an anti-religion book, the focus is on common religious practices harming children. Each thought-provoking page offers a look into this unexamined dimension of modern life.

The Direction of Human Development: Biological and Social Bases by Ashley Montagu, Copyright 1955, Published by Harper Brothers, New York, NY.

Not a Parenting book, this is a scientific study of human development by a leader in anthropology in his time. The book was published in 1955 and becomes particularly interesting now because Montagu's findings, based on research methods of his era, are verified by modern brain research and brain imaging. His conclusions as they relate to the parent-child relationship were this: The most basic human needs are to love and be loved and the most basic human drive is toward cooperation. He postulated pathologies of personality to be the result of the thwarting of our basic needs and/or our basic drive. Alfred Adler, Carl Rogers, and Alice Miller, three influential minds in our work, arrived at the same conclusions through their research and work with troubled and disturbed individuals.

For Your Own Good: Hidden Cruelty in Child-Rearing and the Roots of Violence by Alice Miller, Copyright 1983, 1984, 1990, Published in Canada by Harper Collins, 1990 edition Published by Noonday Press, New York, NY.

This is a life-changing book by a world famous psychoanalyst. Much of her focus is on the childhood and emotional development of Adolph Hitler. We come away from her words understanding many things about nurturing children and knowing Hitler would not have been "Hitler" without having suffered as he did as a child. You will not want to put her book down once you start reading it.

Why We Sleep: Unlocking the Power of Sleep and Dreams by Matthew Walker, Ph.D., Copyright 2017, Published by Scribner, an Imprint of Simon and Schuster, Inc., New York, NY. This groundbreaking book, by an expert on sleep and neuroimaging, gives us newly discovered answers about sleep and the vital ways in which it effects our minds and bodies. This is important information. I highly recommend sharing it with teenagers.

DISCLAIMER

The information and advice in this book put forth a philosophy and type of communication intended as a guide for creating happy, healthy relationships between adults and children. Please seek professional counseling or medical advice for problems not addressed or remaining unsolved. The author and publisher accept no liability nor responsibility for any direct or indirect damage alleged to result from following the advice presented herein.

THE TWELVE COMMUNICATION ROADBLOCKS

ORDERING, DIRECTING, COMMANDING

WARNING, ADMONISHING, THREATENING

MORALIZING, PREACHING

ADVISING, GIVING SUGGESTIONS OR SOLUTIONS

ARGUING, PERSUADING WITH LOGIC

JUDGING, CRITICIZING, BLAMING

PRAISING, AGREEING

NAME-CALLING, RIDICULING

ANALYZING, DIAGNOSING

REASSURING, SYMPATHIZING

QUESTIONING, PROBING

DIVERTING, BEING SARCASTIC, WITHDRAWING

THE TWELVE COMMUNICATION ROADBLOCKS

ORDERING, DIRECTING, COMMANDING

WARNING, ADMONISHING, THREATENING

MORALIZING, PREACHING

ADVISING, GIVING SUGGESTIONS OR SOLUTIONS

ARGUING, PERSUADING WITH LOGIC

JUDGING, CRITICIZING, BLAMING

PRAISING, AGREEING

NAME-CALLING, RIDICULING

ANALYZING, DIAGNOSING

REASSURING, SYMPATHIZING

QUESTIONING, PROBING

DIVERTING, BEING SARCASTIC, WITHDRAWING

Printed in the United States
By Bookmasters